In a Field of Words
A Creative Writing Text

Sybil Pittman Estess
Houston

Janet McCann
Texas A&M University

Prentice
Hall

Upper Saddle River, New Jersey 07458

Library of Congress Cataloging-in-Publication Data

McCann, Janet.
    In a field of words : a creative writing text / Janet McCann, Sybil Estess.
      p. cm.
    Includes bibliographical references and index.
    ISBN 0–13–085035–7
    1. English language—Rhetoric.   2. Creative writing (Higher education)   I. Estess, Sybil
P., II. Title.

PE1408.M165
808′.042—dc21

2001052362

Editor-in-chief: Leah Jewell
Senior acquisitions editor: Carrie Brandon
Executive managing editor: Ann Marie McCarthy
Production liaison: Fran Russello
Editorial/production supervision: Bruce Hobart (Pine Tree Composition)
Prepress and manufacturing buyer: Sherry Lewis
Cover designer: Robert Farrar-Wagner
Marketing manager: Rachel Falk
Marketing assistant: Christine Moodie
Copy editor: Carolyn Ingalls

This book was set in 10/12 Meridien by Pine Tree Composition, Inc.,
and was printed and bound by Hamilton Printing Company.
The cover was printed by Jaguar Advanced Graphics.

 © 2003 by Pearson Education, Inc.
Upper Saddle River, New Jersey 07458

Printed in the United States of America

11

ISBN 0-13-085035-7

Pearson Education LTD., *London*
Pearson Education Australia PTY, Limited, *Sydney*
Pearson Education Singapore, Pte. Ltd.
Pearson Education North Asia Ltd, *Hong Kong*
Pearson Education Canada, Ltd., *Toronto*
Pearson Educación de Mexico, S.A. de C.V.
Pearson Education—Japan, *Tokyo*
Pearson Education Malaysia, Pte. Ltd.
Pearson Education, *Upper Saddle River*, New Jersey

Contents

A Word of Introduction

This book is intended for the beginning creative writer who has perhaps written a few poems and stories but who has not had formal instruction. The book does not expect that its user knows the language of poetry or fiction, or that he or she has read more literature than the average college freshman has read. Its main goal is to provide basic instruction in three genres—poetry, fiction, and creative nonfiction. But its method is to present ways to get started, things to write about, and directions to look for help in all elements of writing including first publication.

The book assumes that creative writing provides personal fulfillment and that most people who are interested in writing have an aptitude for it and can, through creative writing courses and other means, find ways to develop their abilities. Also, it assumes that everyone has a story to tell or a poem to write, and that people learn to write mostly by writing. This book will help beginning creative writers to find words for their stories and to give their stories a shape.

Besides serving as a basic text, this book can be used as a self-help book by individual writers putting forth their first efforts. The chapters of the book need not be used in order, since the organization is flexible and responsive to the user's needs. There is enough material in each chapter to use it as a beginning text for a one- or two-genre course, or the book can be used to introduce all three genres—fiction, creative nonfiction, and poetry—to the aspiring writer.

We have included an abundance of examples of everything that we discuss, and these vary from the immediately accessible to the difficult, partly to enthrall very different new writers in the pleasure of words, but also to underscore our shared belief that good writing is a wide and varied field.

The text was fun to write. We hope that it will be equally fun to read and that it will be an enjoyable guide for those who wish to wander through the word-field, gathering and scattering.

Getting Started

> What is written without effort is in general read without pleasure.
>
> —Ben Jonson

You are taking this class because you want to write. Maybe you have been keeping journals and writing poems or stories for years, or maybe it is only recently that you have discovered, among your other loves, a love of words. Either way, you have decided to explore your interest within the framework of the creative writing class. This takes a bit of courage, because you will be sharing your work, opening it up to others who have different ways of looking at things. You are enrolled in the course because you recognize that you don't write for yourself alone, but for readers, however many or few. (If you really were writing for yourself alone, you would not be in a creative writing classroom; you would be writing in a journal that you keep under your mattress.)

But you are here—in this class, in this book. You want to find your audience and to learn from your readers and fellow writers. You want to make the step from personal diarist to public writer. To do this, you will mine your available sources of material and work on your means of expression. Where does what you write come from? From yourself, of course, and from the world. To do your best writing, you may impose structures of disciplined observation on your experience, so that it is most easily available to you as the raw materials for your writing.

Two useful habits for ordering experience are journal keeping and creative reading. These two practices keep your material new and fresh for you whether you will eventually use it for poetry, fiction, or creative nonfiction. These practices allow you to gain distance on your life events and your reading so as to use these most fruitfully in your writing.

Journal Keeping

The journal is the lifeblood of your writing. What goes into it, I think, should be private, because if it is graded, if someone else has access to it, you are going to write, at least in part, for that reader. But you need the raw power of unedited experience that you will then shape into poetry or prose. Journals work best if the only censor is you, writing down what you find most interesting and sad and beautiful about your life and observations, answerable to no one.

What kind of thing goes into a creative writing journal? Such a journal is not the same as an ordinary diary, which may list appointments and deadlines—"History project due! Don't forget Bobby's b'day." This is not to say that the journal of daily activities cannot stimulate some good writing, as often it does, just by reminding the diarist of something that has happened. The journal isn't like the personal diary of dates and relationships, either, with every detail of a date or a spat. These can generate writing, too. But your *writing journal* consists of things that you might like to write about—events and observations that you think, because of the way they interest you, might have interest for others. They may be the most ordinary of events. Here is an example of mine:

> *Tonight we went to visit J's mother in the Alzheimer's wing. The place is said to be one of the best facilities in the country. I had never been there before—it was bright and colorful, like a kindergarten, with colored leaves pasted on the wall—I guess they were trying to remind the residents it was fall, even though here in Texas the leaves are never those colors. No one seemed to be in communication with anyone else, though one old woman with purple bruised arms grabbed and me and kept saying, "Look what they did to me!" And on the schedule for the day it said "Three o'clock: Memory." Wonder what that is. Hope I never end up in a place like that, although I can't think of many better alternatives for people with Alzheimer's—the other way to go would be to be a tremendous nuisance for your children, and disrupt their lives.*

There's nothing very original or striking here, just an observation and a reflection. But this kind of material is still useful to the writer. Everything seen and thought about may be useful. So, indulge yourself a little. Go out and buy a good blank book—maybe one that is made of lush felt, or one that is bound in wood, or one that is so big you think it must be intended for sketching, not writing. Put your name on it. Leaf through it, letting its very emptiness make you reach for your pen. Then start to write.

I recommend that students make daily entries, although not everyone uses writing journals in this way. But something in each day's experience is poem-worthy, or salvageable for fiction, and if you know that you have to write something daily, you tend to be more observant. For instance, you witness an argument between a gas station attendant and an old lady, and because of the journal, you notice what each says, what each is wearing, what time of day it is, what the weather is. Later you might be writing a short story with a similar argument in it, and because of your journal, you are able to create a true-to-life dialogue. Or you pass a local "adult video store" and notice a crowd there—a group of young people are marching outside bearing signs that read, "BOYCOTT HELL." This situation interests you, so you write it down.

What each person puts into a creative writing journal is different. The suggestions given here are to be considered as advice, not as an assignment.

Make a ritual of your journal keeping, taking a particular time each day to sit down and enter your thoughts and reflections. It is helpful to carry a little notebook with you, to jot down things you want to enter but may forget—an overheard conversation, the colors of new leaves, an expression on someone's face. It is best, though, not to make yourself write a certain amount daily—say, a page—because this is not supposed to be a chore. You love words, remember? But if you have to produce 250 of them every evening before you sleep, you may love them less.

There are styles of journal keeping, appropriate for different writers and different circumstances. Here are a few of them for you to think about. To select one style or to come up with your own, you need to decide why you are keeping the journal and how you want to use it. Some writers keep two journals, or even more, for different purposes. I keep two, an electronic journal and a journal handwritten in a cloth-covered blank book. The electronic one I do automatically as I check the e-mail—jotting down chores, projects, social events, and so on. Sometimes I launch into a mini-essay on something suggested by one of the entries—Thanksgiving, for instance, which is ordinarily my least favorite holiday, or shopping in the mall. The handwritten one is much more personal, containing details of a long-term friendship or musings about intimate family matters. I write in it only when compelled to; one of these little books lasted eight years. Maybe the act of handwriting, the loops and bumps of it that can be identified by a handwriting expert as yours, compels the personal. I don't know. I use both diaries for creative writing, but most of my ideas come from the cloth-covered one.

Following are some styles of journal-keeping:

1. Keep a large spiral notebook as a journal, making entries two or three times a week. On the right side, jot down events that struck you as meaningful or interesting. Use the left as an informal scrapbook. Stick in it quotations, cartoons, or photographs that catch your attention. Look through your family's pile of discarded magazines for intriguing bits to add.

2. Buy two different colored blank books. Use one to record observations or scenes that you observe, and the other to describe reflections or meditations. Write daily in at least one. Every so often, take time to read them both together, to see what your observant and your reflective self made of a certain situation.

3. Create an imaginary addressee for your journal—the addressee may be an imagined counselor, a parent, or a friend. Of course, your correspondent may be based on a real person. When you record events and reflections, imagine yourself explaining them to this individual. Your journal, then, will become a long series of letters, explaining your life experiences to a chosen

reader. You can also simply name your journal. Anne Frank began entries in her world-famous Holocaust diary with a simple "Dear Kitty."

4. A trick to help keep the journal going is to set yourself a daily number of minutes to write, say five or ten. This method works best with electronic journals, in which you can write a great deal in a small time. Set a timer, and then write without stopping until it rings. You don't have to stop if you don't want to or if you are in the middle of a good reflection.

5. Another trick is to keep two journals, a "private" one and a "public" one. Write in the private one daily, putting down thoughts and observations without censoring anything. Write in the public one once a week, selecting thoughts from the private one, shaping them and polishing them slightly. Share the public one with your instructor. This sharing will serve as your first step in the creation of poems, fiction pieces, or creative nonfiction.

6. Keep a journal that you have defined thematically. For instance, if you are particularly interested in environmental issues, keep a journal in which everything that you hear, read, and do concerning the environment is recorded. Sometimes, of course, writers use this technique unintentionally— they are so preoccupied with an issue that the issue shapes their observations. Doing it consciously allows you to be aware of your selection process. This kind of journal is often suited to creative nonfiction writing, when the goal of the writer is not autobiography but commentary.

7. Keep an image journal. On one side, paste any ads, photos, designs, and the like that interest you. Photocopy anything graphic that stimulates your imagination. You may also wish to download interesting images from the Internet. Write a brief analysis on the other side, keeping track of the source of the image and reminding yourself why you liked it or were compelled by it. Photos, paintings, cartoons, diagrams, ads—these may evoke verbal images that will be of value in your writing. A big scrapbook is best for this kind of "journal." In my scrapbook, I have some illustrations from old German children's books that I inherited when they were falling apart. They are magical in their poem-drawing power. The stories in the original were heavily cautionary tales: parents did not shy away from terrifying their children into obedience. One illustration showed a giant with huge scissors who rushed into the rooms of children while they sucked their thumbs and who then snipped off the thumbs. This illustration of what happened to thumb-suckers suggested a sequence of poems on fear and nightmare. "Struwwelpeter," or "Sloppy Peter," was a sort of child demon of disorder—if the German child didn't brush his or her teeth or wash his or her hands all the time, then the child would turn into Struwwelpeter. These figures and others that may have more appeal to you are now available on the net—try some net-surfing to fill out your scrapbook. Some will tap the wells of inspiration. What kinds of threats and images were used to keep children in line during your own childhood?

8. In addition to your regular entries, keep track of your intellectual development in your diary—write down the titles of books read, ideas mulled over, attitudes modified. Now and then ask yourself what individuals or events were most in-

fluential in defining your intellectual growth, and in what ways. This kind of reflection serves well in both creative nonfiction and fiction.

9. Just keep a ratty old spiral notebook around, in which you write anything, at any time.

It is useful to leave your journal, or at least a pen and paper, beside your bed when you go to sleep—then you can write down your dreams before they escape. Often some excellent poems come from dreams, because the dreams contain powerful shared symbols, and you can evoke these figures, or archetypes, in your readers through the representation of those you find in your dreams.

Most professional writers keep journals, if we are to believe what they say in their essays and interviews. Reading the accounts of what they have witnessed and have done brings back the emotion, which is then, as Wordsworth suggested, "recollected in tranquility," or at least with some perspective on the emotion-causing event. You may be able to write better, more subtle, and more rewarding poems and stories if you don't rush to your computer and write out every noteworthy experience as a sketch or poem, but rather first write in your journal, and then reflect on the meaning of the experience and compare it with your other life experiences, and then use it as the source of your essay, story, or poem.

See what poet Ingrid Wendt has done with an experience she recorded in her journal. This poem forms part of her book *Moving the House*, which is a sequence of poems that turns the experience described in the title—the actual transportation of a house to a new location—into a mythic event. Wendt commented that the making of the event into poetry helped her find the positive value in what had been a negative experience—a notion to be discussed later.

.... **Ingrid Wendt**

*Feeling Dry**

> To want to write, but to lack words.
> More accurately, to lack some
> thing to feel.
>
> This unpainted
> desk, cars outside
> proving themselves on the hill,
> smoke from burning fields
> slipping unnoticed under the sun
> until someone drowns
> in his own breath.

*Ingrid Wendt, "Feeling Dry" from *Moving the House*, BOA Editions, Brockport, NY. © 1980 by Ingrid Wendt. Reprinted by permission of the author.

To listen for some wind.

To feel responsible for listening
and be unmoved, an air sock
limp as an unfilled dunce's cap
waiting some change in the weather,
something full as the river
you fished last weekend
without luck

and then swimming saw
the whitefish
grazing on stones

the flickering trout steady
as mobiles suspended
on more levels
than you thought water
could contain.

Look at the images that Wendt finds to describe listening and waiting, and the opposition between dryness and water. Notice also how she links the pictures so fluidly that the poem reads seamlessly, liquidly one might say. The reader is invited to flow through the poem.

  Look, too, at the images in another professionally written poem based on a life experience of the poet John Gilgun.

.... **John Gilgun**

*Zachary Enters**

Zachary Scott Wilson-Long, born June 18, 1999.

Little boy

Entering the great safe pond of your mother's arms
Your butterfly eyes
Your wax white hands

Held by the singing in your blood
Transfixed by visions of a white wall
Rocked in the bee buzz of trance

*John Gilgun, "Zachary Enters" is reprinted by permission of the author.

Your likeness in the mirror
Swans lifting themselves from the horizon
Half glimpses of the sea, of waterfalls

And now time and now machines and now the world.

It's a great trick to be able to get into the sensibility or awareness of someone else; how does Gilgun represent the sensibility of the newborn? What kinds of pictures does he use? What do you think it is like to be a preverbal infant? You might yourself want to try a poem or a fictional sketch on this subject.

In reading poems, look at the way pictures convey the feelings that the writer wishes to share, and then ask yourself what pictures keep cropping up in your journals and which images from your experience have the most power.

So, it makes sense to consider that a good first step to becoming a published creative writer is to work on private writing. For a week, try keeping a journal religiously, in addition to doing your regular assignments. Choose one of the suggestions for journal keeping, and then get started. Use the writing to hone your observation skills and to work on your vocabulary. For example, you are awakened in the morning by birds in the trees: what birds? what trees? Ask questions and look things up, perhaps using the journal's last page to list new words and their meanings. If it is consistent with your class assignments, keep a journal for a week without attempting any other kind of writing. Then use your journal materials to write your first class assignment.

Here is my poem based on the visit to the Alzheimer's ward. It was prompted several weeks later by the journal entry. When I returned to the journal, I wished I had put down more: the name of the place, the impression I got approaching the large building, and so on. But still there was enough for the poem.

··

*In the Alzheimer's Ward**

Well-lit, a giant colorful playpen,
bright fish in huge aquariums
and tropical birds in cages big as windows.

Old children sit in wheelchairs
or on benches, one is curled up tight
in the beanbag chair, like a museum's

*Janet McCann, "In the Alzheimer's Ward" published in *New Letters,* 1984. Reprinted by permission of the author.

display of birth. A posted schedule
presumably for visitors and staff,
announces *3 o'clock, memory.*

After the television hour, after nap,
well before dinner, they will have memory.
This is the best Alzheimer's ward

in the country, a visitor
murmurs. Before nap, after television,
daily, comes memory. A sweet-faced woman

sits carefully upright with an armful of shoes:
They have forgotten them,
I will keep them for them, they leave them

everywhere. Another woman shows her spotty,
flaky arms, pulls at her face, says *Look,*
look what they did to me, it is a crime.

But most are silent. Still, at three o'clock
they will have memory. At three o'clock
the memory cheerleader will come prancing in.

Mother, she will say slowly, gesturing,
Father. Home. Husband. Wife. Children.
But surely, surely it is better not to remember,

to look at the bright wings, the sleek fish,
to hold the teddy bears sitting around on tables
(that belong to no one in this communist country)

and watch the clock hands move? But the memory cheerleader
comes, she will lead them. *Husband, mother, home.*

Looking at the journal entry brought back the experience and reminded me of details I had not recorded. But reading the journal especially centered me on the part of the experience that had most struck me: the notice "Three o'clock: Memory" on the schedule of events.

In addition to journal keeping, creative reading will help you write. You may want to keep an additional journal for responses to reading. Or you can integrate your reading observations with your regular journal, perhaps dividing up the pages as in the seventh suggestion on page 4, but instead of writing an expansion of the daily observation on the right side, you would write about your readings.

Creative Reading _____

We tend to think of reading as a passive activity, but it isn't—it is not the same thing as sitting in front of the television, at the mercy of the screen, even timing Coke and bathroom breaks to coincide with commercials. Reading is active. You determine the pace of the reading, put down the book when you get an idea, go look out the window, and come back to the book, which is patiently waiting for you. You read yourself into the story, if you wish, and on your terms. The pictures that come into your head while you read are your own, evoked by the book but not controlled by it—which is one reason I prefer reading even Stephen King to seeing the movies made from his novels (OK, unless the movie is *The Shining*).

Consider that the reading experience is based not merely on the text on a page but on you—where and how you are as a reader. You can read even more creatively, or actively, by being aware of your freedom as a reader and profiting from it. For instance, you may deliberately pull everything that impinges on the text right into it. You may take note of the circumstances of your reading, the reading environment: lying on a lounge chair on the lawn reading until dark, curled up on a featherbed, or sitting in the library among other people who are studying calculus or making dates. In a restaurant waiting for a friend, accompanied by a book of poetry, you might let the day and time into the book. Images of the poetry may combine with scenes from the restaurant, making a new poem that comments on the old one, on the scene, or on both.

Gary Snyder's "Milton by Firelight" is a poem based on a creative reading experience. What sense of the narrator do you get from his reaction to reading Milton by firelight?

.... **Gary Snyder**

*Milton by Firelight**

(Piute Creek, August 1955)

"Oh, what do mine eyes with grief behold?"
Working with an old
Singlejack miner, who can sense
The vein and cleavage
In the very guts of rock, can
Blast granite, build

---

*"Milton by Firelight" from *No Nature* by Gary Snyder, copyright © 1992 by Gary Snyder. Used by permission of Pantheon Books, a division of Random House, Inc.

Switchbacks that last for years
Under the beat of snow, thaw, mule-hooves.
What use, Milton, a silly story
Of our lost general parents, eaters of fruit?

The Indian, the chainsaw boy,
And a string of mules
Come riding down to camp
Hungry for tomatoes and green apples.
Sleeping in saddle-blankets
Under a bright night-sky
Han River slantwise by morning.
Jays squall
Coffee boils

In ten thousand years the Sierras
Will be dry and dead, home of the scorpion.
Ice-scratched slabs and bent trees.
No paradise, no fall,
Only the weathering land
The wheeling sky,
Man, with his Satan
Scouring the chaos of the mind.
Oh Hell!

Fire down
Too dark to read, miles from a road
The bell-mare clangs in the meadow
That packed dirt for a fill-in
Scrambling through loose rocks
On an old trail
All of a summer's day.

The issue is not whether you share this view of Milton but rather how you understand this poem, in which a particular narrator interacted with a certain text. You get a sense of what the speaker is like, what kind of reading the speaker would find more appropriate to his or her circumstances. (Do you think that this same sort of situation would come about from the speaker's reading Shakespeare by firelight? Would he or she be able to dismiss Shakespeare as irrelevant to someone who lived close to nature, doing hard, rough work? Why, or why not?)

Another kind of creative reading might be thought of as creative research, or spontaneous research. This kind of reading grows from your interests and inclinations; it is not assigned. People of intellectual curiosity do it all the time, and much of your websurfing is this kind of creative reading. Your explorations are unlimited; you follow the links as your imagination and the screen dictate.

This is not the same kind of reading as what you do for your area of specialization. It goes without saying that writers need to read what is being written now in their genre of poetry, fiction, or creative nonfiction. People often do write in a vacuum, writing poem after poem, for instance, without knowing anything about what poetry has come to be. They may think of Robert Frost as being the last poet. This kind of intellectual isolationism usually—granted, not always—results in poetry that has little appeal to a sophisticated reader. But your keeping up with current movements and individual writers is not what this kind of creative reading is about.

Rather, you focus on what appeals to you, set up your own reading program that informs you in your chosen areas, and keep track of this reading so that when you choose to write, you know where to look. You deliberately don't rule out anything as possible source material. For instance, you have an observation recorded in your journal from your trip to a friend's home in Florida over spring break. While you were bird-watching, you saw something fly by so high that you could hardly see it. You picked up the binoculars and took a look—that's quite a bird, you thought, high and fierce like that, and so you looked it up in your friend's bird book and found that it was a peregrine falcon. You had never seen a falcon before, and the book said that there aren't many of that kind of falcon left; DDT and other forms of pesticides and pollution have killed most of them. Now, just this morning, you are reading along in your Modern Poetry class, and the images of destruction in William Butler Yeats's poem "The Second Coming" catch your eye. The poem is about a second coming, not of Jesus Christ, but of a monster, an Antichrist. All sorts of bad omens announce this coming, including a falcon reference—the tamed bird, always obedient to its master, "cannot hear the falconer."

The bird that you saw in Florida arises again in your mind. You realize then, that you want to know more about falcons, so you go to the library after the class is over to find out more about the bird. You check the "falcon" entries in the card catalog or the on-line catalog—and you remember Shakespeare's many references to the sport of falconry, and so you look up a concordance to Shakespeare to find out where some of them are. You check out a basic book on falconry and falcons—maybe Mitchell and Speedy's *Introducing Falconry*. You also look up the falcon in reference works on myth and symbol. You look at poems about falcons—maybe you are especially drawn to Gerard Manley Hopkins's "The Windhover" and Robert Duncan's "I would be a falcon." Although these two poems are radically dissimilar, they both appeal to you.

You read bits and pieces from all these sources, and you look at the available pictures, and you remember how the bird looked in the air, and then you write. This project is a poem. When you have finished your draft, or before, you write down in your reading notebook all the sources you have consulted. It may turn out that you aren't completely satisfied with your poem, so that you want to go back to the sources again. Often a poem written in this way has sections, maybe even with different forms: a section of blank verse, a section of three-line stanzas, a long narrative loop in the most free of free verse. You may want to throw in sentences taken from the descriptions in the book—identifying these quotations, of course. Epigraphs—quotations that begin a literary work—often enrich a piece of writing. (In a poem, the epigraph ordinarily follows the title.)

So—whatever subject catches your interest, look it up. Start with basic, obvious sources: encyclopedias, dictionaries of symbols, mythologies. Move outward in whatever direction feels right. This kind of research is great fun for the traditional researcher, because there are no rules. But do keep a record of all the sources that you consulted. You may want to photocopy bits and pieces of information to stick into your reading journal. After you have looked up some facts, then look into fable, fiction, and poetry. What you are doing is hooking your own experience and interest into history and myth. The sources that you tap in this way will empower your writing.

The writer can easily invent a format for a creative reading journal. One way of keeping the material together is to begin by identifying the motivating incident for the research, then to list the sources read, and finally to clip or paste in the most intriguing of the research results. These steps may be followed by a brief, informal bibliography of other sources that might be consulted if the project is finally followed up and overflows the boundaries of your original sources.

Although I don't ask students for a full-scale creative reading journal, I do require two researched poems over the course of the semester. Also, the students must document the research process and turn in the documentation in the format previously described. Students often find this task—researching poems and writing them this way—either the most satisfying or the most frustrating of the course. The exercise helps new poets realize that poetry is not just the expression of personal emotion, however important emotion is to poetry. Of course, fiction and creative nonfiction writing often demand just research, as is to be expected. But poetry too may benefit from an infusion of facts that you have hunted down and selected.

Your journal keeping and your reading may merge and diverge, both feeding on and nourishing each other. What will profit ultimately, though, from all these exchanges and interchanges, is your writing.

EXERCISES

1. Set up a journal according to your instructor's specifications. Allow yourself a regular writing time.

2. After keeping your journal for a week or so, choose some topic in it on which to do some rough, unstructured research. Find and record ten different sources that you might consult if you were to write on this topic. Make the sources very divergent: try to include poetry, fiction, encyclopedias, and books of very different natures.

3. Write a short poem or prose sketch that uses at least two of your sources.

4. Find a poem written in the last ten years that you find exciting. Write a page in your journal about why you like this poem. Exchange the poem with someone else in the class; then write about your classmate's find.

5. Cut out newspaper stories of events that you find most illustrative of injustice over a two-week period. Put these in your journal, together with a sentence or two of reaction. After you have assembled three or four of these stories, look them over, and then let the one that still has the strongest emotional effect be the basis of a poem.

6. Look at illustrations from an old children's book, either on the Web or in the special collections of your library. Reflect on the most striking image that you find, and then write a poem or a paragraph about it.

Critical Reading

Of course, a writer doesn't read a piece the way that a student would read it for a literature class. The writer wants to know how the piece causes the effect it does, how the nuts and bolts are used to hold the story together. Like anyone else who reads for pleasure, the writer reacts first to what she or he reads. Then, however, comes analysis, a careful deconstruction to see the means by which the story or poem "works"—or why it doesn't work. The reader for a basic literature class is usually looking for theme, symbol, and so forth, and any judgment may be private. You, as a writer, are looking for flaws as well as for successful devices.

READING POETRY AS A POET

First, you may think "Wow," maybe, or perhaps "Ugh." Or I wonder what that was all about? You don't want to become so analytical that you don't allow this first rush of feeling or don't heed what your literary gut is telling you. But you don't want to make your first impression the only one, either.

Being involved in the process of writing, you don't want to be too quick to dismiss something—to say that this poem is too obscure, or is too obvious, or represents a position that you don't like, or—as is very common—that this isn't what you think of as poetry. You should read the poem again as open-mindedly as you can, attempting to enter it. If it is completely closed to you, you might do a little simple research. For instance, if the poem seems to rely heavily on a Greek myth or on a character whom you aren't familiar with or have forgotten, you could look up the story in a mythology book, or even on the Web. Sometimes the key to a simple allusion is all you need to enter the world of the poem. You have to know the story of Leda and the swan to appreciate William Butler Yeats's poem "Leda and the Swan," but that basic information is all you require to enter this complex poem with its variety of rich interpretations.

Readers have a tendency to be more patient with older poems than with new ones, figuring, perhaps, that the works of T. S. Eliot had been tried and tested before they entered the canon of great poetry, whereas a new writer hasn't yet passed any test, the writer just might be producing gibberish. But it is valuable to let the new work have a chance to show its meaning, too.

Here are two short pieces by poet Jan Lee Ande. Read them and just react— and then analyze your reactions.

.... **Jan Lee Ande**

*Contemplation**

A few angels and archangels come here for the view,
and the illusion of time ticking on its way.
On the outstretched concrete arms of Christ the Redeemer
in Rio de Janeiro, they find a familiar perch.

Here the hallowed laws of heaven are above
and the ways of the people below.
Poised on the motionless fingers, they take a good
long look at the world and all of its yearnings.
Should anyone pause and reflect on their presence,
they keep messages tucked in their tidy sleeves
or folded neatly beneath wings.

Some things are named for them and these
they find pleasing: angel food cake light as clouds,
the angel network with its proclamation of good deeds,
and the angel fishes swimming inside a glass globe
with their compressed bodies and sad mouths.

Before leaving this world, they may descend
Angel Falls (a trip to Venezuela quick as a thought
in the mind's eye) and soon they are sailing
over the world's longest waterfall—the rush
of water whipping their wings,
the white froth wild as a multitude of tongues.

*Jan Lee Ande, "Contemplation," Chester H. Jones Foundation, National Poetry Competition, 1999 Anthology. Reprinted by permission of the author.

Jan Lee Ande

*World Tree**

If you are lost in the world, bewildered
in the middle ground between heaven
and earth, stand here. Say: sequoia,
redwood, banyan. Say: El Gigante and
bristlecone pine.

Take off your shoes and let the moist soil
rise between your toes. Your feet
are rootstock and seedling. Listen to the words
thrummed in sap and bark.

Capture daylight in your thin branches.
Green leaves tendril down from your crown.
If you stand very still, sparrows come
to rest. You know them—the grays
and the browns—one by one.

You learn to call the underworld,
all creatures, and the gods your clan.
You have found your way.
For all that wanders, first lost and alone,
and then takes a stand, comes at last
to the center.

What is the poet doing in both of the poems? These two poems are motivated and inspired by the poet's spiritual values. Does her approach speak to you? What would your own sense of the spiritual prompt you to write, in a poem or an essay?

Another way of giving a new poem a chance is either to read it aloud or to listen to someone else read it. Maybe it is a performance poem that needs an audible voice to achieve its full effect. And you may hear things through your physical ear that you missed when looking at the poem on the page, especially if you do not read poetry a lot and have not yet trained your mind's ear.

*Jan Lee Ande, "World Tree," *Nimrod: International Journal,* Vol. 41, No. 1, Fall/Winter 1997. Reprinted by permission of the author.

Once you have done your best to enter the poem, you should ask some questions, not necessarily in any particular order. What is there about the poem that accounts for your reaction? If you liked the poem, you are now well on the way in your analysis. What makes this piece a poem? Traditionally, poetry had rhyme and rhythm, but of course a lot of poetry now is not traditional. Poetry, though, has something condensed about it—it reverberates instead of merely stating. And poetry is in some sense formal, even if it is not in any way traditional. That is, the poet has paid some attention to the positioning of the words on the page. The pattern, or apparent lack of pattern, is part of the poem. Thus, you look to see how the appearance of this poem and the elements of poetry that you can easily identify, such as repetition and rhyme, contribute to its effect.

What is there about the meaning and the surface of the poem that appeals to you? What is the poem doing—sharing an experience, teaching through metaphor, illuminating something hidden, exposing injustice? How do the images in the poem help you experience the theme?

Part of the appeal of a poem is often the thrill of the original: something is being done or shown in some new way, through fresh language and unexpected combinations. Can you find examples of these techniques in the following poem?

.... **Kathleen Hart**

*The Third Way**

Did you see the front page of the *Times?*
Picture of two galaxies colliding. We're
watching it for practice since our own
is also colliding with another. Impact
should occur in about three billion years.
Do I need another death scene to imagine?

Can you look at that picture and imagine
yourself in a galaxy? Can you imagine ours?
Once I'm dust—and aren't I dust now,
floating around in some world? I know I'll die of
1) a disease and know it or 2) suddenly
and not know it.

*Kathleen Hart, "The Third Way" is reprinted by permission of the author.

> But look: This morning the moon followed me
> almost the whole way on my drive to work,
> all belly and not embarrassed, floating
> through the galaxy and tethered to me as if she
> had been expecting me for three billion years
> tugging on me to die a third way,
> to die of fierce love.

Poets often take ideas personally; that is, they look at theoretical concepts and abstract ideas and "see" these as immediate parts of their own lives and those of others—which in a sense, of course, they are. How does the Hart poem accomplish this purpose? Can you think of natural laws that seem to have some personal application?

If you feel that something you have read is a fine poem, a great poem even, you may think, "Oh, if only I had written that!" That is a good thought, because it helps you look at the nuts and bolts. How did the writer create the work? Is there anything that identifies itself as the basic incident, reading, myth, or image that sparked the rest of the poem? One approach to the poem is to write down the most compelling lines and to consider why you like them. And then you might want to use the poem as a stimulus for writing immediately, using a line or two from the original as an epigraph for your poem, or answering the poem in some way.

Consider the following pair of poems, the first being one of the most famous poems in English, and the second, a contemporary response to it. Annie Finch's poem is a highly skilled piece based on creative reading.

.... **Andrew Marvell**

To His Coy Mistress

> Had we but World enough, and Time,
> This coyness, Lady, were no crime.
> We would sit down, and think which way
> To walk, and pass our long Love's Day.
> Thou by the Indian Ganges side.
> Should'st Rubies find: I by the Tide
> Of Humber would complain. I would
> Love you ten years before the Flood:
> And you should if you please refuse
> Till the Conversion of the Jews.
> My vegetable Love should grow

Vaster then Empires, and more slow.
An hundred years should go to praise
Thine Eyes, and on thy Forehead Gaze.
Two hundred to adore each Breast.
But thirty thousand to the rest.
An Age at least to every part,
And the last Age should show your Heart.
For Lady you deserve this State;
Nor would I love at lower rate.
But at my back I always hear
Time's winged Chariot hurrying near:
And yonder all before us lie
Deserts of vast Eternity.
Thy Beauty shall no more be found;
Nor, in thy marble Vault, shall sound
My echoing Song: then Worms shall try
That long preserv'd Virginity:
And your quaint Honour turn to dust;
And into ashes all my Lust.
The Grave's a fine and private place,
But none I think do there embrace.
Now therefore, while the youthful hew
Sits on thy skin like morning dew,
And while thy willing Soul transpires
At every pore with instant Fires,
Now let us sport us while we may;
And now, like am'rous birds of prey,
Rather at once our Time devour,
Than languish in his slow-chapt pow'r.
Let us roll all our Strength, and all
Our sweetness, up into one Ball:
And tear our Pleasures with rough strife,
Thorough the Iron gates of Life.
Thus, though we cannot make our Sun
Stand still, yet we will make him run.

Even if you aren't familiar with every word in the poem, you certainly un-derstand the basic idea—that this is a seduction poem, that the speaker is trying to make his beloved less reluctant to accept his embraces by focusing her atten-tion on the fact that they both must eventually die. In the seventeenth century, this type of seduction poem, called a "carpe diem," or "seize the day" poem, was very popular.

Annie Finch

....

*Coy Mistress**

(in answer to the poem by Andrew Marvell)

Sir, I am not a bird of prey:
a Lady does not seize the day.
I trust that brief Time will unfold
our youth, before he makes us old.
How could we two write lines of rhyme
were we not fond of numbered Time
and grateful to the vast and sweet
trials his days will make us meet?
The Grave's not just the body's curse;
no skeleton can pen a verse!
So while this numbered World we see,
let's sweeten Time with poetry,
and Time, in turn, may sweeten Love
and give us time our love to prove.
You've praised my eyes, forehead, breast:
you've all our lives to praise the rest.

Finch's answer to Marvell argues that some of his basic assumptions are incorrect, especially the one that assumes that a relationship is necessarily a physical thing. How does Marvell's poem imagine women to be? How does Finch's?

Have you recently read an older poem that you found to grate on your sensibilities in some way because of the differences in values between then and now, or more specifically, between you and the writer? If so, your response may generate a new poem.

If you don't like a poem at all, even after a couple of readings, ask yourself why not. If you don't understand a poem, does it still appeal in some way? You don't have to be able to explain a poem away to enjoy it. Perhaps the poem is clichéd in language and thought. Or perhaps it expresses a perspective for which you simply cannot feel empathy. If it is a good poem and if you are a skilled reader, you may be able to enter the poem despite the unsympathetic position. You may, as I do, "like" the Marvell poem without in any way sharing his attitude. But in any case, knowing why you like a poem will help you articulate your concept of good poetry.

*"Coy Mistress" from *Eve,* by Annie Finch, Story Line Press, 1997. Reprinted by permission of the author.

READING FICTION AS A STORY WRITER

Even in the initial reading of a story, fiction writers often tend to withhold something from the experience—they are automatically looking for clues to character, to event. The story writer does not wish to be seduced or tricked into accepting something he or she knows is flawed. But it may be better to try to suspend criticism on the first reading, to see how the story would work for a nonwriter. As you would in reading poetry, first react—then analyze.

If the story works, what is good about it? Which of the elements of fiction seem to predominate? Is the story good because some character is hyperreal, because you feel that you know this character? Then the story is character-driven. Is the story good because of the suspense, the interest in what happened that kept you reading? Then the story may be plot-driven. Ask yourself what the best elements of the story are and how they are put together.

The story may be experimental, postmodern. We expect certain things from stories, and these are the narrative conventions. We expect the engagement, conflict, and resolution to occur in some kind of meaningful time frame; we expect coherence. We expect the point of view to be maintained; we don't expect logical oddities, such as the first-person narrator's getting himself killed on the last page, or even in the middle, muddling the question of who told the story. But in experimental fiction, all the conventions are subject to deliberate violation, bringing up questions about what is narrative, and by extension, what is truth. If you are reading a postmodern story, you may like it for different reasons: the sustained emotionless tone, the intrusion of the author into the story, the violation of expectations. To some extent, the story "Some of Us Had Been Threatening Our Friend Colby," which follows, is experimental narrative. Does this story violate your expectations? Do you like it?

We expect ordinarily to be able to place the characters and their community within our understanding of how society operates.

What have the beginning and ending to do with your appreciation of the story? If the beginning just hooks you in, how does it do so? Is the ending satisfying? Look at the beginning and the end of "Colby." Are you surprised at the ending? How does what is *not said*—play a large part in this story's effect?

After you have read about fiction and analyzed it in class, you will have a lot of specific areas to look at, particularly the techniques that the writers use to draw the reader in, get from one action to another, imply character, subtly fill in needed background events, and maintain a single tone from beginning to end. You will also read creative nonfiction as a writer, but what you will look for depends strongly on the kind of essay you are reading. Mostly, you will look at successful pieces to see how they are put together, what details are chosen to support the overall impression, and how the writer often telegraphs, rather than states, a judgment.

Can you read creatively and critically at once? Possibly not. Therefore, read creatively first, and enjoy the experience of reading and the connection the story makes with your own life experience. Then go back and read critically. In reading as well as in writing, the pleasure tends to come first, with discovery or invention. The work comes next, with analysis or design. This initial fiction reading has been chosen for its odd combination of the real and the bizarre. Discuss it as a writer: How is it constructed? Is it suspenseful? How is character development accomplished, or are these characters totally undeveloped? What do you think about this story?

.... **Donald Barthelme**

Some of Us Had Been Threatening Our Friend Colby*

Some of us had been threatening our friend Colby for a long time, because of the way he had been behaving. And now he'd gone too far, so we decided to hang him. Colby argued that just because he had gone too far (he did not deny that he had gone too far) did not mean that he should be subjected to hanging. Going too far, he said, was something everybody did sometimes. We didn't pay much attention to this argument. We asked him what sort of music he would like played at the hanging. He said he'd think about it but it would take him a while to decide. I pointed out that we'd have to know soon, because Howard, who is a conductor, would have to hire and rehearse the musicians and he couldn't begin until he knew what the music was going to be. Colby said he'd always been fond of Ives's Fourth Symphony. Howard said that this was a "delaying tactic" and that everybody knew that the Ives was almost impossible to perform and would involve weeks of rehearsal, and that the size of the orchestra and chorus would put us way over the music budget. "Be reasonable," he said to Colby. Colby said he'd try to think of something a little less exacting.

Hugh was worried about the wording of the invitations. What if one of them fell into the hands of the authorities? Hanging Colby was doubtless against the law, and if the authorities learned in advance what the plan was they would very likely come in and try to mess everything up. I said that although hanging Colby was almost certainly against the law, we had a perfect *moral* right to do so because he was *our* friend, *belonged* to us in various important senses, and he had after all gone too far. We agreed that the invitations would be worded in such a way that the person invited could not know for sure what he was being invited to. We decided to refer to the event as "An Event Involving Mr. Colby Williams." A handsome script was selected from a catalogue and we picked a cream-colored paper.

Magnus said he'd see to having the invitations printed, and wondered whether we should serve drinks. Colby said he thought drinks would be nice but was worried about the expense. We told him kindly that the expense didn't matter, that we were after all his dear friends and if a group of his dear friends couldn't get together and do the thing with a little bit of éclat, why, what was the world coming to? Colby asked if he would be able to have drinks, too, before the event. We said, "Certainly."

The next item of business was the gibbet. None of us knew too much about gibbet design, but Tomas, who is an architect, said he'd look it up in old books and draw the plans. The important thing, as far as he recollected, was that the trapdoor function perfectly. He said that just roughly, counting labor and materials, it shouldn't run us more than four hundred dollars. "Good God!" Howard said. He said what was Tomas figuring on, rosewood? No, just a good grade of pine, Tomas said. Victor asked if unpainted pine wouldn't look kind of "raw," and Tomas replied that he thought it could be stained a dark walnut without too much trouble.

I said that although I thought the whole thing ought to be done really well and all, I also thought four hundred dollars for a gibbet, on top of the expense for the drinks, invitations, musicians, and everything, was a bit steep, and why didn't we just use a tree—a nice-looking oak, or something? I pointed out that since it was going to be a June hanging the trees would be in glorious leaf and that not only would a tree add a kind of "natural" feeling but it was also strictly traditional, especially in the West.

Tomas, who had been sketching gibbets on the backs of envelopes, reminded us that an outdoor hanging always had to contend with the threat of rain. Victor said he liked the idea of doing it outdoors, possibly on the bank of a river but noted that we would have to hold it some distance from the city, which presented the problem of getting the guests, musicians, etc., to the site and then back to town.

At this point everybody looked at Harry, who runs a car-and-truck-rental business. Harry said he thought he could round up enough limousines to take care of that end but that the drivers would have to be paid. The drivers, he pointed out, wouldn't be friends of Colby's and couldn't be expected to donate their services, any more than the bartender or the musicians. He said that he had about ten limousines, which he used mostly for funerals, and that he could probably obtain another dozen by calling around to friends of his in the trade. He said also that if we did it outside, in the open air, we'd better figure on a tent or awning of some kind to cover at least the principals and the orchestra, because if the hanging was being rained on he thought it would look kind of dismal. As between gibbet and tree, he said, he had no particular preferences and he really thought that the choice ought to be left up to Colby, since it was his hanging. Colby said that everybody went too far, sometimes, and weren't we being a little Draconian? Howard said rather sharply that all that had already been discussed, and which did he want, gibbet or tree? Colby asked if he could have a firing squad. No, Howard said, he could not. Howard said a firing squad would just be an ego trip for Colby, the blindfold and last-cigarette bit, and that Colby was in enough hot water already without trying to "upstage" everyone with unnecessary theatrics. Colby said he was sorry, he hadn't meant it that way, he'd take the tree. Tomas crumpled up the gibbet sketches he'd been making, in disgust.

Then the question of the hangman came up. Pete said did we really need a hangman? Because if we used a tree, the noose could be adjusted to the appropriate level and Colby could just jump off something—a chair or stool or something. Besides, Pete said, he very much doubted if there were any free-lance hangmen wandering around the country, now that capital punishment has been done away with absolutely, temporarily, and that we'd probably have to fly one in from England or Spain or one of the South American countries, and even if we did that how could we know in advance that the man was a professional, a real hangman, and not just some money-hungry amateur who might bungle the job and shame us all, in front of everybody? We all agreed then that Colby should just jump off something and that a chair was not what he should jump off of, because that would look, we felt, extremely tacky—some old kitchen chair sitting out there under our beautiful tree. Tomas, who is quite modern in outlook and not afraid of innovation, proposed that Colby be standing on a large round rubber ball ten feet in diameter. This, he said, would afford a sufficient "drop" and would also roll out of the way if Colby suddenly changed his mind after jumping off. He reminded us that by not using a regular hangman we were placing an awful lot of the responsibility for the success of the affair on Colby himself, and that although he was sure Colby would perform creditably and not disgrace his friends at the last minute, still, men have been known to get a little irresolute at times like that, and the ten-foot-round rubber ball, which could probably be fabricated rather cheaply, would insure a "bang-up" production right down to the wire.

At the mention of "wire," Hank, who had been silent all this time, suddenly spoke up and said he wondered if it wouldn't be better if we used wire instead of rope—more efficient and in the end kinder to Colby, he suggested. Colby began looking a little green, and I didn't blame him, because there is something extremely distasteful in thinking about being hanged with wire instead of rope—it gives you sort of a revulsion, when you think about it. I thought it was really quite unpleasant of Hank to be sitting there talking about wire, just when we had solved the problem of what Colby was going to jump off of so neatly, with Tomas's idea about the rubber ball, so I hastily said that wire was out of the question, because it would injure the tree—cut into the branch it was tied to when Colby's full weight hit it—and that in these days of increased respect for the environment, we didn't want that, did we? Colby gave me a grateful look, and the meeting broke up.

Everything went off very smoothly on the day of the event (the music Colby finally picked was standard stuff, Elgar, and it was played very well by Howard and his boys). It didn't rain, the event was well attended, and we didn't run out of Scotch, or anything. The ten-foot rubber ball had been painted a deep green and blended in well with the bucolic setting. The two things I remember best about the whole episode are the grateful look Colby gave me when I said what I said about the wire, and the fact that nobody has ever gone too far again.

Fiction

Writing short stories and writing essays are similar processes, and sometimes when you are reading a work, it is hard to tell exactly where the boundary lines are between fiction and biographical essay. Many of the techniques of the one transfer easily to the other. We look at fiction first because most elements of fiction also apply to many kinds of essays.

Fiction Fundamentals _____

> Writing fiction has developed in me an abiding respect for the unknown in a human lifetime and a sense of where to look for the threads, how to follow, how to connect, find in the thick of the tangle what clear line persists.
>
> —Eudora Welty

Most recreational readers at least think about writing fiction. If you enjoy entering constructed worlds again and again—if you look forward to getting home from work and/or school to pick up a book—you at least think about creating your own fictional universe and inviting others to share it. But you probably cannot just set down the stack of novels you have been reading and then simply write a novel, even if you have formulated a good plot and have an excellent vocabulary. You need to learn the craft first.

From being a reader, you learn a great deal about writing. You learn what can be gained from the attentive reading of others' work. But you don't learn the scaffolding that underlies the completed work, because that is not what gains your attention, even if it is visible. What you need to do is to begin looking for those things that contribute to a story's overall effect. The writer becomes a more aware reader, first reading the story for the sheer enjoyment of participation that makes us readers, then returning to pick it apart. How did the writer create that effect? we ask. How were our expectations manipulated? Why do we care about this character? What hints did the writer plant that the story would come out as it did—hints we aren't supposed to understand, perhaps, until afterward? Some of the traditional areas of literary analysis are named in the following sections, but we will look at them as writers rather than as general readers of literature. In the subsequent discussion, these elements are grouped together in five general classifications: Plot, Setting, Dialogue, Characterization, and Point of View. No element of fiction, of course, can really be disentangled from the others; they are interdependent. But for the sake of discussing them, we will provide some definitions and general suggestions.

Plot: What happens in the story? How do the events tie together? You might want to summarize the plot briefly when you finish a novel or story, just to clarify plot structure in your mind. What kind of stories are plot-driven—that is, what stories can you think of in which plot is clearly the most important element?

Creative writing classes are often taught to downplay plot, considering it far less important than character, theme, and other elements of fiction. It is true that you don't want a story that is nothing but plot—yet the sequence of events is important to the magic of story. Some of the wonder and delight that we see in a five-year-old's eyes when she asks, "And then what happened?" can be kept for the adult reader through careful attention to plot.

Conflict: What is the story's major conflict? Is it internal—someone struggling with himself or herself—or external—a struggle between people, between one person and society, between two groups? Are there secondary conflicts? How do the conflicts direct the plot? Who, or what, comes out on top, and how does the outcome of the conflict express the theme?

One of the problem areas in first stories is commonly this element of conflict. Often ideas for a story are based on a character, and it is then hard to take this person whom we know and involve him in a clear conflict. But conflict and plot are closely allied. Look at the conflicts in the stories you read to see how conflict operates to advance plot.

Pacing: How does the writer make the events seem to occur naturally—that is, without the reader's feeling that he or she is being rushed through events, or that important elements of the action have been left out? How does the writer get the reader from one scene to the next? How can you avoid making the entire first section into a tedious scene-setting for what is about to happen?

The creation of individual scenes, as well as the movement from one to the next in a natural-seeming way, is not easy. You will need to look to see how it has been done in other stories and then to adapt these methods to your own work.

Setting: What has the writer done to give the reader a sense of place? What does "place" do in the story? How can you hone your descriptive skills so that you can write passages that set the scene at the same time that they characterize your protagonist and advance the action?

Your own personal setting may do much to make your stories rich. Think of the scenes most familiar to you—places where you know the name of every tree, where nothing that occurs is surprising to you because everything is very familiar, and where the people have been formed by their environment. These places may be your best settings for stories.

Cultural considerations: Your personal setting includes elements of who you are as well as where you came from. Who are your people? What physical details come to mind when you think of the words "my people"? Do you think in terms of family, ethnicity, social group, or what else? If you had to explain your identification to someone of another group vastly different from yours and you wanted to make your listener feel what it is like to be one of your people, what would you tell the listener?

Personal setting is nowhere more evident than in details of family life. Your Thanksgiving meal or Chanukah celebration or Kwanzaa gathering or Christmas dinner closely observed, heard, smelled, tasted, touched, will provide a vivid impression of you, your family, and your people.

Character: How does the writer characterize? In a good short story, you get a clear impression of what someone is like. How does the writer communicate to you both easily distinguishable character traits, like generosity or stinginess, love of order or tendency to live in disorder, and all the subtle nuances of character? Often when you are reading a story or a novel, especially a novel, you will be able to guess how a character will react. How do you know this—what are the keys hidden in the narrative?

Often a story idea will start with a character, a person you know either well or slightly, or even someone you merely observe. Having come up with a notion of "what she's like," you may then proceed to formulate your plot on that basis: "what she would do if . . . ?"

Dialogue: What part does dialogue play in the story, and how does the writer use dialogue to characterize and to advance the plot? How does a writer make the characters speak differently—if a professor is talking to a high school student, for instance, how does the author show the difference in age and education? How do you make characters sound as though they are speaking normally? Should you try to attempt dialect in your writing?

Theme and meaning: What statement is this story making about how people live (and sometimes die)? What values underlie the story? How does the writer make the presence of these values known? How can you make a short story support your value system without turning it into a sermon? What symbols carry the meaning of this story, and how are these symbols handled—that is, how does the writer make them seem a natural part of the narrative?

Style and voice: What makes it sound as though the same person is telling the entire story—that is, that there is a unified intelligence behind the narrative? What methods does the writer use to sustain the sense that there is "someone home" in the story? Sentence structure is one element of style, of course; you might compare William Faulkner's sentence structure with Ernest Hemingway's, or Adrienne Rich's with Lucille Clifton's to see how important style is in establishing voice.

Point of view: Who is telling the story? Is it told in the first person singular "I" or the third person singular "he" or "she," or even, as is occasionally the case, in the second person "you" or the first person plural "we"? Then, if (as is most common) the story is told in the third person, through whose consciousness are the events slanted? Do we see one person's thoughts? Everyone's thoughts? No one's thoughts? Most modernist fiction sustains a single point of view. Postmodernist, experimental fiction tends to have multiple points of view. You will look at the benefits and disadvantages of both.

Diction: This aspect of fiction writing is, of course, related to all the others. The words that you choose have an important bearing on voice, characterization, setting, symbolism—you name it. Since some considerations of diction are the same whether you are writing either poetry or prose, it may be useful to read about diction in both sections of the text at the same time. When you are reading a favorite story, what distinctive elements of diction can you identify?

Allusions: Just as in poetry, works of fiction often refer, or allude, to other fictional works, to events in history or myth, or to other arts. You need to heighten your awareness of these references in the fiction that you read and to be aware of how you can use allusion profitably in your own work. Sometimes recognizing a reference may simply enrich your appreciation of a work; sometimes, for instance, if you are reading a contemporary representation of the Oedipus story, the allusion is the key to the whole experience.

These considerations, in various combinations, play a part in our discussion of fiction. As you work toward building a short story, it is of major importance to keep reading fiction, all the time. Read whatever you normally read—serious novels, detective stories, science fiction (yes, these three categories sometimes overlap), but read as a writer. Look for the hidden structures that underlie the surface of the story, and then see if you can apply the scaffoldings that you uncover to your own ideas and experience.

EXERCISES ....

What is your favorite short story? Just think about the question for a moment. Don't limit your choices to what you've read in college—look back at the short stories that set you afire earlier, that made you look for more books by that author. Think about stories that you discussed with others, stories that made you want to write your own.

Now, make a list of three favorite works of fiction, either short or long, and for each one, jot down why you like it. Then look at the list of elements of fiction and see whether you can connect specific things that have been done in one or more of these areas with your reasons for liking a particular work. For example, many readers find J. R. R. Tolkein's *Lord of the Rings* trilogy, either with or without the prefatory novel *The Hobbit*, extremely powerful and moving. Why? There is a marvelous plot, of course, as well as the precise, memorable description of a complex invented world. Characterization is detailed and consistent. Although the main characters are hobbits, not humans, they are very humanlike. The sweep and scope of the Tolkein universe is awe-inspiring. Moreover, many readers find something very morally satisfying about the complex adventure and the definitions of good and evil played out in it.

Now, choose one of your selections, preferably one for which you are not familiar with the writer's other works, and then read something else by that author. See whether you like this work too, and if so, determine whether there are any characteristic strengths you can identify in the two works. For instance, if you like Ernest Hemingway's "Hills Like White Elephants," which is included in this chapter, and if the characterization done through understated dialogue is an important element of its appeal, try reading Hemingway's "A Clean, Well Lighted Place," and see whether it has a similar effect, and for the same reasons.

For a first story for you to write or even just to plot out, consider the buddy story. Who has been your longtime best friend, and when did the friendship start, and what has happened to it over the years? Why did you and this individual become friends? Why have you stayed friends? What do you imagine will happen to this friendship—do you think that both of you will stay in touch over the rest of your lifetimes, or not? Why, or why not?

Now, think of an event that strained this friendship. Could you find a story in that? Write the scene that crystallized the strain or tension. It could involve a betrayal or a joking argument that got out of hand or a discovery one of you made about the other that may have strengthened or weakened the bond between you.

Now, this is the hard part—instead of considering what happened as a result of the conflict, think about what, according to the scene you just wrote, you believe would likely have happened. That is, given the personalities of the people involved and the events you have described, create a sequel to the scene that may or may not have any relation to what originally happened.

The most difficult part of writing stories based on reality is letting go of "what happened." It isn't necessarily the case that "what happened" is more realistic as narrative than what you invent, and it usually isn't better fiction. "But it really happened!" is often the novice writer's complaint when accused of lack of realism. Unfortunately, fictional realism is not based on "what happened" but on what would seem likely to happen.

E X A M P L E

Martin and Bob have been best friends for years. Bob undergoes a religious conversion, and after that he feels the need to convert Martin. They still do the same things together, but Bob keeps working religion into it, and Martin starts finding ways to avoid Bob instead of looking forward eagerly to their shared activities.

What happens? The friendship just stops. Both are unhappy with this result. Bob converts Martin. Bob slips back into his old ways, and they pick up the friendship again just as it was. Something else happens.

In this story under consideration, which was written by a sophomore and was based on material in his journal, the two are placed in a dramatic situation in which Bob, forced to choose between his new church and his friendship, chooses the church and suffers greatly because of this choice. In the last scene, Martin attempts to talk Bob back into the old fellowship, but Bob remains a stranger. But in the real situation, nothing dramatic happened: the friendship continued, but somewhat less-ened, and Bob learned to moderate his conversion efforts.

Do you have a buddy story to tell? Most of us do. We are social beings, and at a time when the stability of the family is uncertain, many find much of their security and sense of continuity in friends. And wherever emotion is invested, there are sto-ries. Write out your idea not as a fully developed short story but as a tale. Then you can examine it to see what can be done with it.

In summary, you may think of your first short story as a buddy story. You might consider the following arrangement of events: There will be a dramatic scene that outlines the conflict and introduces the characters. Then there will be another scene that shows what happened as a result of this conflict. Finally, make an outline of this story, so that you and your instructor may then determine whether the story should be written or whether the outline should just be considered an exercise in planning.

Plot

Persons attempting to find a motive in this narrative will be prosecuted; persons attempting to find a moral in it will be banished; persons attempting to find a plot in it will be shot.

By Order of the Author
—Notice beginning Mark Twain's
The Adventures of Huckleberry Finn

Often we begin our project of writing a short story with a plot, which may be what someone has in mind when he or she says, "I have this great idea for a story . . ." This story line may be incomplete, perhaps the merest outline of an event that happened to us or almost happened to us, or that we witnessed. Something in a real situation sparks the imagination. An observation of some odd bit of behavior might lead to the question, "What was that all about?" and the question might be answered by the beginnings of a story.

One student wrote a story based on a two-minute conversation that she overheard at a supermarket, in which a rather grubby cowboy asked an elegantly dressed and coiffed woman how to cook a beef brisket, and she answered him in detail, even writing the cooking time and the required spices on an envelope. The student made the event into a little encounter-between-lonely-people story, ending with the two deciding to terminate what had been a possible friendship because there were so many dangers, and both were, in different ways, afraid.

You might want to make a connection between two events, and this connec-tion may spark a short story. Watching a friend's child play soccer might remind you of your own soccer-playing days, and you might telescope the details of the game with a long-ago game of your own, developing a story about parent-child relationships and the ritual of sports.

Once you have started to write the story, then all the other elements of good writing come into play, and it may be that you must alter the plot that you started with. Your workshop leader might comment, "It was a nice dramatic ending to have her jump out the window that way, but she just wouldn't have done that." It is difficult even to discuss all the elements of the short story separately, because they are so independent. You have to have a plot of some sort, though, or you may write a sketch or vignette—not a short story. Your plot may be subtle and quiet, deliberately not calling attention to itself, or it may be a structure built to spring like a mousetrap. But you have to have one—Mark Twain did too.

What makes a good plot? For a piece of short fiction, say ten to fifteen pages, what constitutes an acceptable sequence of events? It is not easy to generalize; some stories are plot-driven, whereas the plots in others are a minor element in their makeup. Some stories have suspenseful plots, whereas others do not. There aren't any unities that can be followed absolutely: a short story plot may cover a single hour or several years. If the time covered is long, though, the writer will have to use some fancy footwork to keep the story from seeming awkwardly paced.

Let us start by defining plot. One famous definition points out the distinction between plot and simple narrative thus: "The king died and then the queen died is narrative; the king died and then the queen died of grief is a plot." In other words, plot involves a sequence of events with the emphasis on causality. You will be showing the causal relationships between events in your story. If you are a successful plotter, the events will seem naturally to follow from one another, and the outcome, even if a surprise, will seem motivated. But you won't be just "making up a plot" in a vacuum; your plot will be tied in with the whole goal of your story, its theme, its characters, what emotional effect you want it to have on the reader. You should remember that your plot isn't set in stone; it needs to be flexible, responsive to the demands of character and tone.

It is sometimes useful to begin by choosing three of your favorite short stories and then writing brief paragraphs summarizing the plot of each. Never mind if the summary isn't fully complete. For Hemingway's "Hills Like White Elephants," for instance, you might prepare something like this: A man and a young woman are waiting for a train in northern Spain; it is the express from Barcelona to Madrid. She is imaginative, but he is not; she claims that the hills look like white elephants, but he is not entertained. They are clearly expatriates. They drink exotic drinks and wait for the train; as they converse, it is clear that the woman is unhappy, because the man wants her to have an operation that she does not want. Each of the two tries to manipulate the other, but it is suggested by behavior and speech that the man will have his way and that the gap between them is widening.

Now look to see what the actual sequence of events has to do with the story as a whole. Often its main effect is to illuminate character; there is an interplay between the events and the people who experience them so that the reader feels that he or she "knows" the character and that the reader's experience is enriched by the acquaintance. Plot and character together may illustrate some basic truth the writer wishes to represent as a theme. In the case of "Hills Like White Elephants," one might say that plot is very closely dependent on character. Little happens: two people wait for a train. Much is implied about their relationship and about the life they have chosen as expatriates, citizens of everywhere and nowhere. Sometimes in the short story, this truth takes the form of an epiphany, or discovery, made by the main character from the events. This discovery affects the main character in a positive or negative way. In the Hemingway story, nothing much is learned by the main characters, but it is a part of the point of the story that they learn nothing from their experience.

In "Hills Like White Elephants," the relationship between the two characters is perceived as a sterile one, an attraction that provides no real satisfaction to either. Everything the two say and do emphasizes this sterility. As mentioned, nothing much happens in the story, nothing is really decided, but in the conflict between the man and the woman, it is clear that the man wins.

Now it may be time to look at your journal to see whether there are seeds of short stories waiting there. Very often the best sources for short stories are our own lives, rather than something more obviously "made up" or researched. (If you start writing a story set during the Civil War, there are all sorts of ways you may go astray that won't present themselves if you are writing about what is happening here and now, and to people you know.) What have you witnessed recently that is worth writing down? An altercation on the street, perhaps, or an argument between roommates? Why did you find this event noteworthy?

Some events from your journal that might suggest stories are awesome or life-changing, like family deaths. Others are apparently trivial. A really wild party might be an opening, or being falsely accused of something, or some embarrassment—like a situation in which you acted badly through ignorance. (Hasn't that happened to everyone?) These events are just events, though—they are not plots. They become plots when you trace out their chains of causality and show their effect on character. When you do trace them out, you usually find that you have one or more conflicts, which are then resolved one way or another, with certain specific results.

The conflicts generally examined in fiction classes are often divided into groups: conflicts between two people, between one person and society, between a person and nature, and between two aspects of oneself. Of course, more than one conflict can be present in a single story. However, one conflict usually dominates. The story usually begins with some kind of motivating incident that sets the opposing forces in motion, and then the conflict escalates, sometimes in a series of crises, until it is resolved in the climax.

The question that comes up first, though, is this: which of all the events that constitute your "plot" do you put in the story? Do you start with the main character's experiences in childhood? How do you fill in the background necessary to make the narrated events meaningful? Analysis of various stories is likely to produce various constellations of events. But a formula that works is to include a single main scene that describes a sequence of actions taking place in a short time. Examples might be a family fight, a romantic picnic, an ill-starred restaurant dinner. Then you describe another scene that shows what the events in the first scene caused. In the main scene, you can include memories, even flashbacks, to fill in the missing exposition. For a professional example of this method, look again at Donald Barthelme's wonderfully strange and ominous story "Some of Us Had Been Threatening Our Friend Colby" in Chapter 1. Note that the concluding scene actually asks more questions than it answers—but it does conclude the plot. Reread the story, looking at the means by which Barthelme develops suspense—a primary function of plot. Notice the details that propel the question, "And then what happened?" Do you as reader following along the action decide that some turnaround will occur, some revelation that will make sense of the action? What is your response to the story's end?

Now let us consider a plot that came from a student's journal. His journal states that he played his trumpet again, after having set it aside after he finished high school three years ago. His playing was rusty at first, but his old ability began to come back after a while. This in itself is hardly plotworthy, but the student begins to reminisce about how the high school band was very important to him and how his band experience was associated with his first real love, who painfully dumped him for another student during the band trip. He decides to write about that experience, and then about discovering the old trumpet again and finding that he could still play it.

The student now has the beginnings of a plot. Yet he still has work to do. What does he want to do with this sequence of events? What will the theme be? Where will the story end up? But he has a good start. It would help him to look at his conflict. What is it? It may turn out that there are two conflicts: one in the past, between himself and his rival for his girlfriend, and he loses. The other is in the present of the story, and it is between his two selves. One self is optimistic and confident, but the other is negative. The negative self is associated with the loss of the girl, and the negative self doesn't want him to play the trumpet (or do anything well). It is a triumph that the positive self wins out.

You may not want to make your story quite so close to home. To distance it, you can take an area you know well, and then people it with invented characters; or you can take people whom you know well and put them somewhere different. You can begin from a "what if" premise. What if technology takes over in a certain way? What if everyone has a "smart house," in which computers control all the elements of its inhabitants' existence? Your "what if" may even come from your journal—speculation about controlling computers, for instance, might come from a case in which the university computers went down and caused problems for everyone.

Many students want to write science fiction, which is surely an intriguing genre. Its writers need to realize, though, that dialogue, characterization, and the like are of major importance here too—in other words, that a provocative situation or premise does not in itself make a story. If you don't trace out the thread of the plot before beginning the story, you are likely to find that you are stuck in the middle and—if the story isn't due the next day—that you then abandon ship. If the story is an assignment that is due the next day, you may be tempted to write a very bad or an artificial development as an ending. It is usually more satisfactory to begin with the close-to-home story and work outward as you gather experience.

To make a plot out of an incident, you might try following these steps. First, write down the incident. Next, develop characters who are based on the nature of the incident. Then, trace out the plotline on the basis of the characters and incident. Finally, write.

Here is an example, which is adapted from a student's notebook and story. You saw a young woman campus police officer attempt to give a ticket to a tough-looking biker. The biker grabbed her pad of tickets, threw them into the gutter, and sped off. She was calling someone on her cellular phone as you rushed by, late to class, and she did not look happy. As you sat in class, the incident made you think about authority and about male-female relationships. You therefore decided that you would write a story about what had happened.

Fine. Now what?

First, you write down all the details that you remember about what happened. The police officer at first looked very polished, with a lacquered hairdo and a spruce uniform. The biker did not look like a student, but instead like a hoodlum just cutting through campus. The actual action took about ten seconds—the biker stopped not because the officer had whistled but because a car was in the intersection ahead of him; when he saw she was giving him a ticket, he gave her a look of rage, grabbed the ticket book and threw it into the muddy gutter, and then roared off. When the officer was calling for a backup, she looked assaulted—hair in disorder, uniform less sharply pressed—although the biker had not even touched her.

So—why do you want to write a short story about this event? Well, you say, it was amazing that this punk's mistreatment of the officer had so changed your perception of her. But you decide that this change isn't a story. Not enough happened in the incident that you could simply write it down. You have to take it beyond the end of what you saw to make it a story. What could happen, then, to make it a story? You have an incident with a conflict: officer versus biker; biker shows contempt for officer, and apparently wins out. There is less than a story here. Nothing is learned, nothing is demonstrated. But, of course, the adventure doesn't end there. The real-life events will have some consequences that the student will never learn. What might have happened?

The outcome of events is partly determined by the characters involved. What are these two characters like? Let's say that you decide the officer is a sensitive person who has gone into this field for unselfish reasons; she would like to help straighten out young people before it is too late. You name her Clara Wilburn. You decide that despite his looks, the young man, Mike Ripley, is a student—someone with a lot of energy and a hair-trigger temper, abused as a child, always in trouble. He is someone whom the officer would think about as retrievable, if she knew him. Ripley is a person she would particularly want to help.

Now you return mentally to that scene. You imagine that the officer has successfully called in the license plate number and that the young man has been arrested. It turns out that he is out on probation; now the charge against him of interfering with a police officer will send him to jail for years. There is a hearing at which the campus police officer is present; she testifies, and although she recommends that he be given another chance, he is put away. Now, though, she doubts her ability to help people; she decides to give up her position as a police officer and try something else, something without authority.

You have the makings of a story now, since you have two scenes: the scene of the event you saw, and the hearing scene. You decide on a final brief scene to illustrate the effect of the event on the young woman. You are ready to write. You decide to write the scene as an outsider—in the third person, from the officer's point of view. You describe what you saw but eliminate the picture of yourself as observer. You jump in.

Clara looks at the two girls approaching the intersection. Both are wearing shorts; one has a faded tee-shirt advertising some heavy metal rock group, Clara can't tell which, and the other is wearing Bill the Cat. They are clearly going to jaywalk across the intersection right in front of her, Clara decides, and she will have to be looking carefully elsewhere if she doesn't want to write a ticket for jaywalking.

Then something does pull her attention in another direction. A man in a denim jacket and with wildly flying hair is darting around the cars in his Harley, even jumping up on the sidewalk and back into the street.

*Clara reaches for her whistle . . . ***

You're off! Try to stay on the road.

This example skips lightly over one of the biggest problems related to plotting in short story writing—pacing the events so that they read naturally. An easy-to-use approach is simply to limit the action to between two and four scenes, trying to bridge them with smooth, brief transitions. The veteran short story writer will have all kinds of other methods at her or his disposal, including flashbacks, telescoping of events, and nonchronological development. The new short story writer will find it much more satisfactory to proceed chronologically by scenes, with just enough transitional material so that the reader does not get lost. And often there are two scenes—one, an extended scene, that sets up a dramatic situation, and a second, shorter scene that resolves it.

The preceding short story, for instance, might have the first scene end with the arrival of Clara's superior and his telephoned instructions to another officer to arrest the biker. A space on the page might indicate the passage of time.

*Clara has almost forgotten the incident when the daily reminder page on her computer reminds her of the hearing. The past six weeks have brought nothing but traffic tickets and dirty looks; no real abuse; no attempted escapes . . . ***

You have smoothly skipped perhaps a month, and no one will wonder what happened to the time, since it is not relevant to the thread of your story. Now you need just quickly to transfer Clara to the hearing for your second scene.

*Paragraphs from student story by Janie Grace, are reprinted by permission of the author.

When you have finished the whole draft, take a good close look at your conclusion. Does it seem natural and in character? Maybe the experience would have a hardening effect on Clara, and instead of quitting her job, she would be less sensitive in the future. The end of a story is, of course, of utmost importance, and yet there are no sensible guidelines for endings, except to make sure that the conclusion is motivated. The student who wrote Clara's story finally ended by having Clara prick herself with the badge as she shoved it deep into her purse after the hearing. This was a third attempt: it seemed to suggest a lot in a swift, clean closure.

There is a question that is always raised here, or somewhere else along the way: "Do I have to write about my life?" Well, no. Well, yes. You can't help writing about your life. Even if you transport your characters to Mars, their experience will come in some sense from your own. Writers are often asked about a "realistic" story, "Did this happen to you?" The answer is usually both an affirmation and a denial: "Well, the people are like those I knew growing up in rural Pennsylvania, but no one ever actually . . ."

EXERCISES

1. Read a well-known short story, one that has been widely anthologized. Some good possibilities are as follows: Ernest Hemingway's "Hills Like White Elephants"; Jane Smiley's "Long Distance"; Franz Kafka's "Metamorphosis"; D. H. Lawrence's "The Rocking-Horse Winner"; James Joyce's "Araby"; and Tillie Olsen's "I Stand Here Ironing." Now write one paragraph summarizing the plot of the story. Then answer the following questions.

   a. What is the major conflict, and how is it resolved?

   b. What is the position of the main character both at the beginning of the story and at the end? Is there a loss or gain?

   c. How is plot entwined with character in this story? That is, do the characters appear to react naturally to what happens? Do their character traits help determine what happens?

   d. Can you imagine another appropriate ending for this story? Why, or why not?

   Consider these questions in regard to your own planned, drafted, or finished short story.

2. Take an incident from your journal, and turn it into a plot for a short story, using the method described in this chapter. Make photocopies of the journal entry and of the plot summary to bring to class. Share these in class, pointing out any problems you see in the plots. Does the outcome seem likely or unlikely on the basis of the characters and of the event? If unlikely, how might the ending be changed to make it fit the story better?

3. This is a collaborative exercise involving several elements of the short story: plot, character, and dialogue. Your instructor may assign you a partner, or you may choose one.

   a. Invent a character who is not like you. Try to make this person's experience far from your own. Name the character, and list his or her characteristics.

b. Invent another character, one who is similar to you in experience and nature. Name the character.

c. Now, narrate an event that has happened to you recently or that you observed.

In this exercise, you will pair up with another member of the class. You and your partner will read each other's narratives. Then you will adopt your invented characters and briefly discuss the two events in their voices as two brief dialogues.

When you are discussing your partner's event, you will speak in the voice of the character who is like you. When you are discussing your own event, you will speak in the voice of the character who is unlike you. The event will be reported as having happened to that character.

EXAMPLE

Student Sarah, a nutrition major who hates dirt and disorder, invents Lula Mae, a mud-wrestler, and Karen, an accounting major. Her partner Jim, who is in engineering right now but intends to drop out and major in something more compatible with his music interests, invents Mike, a rock band player who is going to school part-time, and Stickney, a would-be CEO who spends every minute on his studies. Jim's event is that he gets mugged and has his wallet stolen. This incident would be discussed in a dialogue by Stickney and Karen. The event would be reported as having happened to Stickney. Sarah's incident is her winning $500 in the lottery. This would be discussed by Lula Mae and Mike, as though it had happened to Lula Mae.

4. Choose a short story with which you are thoroughly familiar, and write a different ending for it. For instance, write an ending for "Hills Like White Elephants" in which the man loses the argument. Ask whether your ending works—does it seem motivated? Why, or why not? Can you imagine the man's yielding in this situation? Is there any believable conclusion that would allow the woman to triumph? (If you have truly fallen in love with your ending, you can always change the characters' names and can write a new beginning for the story.)

5. This class group exercise is mostly for fun, but it does illustrate some of the problems of plotting. Although it is a children's game, if played by adults, it can give some insight into the nature of story-making. Form groups of four or five. Let the first student invent a main character and begin a story. At any point the student may discontinue, and the next student then adds an episode to the story. Continue this process around the group, stopping at points of greatest suspense. No fair killing off the main character!

6. Choose a family narrative—a story about something that happened to a grandparent, perhaps, or something that happened to you as a child that has been retold over the years and embellished in the retelling. See whether you can form this incident into a plot.

7. Create a plot that has nothing at all to do with your life. Now ask yourself how or where you would get the material to fill in the plot and make it into a story. Through research? In an interview?

8. Write a one-paragraph summary of the plot of the story "Hills Like White Elephants," by Ernest Hemingway. Now write a one-paragraph summary of another version of this story in which the woman gets her way.

.... **Ernest Hemingway**

*Hills Like White Elephants**

The hills across the valley of the Ebro were long and white. On this side there was no shade and no trees and the station was between two lines of rails in the sun. Close against the side of the station there was the warm shadow of the building and a curtain, made of strings of bamboo beads, hung across the open door into the bar, to keep out flies. The American and the girl with him sat at a table in the shade, outside the building. It was very hot and the express from Barcelona would come in forty minutes. It stopped at this junction for two minutes and went on to Madrid.

"What should we drink?" the girl asked. She had taken off her hat and put it on the table.

"It's pretty hot," the man said. "Let's drink beer."

"Dos cervezas," the man said into the curtain.

"Big ones?" a woman asked from the doorway.

"Yes. Two big ones."

The woman brought two glasses of beer and two felt pads. She put the felt pads and the beer glasses on the table and looked at the man and the girl. The girl was looking off at the line of hills. They were white in the sun and the country was brown and dry.

"They look like white elephants," she said.

"I've never seen one," the man drank his beer.

"No, you wouldn't have."

"I might have," the man said. "Just because you say I wouldn't have doesn't prove anything."

The girl looked at the bead curtain. "They've painted something on it," she said. "What does it say?"

"Anis del Toro. It's a drink."

"Could we try it?"

The man called "Listen" through the curtain. The woman came out from the bar.

---

*"Hills Like White Elephants" is reprinted with permission of Scribner, a Division of Simon & Schuster, Inc., from *The Short Stories of Ernest Hemingway*. Copyright 1927 by Charles Scribner's Sons. Copyright renewed © 1955 by Ernest Hemingway.

"Four reales."

"We want two Anis del Toro."

"With water?"

"Do you want it with water?"

"I don't know," the girl said. "Is it good with water?"

"It's all right."

"You want them with water?" asked the woman.

"Yes, with water."

"It tastes like licorice," the girl said and put the glass down.

"That's the way with everything."

"Yes," said the girl. "Everything tastes of licorice. Especially all the things you've waited so long for, like absinthe."

"Oh, cut it out."

"You started it," the girl said. "I was being amused. I was having a fine time."

"Well, let's try and have a fine time."

"All right. I was trying. I said the mountains looked like white elephants. Wasn't that bright?"

"That was bright."

"I wanted to try this new drink. That's all we do, isn't it—look at things and try new drinks?"

"I guess so."

The girl looked across at the hills.

"They're lovely hills," she said. "They don't really look like white elephants. I just meant the coloring of their skin through the trees."

"Should we have another drink?"

"All right."

The warm wind blew the bead curtain against the table.

"The beer's nice and cool," the man said.

"It's lovely," the girl said.

"It's really an awfully simple operation, Jig," the man said. "It's not really an operation at all."

The girl looked at the ground the table legs rested on.

"I know you wouldn't mind it, Jig. It's really not anything. It's just to let the air in."

The girl did not say anything.

"I'll go with you and I'll stay with you all the time. They just let the air in and then it's all perfectly natural."

"Then what will we do afterward?"

"We'll be fine afterward. Just like we were before."

"What makes you think so?"

"That's the only thing that bothers us. It's the only thing that's made us unhappy."

The girl looked at the bead curtain, put her hand out and took hold of two of the strings of beads.

"And you think then we'll be all right and be happy."

"I know we will. You don't have to be afraid. I've known lots of people that have done it."

"So have I," said the girl. "And afterward they were all so happy."

"Well," the man said, "if you don't want to you don't have to. I wouldn't have you do it if you didn't want to. But I know it's perfectly simple."

"And you really want to?"

"I think it's the best thing to do. But I don't want you to do it if you don't really want to."

"And if I do it you'll be happy and things will be like they were and you'll love me?"

"I love you now. You know I love you."

"I know. But if I do it, then it will be nice again if I say things are like white elephants, and you'll like it?"

"I'll love it. I love it now but I just can't think about it. You know how I get when I worry."

"If I do it you won't ever worry?"

"I won't worry about that because it's perfectly simple."

"Then I'll do it. Because I don't care about me."

"What do you mean?"

"I don't care about me."

"Well, I care about you."

"Oh, yes. But I don't care about me. And I'll do it and then everything will be fine."

"I don't want you to do it if you feel that way."

The girl stood up and walked to the end of the station. Across, on the other side, were fields of grain and trees along the banks of the Ebro. Far away, beyond the river, were mountains. The shadow of a cloud moved across the field of grain and she saw the river through the trees.

"And we could have all this," she said. "And we could have everything and every day we make it more impossible."

"What did you say?"

"I said we could have everything."

"We can have everything."

"No, we can't."

"We can have the whole world."

"No, we can't."

"We can go everywhere."

"No, we can't. It isn't ours any more."

"It's ours."

"No it isn't. And once they take it away, you never get it back."

"But they haven't taken it away."

"We'll wait and see."

"Come on back in the shade," he said. "You mustn't feel that way."

"I don't feel any way," the girl said. "I just know things."

"I don't want you to do anything that you don't want to do—"

"Nor that isn't good for me," she said. "I know. Could we have another beer?"

"All right. But you've got to realize—"

"I realize," the girl said. "Can't we maybe stop talking?"

They sat down at the table and the girl looked across at the hills on the dry side of the valley and the man looked at her and at the table.

"You've got to realize," he said, "that I don't want you to do it if you don't want to. I'm perfectly willing to go through with it if it means anything to you."

"Doesn't it mean anything to you? We could get along."

"Of course it does. But I don't want anybody but you. I don't want any one else. And I know it's perfectly simple."

"Yes, you know it's perfectly simple."

"It's all right for you to say that, but I do know it."

"Would you do something for me now?"

"I'd do anything for you."

"Would you please please please please please please please stop talking?"

He did not say anything but looked at the bags against the wall of the station. There were labels on them from all the hotels where they had spent nights.

"But I don't want you to," he said, "I don't care anything about it."

"I'll scream," the girl said.

The woman came out through the curtains with two glasses of beer and put them down on the damp felt pads. "The train comes in five minutes," she said.

"What did she say?" asked the girl.

"That the train is coming in five minutes."

The girl smiled brightly at the woman, to thank her.

"I'd better take the bags over to the other side of the station," the man said. She smiled at him.

"All right. Then come back and we'll finish the beer."

He picked up the two heavy bags and carried them around the station to the other tracks. He looked up the tracks but could not see the train. Coming back, he walked through the barroom, where people waiting for the train were drinking. He drank an Anis at the bar and looked at the people. They were all waiting reasonably for the train. He went out through the bead curtain. She was sitting at the table and smiled at him.

"Do you feel better?" he asked.

"I feel fine," she said. "There's nothing wrong with me. I feel fine."

Setting

> Without [a sense of place] the work is often reduced to a cry of voices in empty rooms, a literature of the self, at its best poetic music; at its worst a thin gruel of the ego.
>
> —William Kennedy, on winning the Pulitzer Prize, *Time*, 1 Oct. 1984

"A sense of place" has become more and more important in creative writing of all kinds. Popular novels of the nineteenth century often had only the vaguest hints of the environment in which the events took place. Sometimes obvious errors of fact occurred—the Acropolis, for instance, might turn up in Rome. Readers, even when they noticed, seemed not to care much. Now that so many facts are at our fingertips, accuracy and precision are demanded from writers.

Often the first couple of paragraphs of a short story provide some kind of setting. Sometimes the beginning introduces the main character, with only a subtle, indirect evocation of place. In some way, though, the first few lines of a story establish the scene. We are introduced to the main characters and the location of the events. Relationships are defined; expectations are set up. Something significant is happening, and the events are taking place in a particular time and place.

The first paragraph is of crucial importance, because it often determines whether an editor will read further or look hastily around for your stamped, self-addressed envelope to send your story back. You will find all sorts of suggestions of what to include in the introductory few lines to entice the wary reader, but these suggestions are usually worthless, because any serious suggestions would have to take into consideration the particular story. Some of the general "don't" instructions are worth examining, although it is true that any rule may profitably be violated in some unusual case. In the beginning, it is best not to try to fill in too much background or to start the story too soon; also, it is wise not to begin with a visible appeal to attention.

Looking at it from a broader perspective and considering elements other than the maintenance of an editor's attention, the beginning of the story becomes even more important. It sets up the premises of the fiction, telling the reader what foundation must be accepted as the basis of the story. Or you might see it as the front room of your narrative house, and visitors will either want to enter, or they will not. Many student and professional short stories have been immeasurably improved by their authors simply by replacing the first paragraph with something more tightly drawn, more relevant, more telling.

A good beginning is economical, terse. Consider the following opening to "A Conversation with My Father," by the well-known writer Grace Paley:

> *My father is eighty-six years old and in bed. His heart, that bloody motor, is equally old and will not do certain jobs any more. It still floods his head with brainy light. But it won't let his legs carry the weight of his body around the house. Despite my metaphors, this muscle failure is not due to his old heart, he says, but to a potassium failure. Sitting on one pillow, leaning on three, he offers last-minute advice and makes a request.*
>
> *"I would like you to write a simple story just once more," he says, "the kind de Maupassant wrote, or Chekhov, the kind you used to write. Just recognizable people and then write down what happened to them next."*

We are drawn into the scene. We see the daughter as mobile, perhaps even wandering about, and the father lying there, at the end of his life term. We immediately sense a kind of conflict—that the daughter loves her old father is clear from the description, but it is also clear that there is a reason why she hasn't been writing his kind of story. We want to know what will happen. Will she humor her father, thus patronizing him? Will she try to explain her point of view? Will, in fact, this very story turn out to be the kind that he wanted her to write? Clearly too, the specifics of a particular part of the country do not play a major part in this story—the important elements, the aged father, his daughter, the space that houses the relationship between them, are the real setting.

This Paley story is told in the first person, and thus the narrator's details are chosen by the author to express the narrator's sensibility. Setting, or description, is inextricably tied up with point of view—and this fact is easy to forget when you are writing with third-person limited omniscience. Here is the beginning of a novel, *Who Is Mary Stark*, by Lloyd Kropp. The section starts with the words "Mary Haywood, Summer of 1972":

> *On that dry, warm day of that season Mary Haywood turned thirteen and to mark the occasion Mrs. Haywood had taken her to see her father. She stood now beside his grave, listening to the far drone of speeding cars and trucks on the highway beyond the high fence at the western edge of the cemetery. Her mother was sitting on the grass. She had placed a wreath of orange roses in front of the grave, and now she reached forward and touched the white gravestone with her fingers. Mary could not read the meaning in that simple gesture. It was as if her mother had reached out to touch something cloudy or insubstantial. It made her think of swimming in the lake the previous summer. Opening her eyes underwater and reaching down to touch weeds waving among lines of shadow in the white sand.*
>
> *Mrs. Haywood withdrew her hand from the gravestone. After a moment she looked up at Mary and smiled. "This is the last time we'll come here," she said.**

**Lloyd Kropp, brief quotation from *Who Is Mary Stark* is reprinted by permission of the author.

Notice how Kropp has chosen the details. There are no tufted titmice soaring about, nor are juniper bushes identified, even though these birds and bushes might easily have been near the cemetery. Instead, we get what the thirteen-year-old Mary sees, mixed in with what she thinks and the associations she makes. The first sentence sets us up for a surprise: the father she is going to "see" is dead; he is not visible. This "visit" is obviously one of many, but the passage identifies it as the last. Mary does not feel intense emotion at these graveyard visits. What she experiences is subtle—mostly, she observes, and the reader is given the sense that for her, the graveyard is some kind of threshold between the living and the dead. This impression is communicated through the details and the comparison in the last half of the first paragraph. Mary herself is on a threshold between childhood and adulthood. What she observes will turn out to be the first thread of the novel's central issue, which has to do with the borderline, or threshold, between reality and imagination.

Sarah Orne Jewett's story "A White Heron" begins with nature detail:

The woods were already filled with shadows one June evening, just before eight o'clock, though a bright sunset still glimmered faintly among the trunks of the trees. A little girl was driving home her cow . . . They were going away from whatever light there was, and striking deep into the woods, but their feet were familiar with the path, and it was no matter whether their eyes could see it or not.

Here it does turn out that the part of the country, New England, features largely in the story, but the main conflict has to do with the girl's loving relationship with nature and a challenge to it. Thus, the bond of union is represented in the details of the opening scene. The fact that the cow is represented as a consciousness like that of the child, and the familiarity of the child with the whole scene, gives the impression of a natural unity of which child, cow, trees, and path are all a part.

Setting may be a major or a minor element in your short story; in some of the finest literary stories, there is a dynamic interaction among the place where the events happen, the characters, and the plot. Thomas Hardy's stories embody this interaction: the bleak English moors he describes have an obvious effect on the people who live there. Regionalist stories, essays, and poems capture significant elements of place to make a region real to the reader, and sometimes to make a statement about that region.

One kind of setting-driven story is what is called local color—a regionalist story that attempts to capture the specifics of a particular area of the country and of the people who live in it. Sometimes the local color story sensationalizes or sentimentalizes the element of place, leading people to use negatively the tag "local color." Often the place is already changing, its distinctiveness disappearing even as the writer attempts to describe it. A good example of the local color story is Mary E. Wilkins Freeman's "A New England Nun," which describes a woman's choice to stay single after growing into a narrow, single life while her fiancé was away. The local color of the story derives from the specifics of life in her small New England town.

If your themes are closely related to place, you may be writing a setting-driven story. You will want to represent not only the most superficial elements of the setting but also the deeper nuances of what makes a place itself and what makes its inhabitants natives of that place. To do this, you need to hone your descriptive skills—something that you will need to do, in fact, no matter how much weight you want setting to have in your story.

To create a sense of place, visualize. Awaken your senses. Try to build an image in words that will create a lasting impression, and try to do this in such a way that you are not leaving behind the other elements of the story. This task is not easy to accomplish. Description, like dialogue, can become an end in itself and can run away with you. When description is part of effective fiction, it is interwoven with other facets of the story. Every line, every image relates to plot, character, and theme.

One way of visualizing and recording is to cultivate a reporter's eye. The reporter wants the most telling, most relevant details of the scene in which the murder takes place, in which the old criminal is interviewed, in which the charity ball will be held. The reporter has no time for the trivial. You might try looking at a scene as though you were going to write a news story about an event that happened there. Ask yourself what you would see and what you would overlook, in the drawing room of a Victorian house where a murder was committed, or in the forest clearing where a helicopter had landed illegally.

It's hard to describe in a vacuum. In the past, creative writing teachers often asked the students to describe a scene—even the scene from a classroom window. Often the students would stare unhappily at this scene—maybe a square concrete building, a few trees, students walking and biking on sidewalks and streets—and then finally, aware that fifty minutes was not forever, would begin to jot down details. But these word pictures seldom added up to much. In the best ones, the student would provide a thesis. The scene was one of haste or leisure, of changing weather—of something in particular. This thesis, often unstated, would organize the details into a meaningful picture.

When you write your descriptive sections, however, you will not have this problem. Your setting is a functional part of your story, and what details you use will be determined by what is happening and through whose mind the events are slanted. One character might be very aware of all the specifics of a forest backdrop—what birds and animals are present, what sounds and images characterize the scene. Another might be aware only of unpleasant things, such as brambles, insects, and snakes.

Consider the setting in "Some of Us Had Been Threatening Our Friend Colby." Here there is a deliberate use of an indefinite setting, but why? Notice, however, that although this setting is not identified, it is very specific. What are the details being used for? Look at the briefly sketched setting of "Hills Like White Elephants." Why are the details of the setting important?

What makes for a good setting? The physical detail—the surface of a place—is becoming more important even in popular literature. Earlier it was mentioned that nineteenth-century popular novels paid little attention to setting and even got details wrong, putting the flora and fauna of Africa, for instance, into Louisiana; and earlier detective novels often had little description beyond a vague impression of "the mean streets" of some unidentified city. But now place is paramount—and the subtler the place details, the better. Writers can no longer rely on a vague backdrop that is supplemented by the reader's limited awareness of a particular setting. Setting is dynamic; the relationship between character and location may determine the outcome of action. The more a place is represented as its own unique self, the better. The Texas of dead armadillos and of pickup trucks is cliché. Even the notion of Texas is too vast a generalization. The details and language of Austin will differ from those of Houston, and those cities are located just within central Texas.

The true goal is not description for its own sake but rather a portrayal of the interaction between the place and its people. In the stories studied as local color—such as those written by Sarah Orne Jewett, Bret Harte, and Mary E. Wilkins Freeman—the tales represent the interplay between people and place. The physical surroundings are intertwined with the characters' lives, so that the exterior landscape is a mirror of the interior.

This brings us to the notion of "personal setting," the way in which you create characters and setting at once so that they comprise one thing. Your sense of self, the people you know, your genetic background and roots, the town or city where you grew up, your religion, what you saw from your old bedroom window, the things your parents say over and over again, what they serve for dinner—all these things and so many more are part of the resource from which you create person and place.

It is difficult to gain enough distance from the elements of personal setting to use it effectively, especially if you are still more or less completely surrounded by your origins—that is, if you are still living at home or have just left home, if you have nothing with which to contrast your setting and to help you identify its particulars. James Joyce had to leave Ireland in order to define it. *Dubliners* and *Portrait of the Artist as a Young Man* derive not only from Ireland but also from the difference between Ireland and elsewhere. Similarly, Toni Morrison's portrayal of historical Ohio has come from her growing up there, her studies, and the distance she has gained from being elsewhere. Nevertheless, you have some perspective on your origins, and reading as well as experience will increase this. One good way to become aware of your personal setting is to read contemporary regional literature and to try to see what is "different" about the place and people described. Look at the clothing, language, and details of people's lives. Then compare the scene with your own. Look at Toni Morrison's portrayal of Ohio in some of her stories, and examine how she arranges the interplay between people and place so that every element of the story seems natural and organic.

To exploit personal setting, start writing down its particulars: language, clothing, food, religious attitudes, political attitudes, ways of expressing affection, ways of teaching. And when you come to a broader area, like political attitudes, ask how these are expressed in everyday life. What kinds of sayings or actions communicate attitude? Are there actions or expressions that belong to you in a way that they do not belong to others? Again, to help you get at how to describe, read regionalist stories written by natives of the region described; see what there is about the place that makes it different from other places, and what the characters who live in this locality share.

You will profit from trying to be objective when thinking about your personal setting. Some things will seem comforting, familiar, endearing. Others will seem disturbing. What are you proud of? What do you wish you could change?

When you write either fiction or personal essay, you will want to consider these issues—preferably in front of a word processor, so that you can easily freewrite anything that occurs to you.

A good way of getting a handle on your own personal setting is to investigate that of others—read ethnic fiction and poetry, and listen to music that helps define a group or a people. Observe what the writer does to get across the feel of being a member of this group. Respond to the work by evoking the particulars of your own life that parallel those of the life described. See how Kelly Zayas, a young poet, has responded to the Celtic songs by Bill Whelan, producing an exciting poem that is cross-cultural and about cultural crossing. (Sometimes the most immediate access to cultural knowledge is poetry—but fiction may follow.)

.... **Kelly Zayas**

*Wake Ancestors**

Inspired by Bill Whelan's "America Wake"

slow motion laughter
arms fly beer   on my dress   I partner you
make me fly   I am as Irish as you   young as
your breath   exhausted
I exist   with a salsa in my jig
old men blushing like wine want me   my curves bite their lust
beer in my hair   and you
believe in gods that have vices more powerful than virtue
I believe in you

sweat and chickens
my feet dirt the floor   you smoke cigars
island foreshadowing my smile   Caribbean nights
and me   wisps of ocean breeze   your cheeks are copper soft
I exist   with a jig in my salsa
follow feet to cathedral   pray for sinners
hope pounding out rhythms   my feet   slaves
callused from dancing
they pick the song   lead   me to sweetness

Kelly Zayas's poem shows the effect that one form of art, particularly culturally rich art, may have on another.

*Kelly Zayas, "Wake Ancestors" is reprinted by permission of the author.

Here are some do's for description:

1. Let your nouns and verbs do as much of the work as possible. Avoid pileups of adjectives and adverbs. When you can, incorporate the adverb or adjective into the verb or noun. You might, for instance, substitute "The moon silvered the pines" for "The moon was silver in the pine trees." When you have finished your description, look at every one of your -ly adverbs, and ask, "Is this word necessary?"

2. Keep in mind the goal of your description. Let's say that you are describing a high school picnic that took place in a field outside a small town in Texas and that part of its purpose is to establish that the action took place in a particular area, and another part of its goal is to show that this place is somehow outside the mainstream—the people are relatively unsophisticated. You will then choose details of action and of place that subtly demonstrate your point. You will not want to get involved in elaborate nature descriptions that have little to do with your characters and events.

   Regionalism is a very strong element in Larry McMurtry's *The Last Picture Show*, and he begins the novel with a description of the main street of the fictional Thalia, Texas—but the first sentence determines what is in that description. The story begins, "Sometimes Sonny felt like he was the only human creature in the town." Details of Thalia in November—the cars, the pool hall—but they are selected and organized so as to communicate the essential loneliness of the main character. This loneliness, which is partly caused by the place, is a part of the central theme of the novel.

3. If you are after precision in your description, do some research. If you are going to describe the wildflowers of an area, for instance, be sure those particular flowers grow there. Even if you are writing about your own area, you may want to do a little reading to make sure you have everything correct.

4. When you can, intersperse dialogue and action with setting, rather than having long chunks of description. Often brief details can be offered as dialogue tags, avoiding the awkwardness of synonyms for "said" while providing glimpses of the surroundings:

   "You don't know that's true of me. You're generalizing again," she said angrily.

   "You don't know that's true of me. You're generalizing again." She jabbed her fork into the last piece of steak . . .

EXERCISES

1. Examine four postcards of your hometown, and set a brief sketch in the main street. If you come from a city, bring pictures of a major shopping area, and set your sketch there. Don't worry about plot. Instead, invent two characters and have them window-shop and/or make purchases, and then go into a restaurant and eat. Describe what they see, what they order, what kind of interactions they have with their surroundings, and what they say.

2. Bring to mind a person you think is in some way typical or representative of the place where you live. Now make a data sheet for this individual, providing him or her with name, occupation, family, typical clothing, habits, hobbies, car, education, and pet phrases. Now write a sketch based on the person. See whether you can find a name that subtly suggests the person's character.

3. This exercise is to be done as a class. From old magazines, cut out pictures of two people from the illustrations. Now bring these clippings to class. From the shuffled deck of human images, each class member will draw two people. Now, describe a scene where these two characters might be found.

4. Develop one of the following sentences into a paragraph by supplying details that locate the act in time and place. Your instructor may assign one of them to the class, in order to be able to compare the results.

   a. She left the freeway and drove into a small town, where she stopped at the first restaurant she saw and ordered lunch.

   b. His college football team lost the game in the last thirty seconds of play.

   c. I went shopping for something to wear to tonight's party.

   d. The dentist pulled his tooth.

   e. I woke up in total darkness.

5. Consider the first paragraphs of several short stories you are familiar with. Ask yourself what is implied by these first paragraphs. Now read the first paragraph of another story, this time one that you have not read. Jot down what is implied, and by what means. (In the Paley passage, for instance, how does the writer imply that the relationship between father and daughter is a good one?) Now read the new story. Are your expectations met? If they are violated, how and why? If the story took a different turn from what you expected, do you think that you were deliberately misled?

6. Go somewhere you have never been, and then describe the place. Give as many details as you can of what you saw, heard, smelled, touched, and tasted. This may be a different town, or a kind of event or enterprise: a pawn shop? a fashion show? a dog show? a chili cookout? the annual Texas Smelly Sneaker celebration and judging? How did the newness of the place help you, and how did it hinder you, in your description?

7. Do a little research on a place you know well and may use as a setting. If it is a country setting, what kinds of birds and animals are native, and what plants and flowers are common there? If it is a city, what are the buildings like? In what part of the city would you set the story? What kind of businesses or residences do you see as you walk down the street?

Dialogue

> What I like in a good author isn't what he says, but what he whispers.
>
> —Logan Pearsall Smith

Dialogue is difficult. One often says of a writer that he or she has a good ear, meaning that the writer sees, hears, and records all the elements of speech and associated behavior that characterize. You might think of someone, "He's just like that; that's the way he is," meaning that he is likely to say and do certain things predictably in response to circumstances. To write dialogue, you have to focus on all the details of an exchange of words, in order to catch what is unsaid, or whispered, as well as what is said aloud.

From your favorite story or novel, what scenes do you remember best? Many of us recall our favorite lines of dialogue, spoken by characters we remember as being illuminated by those lines. Hemingway was a master of the tip-of-the-iceberg communication. We see Brett Ashley saying to Jake Barnes, "We could have had such a damned good time." We revisit his answer, "Isn't it pretty to think so," and the whole complicated and painful story of *The Sun Also Rises* returns to us in those lines. Although Hemingway is one writer famous for his dialogue, there are others past and present. And even those writers whose dialogue is not singled out and quoted by critics know how to use this major element of fiction.

Good dialogue is crucial to short fiction, but it is a stumbling block for many beginning writers, who are good at observing details and are comfortable writing them down but who have not developed an ear for speech. A way to begin developing an ear for speech is to read current plays, thinking about what makes a character's speech particularly his or hers. Are there certain phrases, turns of speech, that seem to belong to the character? How is the character's education level represented?

In constructing dialogue, the writer needs always to consider both the importance of the sound of the voices and the purpose of the dialogue to the story as a whole as well as to the development of the characters speaking. If the dialogue is to sound natural, it needs to be appropriate for the age group, educational level, and other characteristics of the speaker. It has to sound right, not necessarily be real. You may, for instance, notice a young man with a partly shaved head and wearing a Curt Cobain tee shirt talking to another similarly dressed person at McDonald's. He might say, "If that's a serious request, then we should do our best to accommodate him." The dress might say one thing, the voice another, and the matter might seem very mysterious to you. You might prick up your ears and listen for the rest of the conversation. But you would not use that character and comment in your story unless you could figure out a logical reason for doing so. Something in the plot would have to account for the discrepancy. In real life, it's quite possible that he just happened to talk like that. If you stayed around McDonald's a while, you might hear a long argument between two mothers about whether the new supermarket was any good. Everything they said might seem appropriate to you—even the pauses. You would keep listening only because you are a writer, developing an ear for dialogue.

As you listen and record, you well may wonder—what about profanity? People use it all the time, of course, in real life. The use of profanity in student works often results in the most interesting class interchanges. Some students will respond to a story, "I am so turned off by the language that I cannot get interested in that story." This is an honest response; but a writer may also find strong language is necessary for some reason. One class was instructed to write a dialogue for a group that the writer could not be part of. One student had the inhabitants of the men's Corps of Cadets dormitory saying things like, "Shucks, my algebra book seems to have been stolen." This somehow did not re-create the aura of the dorm.

On the other hand, too much strong language is a turnoff for many readers. Although Mark Twain reportedly had some profanity in *The Adventures of Huckleberry Finn,* his wife Olivia removed it before publication. Do the dastardly characters in this novel need the profanity? One would think not—and this novel has been read as a children's story by many thousands. Scattering profanity throughout the novel would make it much less desirable as family fare. Moreover, the language that the villains use is adequately wicked so that the reader is not surprised at their actions. You need to ask whether strong language is needed for characterization or for intensity and whether your intended audience will accept it, and then to use it sparingly.

In the following section of an undergraduate story, a student is writing about a high school relationship, and is attempting to use the language that would have been used:

> *I rubbed the sore red ring around my lips, put the well-oiled silver brass Bach trumpet on my lap, leaned over and stared at the sheet music for "Since I Fell For You." April sat in the opposite corner of the small rehearsal room pulling wads of string from her sweater. "That solo is beginning to sound real nice, Zach."*
>
> *"No it doesn't. I suck. I've been here every lunch break trying to get it right for the competition but that bitch principal Harvis keeps chasing me back into the cafeteria."*
>
> *"I'm sure you'll do fine."*
>
> *"It's the only solo I've ever had. This is my senior year and I want it to be perfect."*
>
> *"I wouldn't worry about it. You're a much better trumpet player than you give yourself credit for."*
>
> *There was an awkward moment of silence. I fumbled and clicked the valves of my trumpet, staring into the abstract designs of the maroon and white carpet. (from "Where the Balloons Fly," by Paul McCann)**

This writer has his high school students talking like high school students; the purpose of this snatch of dialogue is to show a moment in a relationship between two band members that is much more important to Zach than to April, who is trying to let him down gently.

*Paul McCann, excerpt from short story is reprinted by permission of the author.

The only way to create realistic-sounding dialogue is to listen and read. Listen in libraries, in restaurants, on buses, wherever you can do so unobserved. See what phrases are particular to what group. Correlate people's words with their observed behavior. Read Ernest Hemingway, Toni Morrison, John Updike, Flannery O'Connor, Mark Twain, Alice Walker, Sandra Cisneros, Eudora Welty—any author known for capturing the rhythms of speech. And, as mentioned before, read plays. There are books of practice exercises for speech and drama classes that include passages from a number of plays and that are great resources for those who want to study dialogue.

Alas, the dialogue must not only sound natural but must also advance the plot. It is easy for a writer to get carried away with page after page of witty interchanges while the plot stalls in a side street. Dialogue characterizes, but it also fills in necessary background and advances the action. All the dialogue in a short story should be directed toward these multiple goals. One way to work with a story is to begin by outlining the plot and then to write some of the dialogue scenes. In this way, it is easy to keep the goals of the dialogue in mind.

In the following snatch of dialogue from the work of Michael Stockham, an advanced graduate student writer who began publishing while still in school, the dialogue both characterizes participants and directs the action. In this story, the character P. W. has given a lift to the hitchhiking Cratie; this is the end of the conversation as P. W. drops Cratie at a filling station and Cratie steps from the truck.

I step out and peer back at P. W. through the door window. His beard changing colors in the light of a neon beer sign flashing behind me. He pushes back his cap and smiles.

—Sure you don't want me to take you where you're headed? he asks. It really isn't any trouble and I'd be glad to do it.

—No, I say, and flush around for something else to add but there isn't anything, just the sound of the signs buzzing around me, a single tumbleweed rambling across the lot. Thanks for the beer, I say, and then just, thanks.

—Likewise Cratie, he says. Then he goes on, he says, you might think of taking a shower or something before you see her.

—I hope Elise doesn't mind me grubby. I can picture her now, waiting in that front room, a small candle on the dining room table, couple of plants and my favorite meal in the oven.

—What meal is it? he asks.

—I don't know, I say.

Dropping his truck into gear, P. W. says, good luck, and heads out onto the road and up a hill. He hits his brakes twice around a curve and disappears. (from "So Much a Circle," by Michael Stockham)*

Note that Stockham uses his own nonstandard method of presenting dialogue, which has specific effects. He uses dashes instead of quotation marks to

*Michael Stockham, dialogue from student story "So Much a Circle" is reprinted by permission of the author.

indicate speech, and as a result, the dialogue is less set off from the description and action that accompany it. Speech and action become one thing. However, it is best to stay with the conventions until your style has developed enough so that if you violate them, you do so with a purpose. In this case, the merging of character and scene is an important part of the effect of the story.

Dialogue characterizes, adds to the plot and setting, and is interesting for itself. Notice how complex is the simple dialogue offered by writer Trent Masiki in the following story.

.... **Trent Masiki**

Winners Go First*

Anthony and I didn't want to start the contest without our cousin, Kevin. But he took too long to make it over. So, we started anyway. Big Mama must have found some more work around the house for Kevin to do. Somehow when Anthony and I visit our grandmother, we get fewer chores or we get out of them altogether. I guess Big Mama expects more out of Kevin since he lives there and me and my brother don't. Kevin tells me all the time how lucky I am to have both my parents. His mother died a couple of years ago from a bad liver, and his father left town two days before he was born. I guess that's why he adores my dad so much, why he thinks I'm so lucky to have him around. But he never had a father. So, he really doesn't know if I'm lucky or not.

The wooded field across the street from my grandmother's house is where the three of us, Kevin, me, and my brother, Anthony, hunt birds and rabbits. We've downed plenty of cardinals, bluejays, and mockingbirds with our pellet and B-B guns, but we haven't been as lucky with rabbits. They're smarter, more alert. Half of the field is tall dry grass yellowed by the summer sun. The blackberry vines it hides prick your ankles. The other half of the field is wooded with oaks and maples. That part isn't very big, but it's just large enough to make you feel that you've left the world behind, that you've gotten away from people and problems. Yet, it's still small enough to be heard if you had to call for help, if you got into trouble. It can be a scary place. There are some parts the sun never seems to touch. They're calm spots, but they're not quiet. There's always something rustling in the brush just behind or just ahead of you.

Young pines border the entire length of the back of the field. On the other side of this line of trees are two sets of railroad tracks that lie between the field and the back of a warehouse. Gray, creosote splattered rocks and dry grass fill the set of tracks nearest the building. The railroad cars don't unload often on these, so the grass grows unchecked between them. The rocks look as if they fell from the asteroid belt. They're small and full of holes. Because they're such a dark gray color, they look a lot heavier than they actually are. They're not good for throwing. The good rocks, the big chalky ones, line the set of tracks nearest the pines. Anthony's sitting on one of the ties in that set now, piling together rocks between his legs. I've already gathered mine. They're for the bottles and cans lined up on the set of tracks nearest the warehouse. I have the best rocks I could find. They have a shape and weight just right for throwing.

"Hey, Torrie, go back over there and move them cans over some. You got 'em too close together." I'm halfway between my brother and our targets when he halts me with this command. "And put some dirt in 'em too," he yells, "so they don't blow down."

"I already did that," I protest. "Weren't you looking?"

Anthony looks at me as if I'm lying. "Well, go on back over there anyway. They still too close together."

Anthony gives orders like my father. It's not surprising. He's named after him. He even walks like him. My father is a big man. He used to play baseball in college. Anthony is good at baseball, too. He can hit home runs all day long. He's good at everything. He makes baskets from anywhere on the court and throws football passes with precision. My father calls him his "little Olympian."

"Anthony, why don't you do anything?" I say, refusing to realign the cans. "I had to get that beer bottle out of the ditch." I wipe my muddy hand on the back of my shorts for emphasis. "And I had to find all the rest of the other bottles and things."

"You a 'find' lie. We brought that milk carton with us."

"But . . . "

"But nothing. Go on now, Torrie. I'll set up for the third round if you win this one. Two out of three, remember. After that I'm going to the court and shoot some ball."

I walk back over to our line of targets. The first one in our throwing contest is a dark green 7-Up bottle. I found it in the brush when we were crossing the field. I got several nicks and cuts untangling it from the blackberry vines. A red and white milk carton sits to the left of the 7-Up bottle. Anthony brought it with him from Pak-A-Sak, the corner store. Beside the milk carton is the forty ounce beer bottle I found in the ditch below the young pine trees at the edge of the field. It's half filled with dirty, rust-colored water, and I have red-orange clay under my nails from pulling it out of the ditch. Two soda cans are last in the line up. I found them in the grass along the warehouse. One side of each of the cans is washed clean of color from having laid too long in the summer sun.

Bending over the faded soda cans, I scoop up more gravel with the cup of my hand and funnel the pebbles into their mouths. It's good to be humble I tell myself. The monks always make their students perform humble tasks in kung fu movies. I watch Kung Fu Theater every Sunday after church. There's usually some Shaolin priest or some drunk, but wise, martial arts master in the movie that takes on a student to teach him a secret fighting style. But the student has to humble himself by cleaning his teacher's home for many weeks and he has to perform a hundred painful training exercises before his master will show him even one move of his style.

The book I have from the library says the best Shaolin fighters have Buddha-mind. Because they don't want to win, they do. It doesn't make sense to me. I mean, why do fighters practice if they don't want to win? What's wrong with wanting?

My father says people win because they're born to and that my problem is I wasn't. He says I don't have a "winner's heart" like him and Anthony. But I do. I come out here across the field alone and practice throwing when Anthony's at the school's outdoor court shooting ball. Almost every target I aim at, I hit. And I don't have to think twice about it. Anthony says he never thinks about winning. He just plays his game and when it's over he finds that he's won. Maybe he has Buddha-mind and doesn't know it.

After I finish funneling dirt into the cans, I set them back on the railroad tie farther apart than they were before. I walk back over to my pile of rocks and inspect them to make sure Anthony hasn't stolen any while my back was turned.

Anthony rises from the railroad tie he's sitting on. "Torrie, you ought to give up. You ain't gonna win this round either."

"You ain't God. You don't know that," I say, trying to be confident and humble at the same time, but more of the first. "I've been practicing with Chris and those seventh grade boys at school. I can beat them almost every time. And you know they're good," I tell him as I take two of the best rocks from the top of my pile.

"Yeah, well that don't matter," he pokes me in my chest with his index finger. "'Cause I'll out throw your little tail every time."

I slap his hand away. "Just throw."

"That's right," says Anthony. "Winners go first."

Anthony downs the first two targets easily. His aim is fierce. He hits the 7-Up bottle at its base. It falls forward on the railroad tie and breaks at the neck. Thrilled with his success, he lets out a loud yell that echoes off the side of the warehouse. He sends the milk carton spinning into the dry grass with his next throw. There's only the beer bottle and the two soda cans left now.

Anthony smiles at me. "This contest is over. You lose again little brother." He says "little" in the same ugly way my father does when he introduces me: "Meet the boys. My son Anthony and little Torrie."

"Look. Just go ahead and throw, and stop clowning," I tell him.

He calls me some name and hurls his rock at the fat beer bottle. The rock grazes it, making a kind of plunking sound. It's hard to believe he didn't topple the bottle. It's the easiest target in the group. He curses himself and slings the sweat away from his face. I want to laugh, but I don't because I need to be humble. My hands are together like they're in prayer, my best rock between them. I stand straight and still as possible, head bowed. My eyes are closed, and like a student of a Shaolin priest, I focus only on my breathing.

"Boy, you oughta quit," Anthony says. "You been reading too many of them kung fu books." Anthony doesn't like kung fu. He watches wrestling. He thinks it's real because it's live on TV. Anthony sings his version of that song by Queen that's played when wrestling comes on, the song that goes "We are the champions my friend. And we'll keep on fighting till the end. . . ." But he replaces "champions" with "champion" and each instance of "we are" with a boastful "I am" or "I will."

I don't pay any attention to him. I concentrate on my rock, putting all my hopes on it. Eyes closed, I imagine myself smashing the bottle, smashing it like the ones I have hit when I've practiced out here alone.

Anthony's up in my face when I open my eyes, pulling the corners of his so that they become tight slits. "You through praying, China Boy?" he asks.

I push him back. "I wasn't praying. I was concentrating."

"Well, you shoulda been praying 'cause as sorry as you is, you gonna need some prayer."

He thinks he's real funny. I focus on the bottle's peeling label. Then I throw the rock as hard as I can. Even after it has left my hand, I twist my body forward in an effort to guide it toward my target. But the rock has a mind of its own. It goes wide and high, hitting the side of the warehouse.

Anthony laughs. "Go 'head, Mr. Kung Fu. You really put a hurting on that big old building." He takes a rock from his pile. "Now watch this," he says.

I balance myself on one of the railroad ties and walk down it and away from him. But I pick up another rock just in case he misses.

"Hey, c'mon now. You got to turn 'round and see this, little brother," insists Anthony. When he has my attention he throws. He hits the bottle dead on. The glass and water explode into the grass.

Anthony's starts to gloat, but he's cut short.

"Hey, y'all through already?" Kevin asks as he comes stumbling down the path between the pines.

"Yeah, we just finished," I say.

"Who won?"

"Who you think won?" answers Anthony. "Torrie ain't hit nothing the whole time we was out here. I don't know why he keep trying to beat me when he know he cain't."

Anthony's words are hard and biting. He kicks some loose gravel in my direction. I jump off the railroad tie before it can hit me. After I get my footing, I throw the rock in my hand at him.

He dodges it and spits an insult at me. "Missed me, punk!" he says.

I move forward with clinched fists. Kevin grabs me. He has one hand on my shoulder and the fingers of the other placed lightly on my chest, holding me back.

"Let that punk go," says Anthony. "Let him go."

Kevin takes hold of my arm. "Torrie, don't start that fighting out here. I'm gonna tell your daddy if you do."

That threat immediately sobers both me and my brother.

"I ain't got time to fight him no way," Anthony tells Kevin. "I'm going go shoot some ball up at the court."

Anthony turns away from me. He departs, pushing aside the young pines as he crosses the ditch at the edge of the field. He ascends the path Kevin came stumbling down. Like fire, the dry grass crackles under his feet, snapping, popping, yielding to his stride.

Kevin jumps the ditch after him but doesn't quite make it. One foot slips into the red mud. "Damn!" He wipes his shoe on the grass. "Torrie, you coming?" he asks, irritated with himself.

"Naw, I'm gonna stay here. I'll be up there later."

"All right then." Kevin turns to catch up with Anthony.

I watch them cross the field and then the street. They finally disappear around the corner. The faded soda cans are still standing. I take two rocks and throw at one and then the other. I knock each of them over on the first try.

The sun's heat pressed tight against my face, I walk back across the field. The blackberry vines prick my ankles, and I know that it's Kevin who's the lucky one.

Note how much of Masiki's dialogue is embedded in action, which helps impel the story forward and keeps the reader involved.

Here are some dialogue don'ts: Avoid using multiple synonyms for "said," such as "she retorted," "he commented," and so on. It is best not to use a lot of adverbs, either, in showing how the characters speak: "Priscilla hissed angrily." Accidentally appropriate combinations used to be called Tom Swifties. The old Tom Swift books, which are boys' adventure stories, use these synonyms and adverbs constantly, resulting sometimes in statements like "'I feel A-1,' he said saucily." It's better to give an action that punctuates the speech rather than an adverb qualifying it. "'Am I late?' he asked anxiously" might be replaced by "'Am I late?' he asked, throwing open the door."

Don't use dialogue just to get facts across to the reader. A character in a weak soap opera may say something like, "Mindy! That dress reminds me of Venus, my dead wife." Unless Venus's life and death are intended as a revelation to Mindy, this is an awkward line. One knows that Agatha Christie just wasn't paying attention in her last Thomas and Tuppence novel, when she has Tuppence tell Thomas that she has just received a letter from Betty, "our adopted daughter, who married and moved to India." Such details are not likely to have slipped Thomas's mind.

Don't attempt to represent dialogue by spelling. Many of us say "of" for "have" and leave off final consonants, but seeing these things in print tends to suggest that the speaker is ignorant. Readers may find this usage insulting, even if you want the character to seem ignorant. And even if the readers don't find this treatment condescending, the use of "wuz" for "was," and the like, slows down the flow of the story while the reader stumbles over the unfamiliar words. In the early part of the century, there was a fad for humorous sketches written in dialect, from the point of view of some "naive" speaker; now these sketches seem virtually unreadable. An attempt at dialect, unless the writer is very sensitive as well as skilled, is likely to prove unfortunate.

However, read the dialogue aloud. Is it speakable? Does it have too many clauses and phrases? Would anyone actually say it? True, some people always speak in complete sentences—but not very many. If a character speaks with more formal phrasing than most other people and uses better grammar, this difference should be meaningful to the characterization and plot.

Also, do work the dialogue smoothly into the story. There are all sorts of possible combinations of dialogue and other material, from a story that is almost exclusively dialogue, like Hemingway's "Hills Like White Elephants," to a story containing only a line or two of dialogue. But the dialogue should seem natural and functional no matter how much of it there is. The actions accompanying the dialogue should not seem like obvious stage business but should be appropriate to what is said, and action and speech should complement each other.

PRACTICE IN WRITING DIALOGUE ···················

Find a newspaper advertisement containing two people. Write a dialogue between them. Briefly define the scene in which such a dialogue might take place. Then do one of the following three tasks: (1) Write a dialogue between a child under twelve and his teacher, indirectly indicating the age level of the child. (2) Write a dialogue between an old woman and a young man. (3) Write a dialogue between two freshman roommates, either men or women; decide on some major difference between them, and let this difference appear in how they speak; differences could be contrasts like being city-bred or country-bred, wealthy or financially disadvantaged, liberal or conservative.

Invent a brief discussion among members of a group that you could not possibly belong to at this time (for example, residents of a retirement home; soldiers in the French Foreign Legion; children in a ballet class). Read the discussion to class members, and talk about any problems you had in preparing it.

Go somewhere and listen to a brief conversation between strangers. Attempt to remember every word, or else write down the dialogue if you can do so unobserved. Write out the dialogue if you have not already done so. How does it differ from the dialogue in books?

Now, try to imagine a situation in which such a dialogue might have significance. This may not be easy. For instance, two students may be talking about whether to go to McDonald's or Wendy's, and then may decide one way or another. This exchange isn't promising, but you might think of a situation in which one member of a couple had too much power over the other, and every decision, no matter how small, was an issue of dominance. Now rewrite the dialogue so that it is cleaned up—that is, the "ums" and needless repetitions are gone—and also so that it does what you have decided it should do. In this example, for instance, show one character's attempt to dominate and the other's desire to resist domination.

Write a dialogue in which you are characterizing a type—sophomores in a dormitory, muggers, executives, lawyers. Work mainly on capturing the language of the type. After you have finished, go back over the dialogue and add individualizing characteristics of your type. People don't usually write short stories this way, of course, but doing this exercise will help you see the different factors that make up an individual's language. And of course this method is used sometimes, when, for instance, in a detective novel, the writer is presenting some atmospheric chatter among insignificant characters. The goal of such chat may be dual: to create an impression of the place and to telegraph to the reader an important fact without drawing the reader's attention to its importance.

Turn the TV on mute. Observe the action for five minutes. Write the dialogue that you don't hear.

Characterization

> We never knows wot's hidden in each other's hearts; and if we had glass winders there, we'd need keep the shutters up, some on us, I do assure you!
> —Mrs. Sairy Gump in Charles Dickens's novel *Martin Chuzzlewit*

A lot of our previous discussion refers to character; in fiction writing, of course, there are not clear-cut divisions between elements. Setting and dialogue characterize. But there are some other considerations concerning character that we may look at, if we are trying to force our created people to keep their shutters up.

Characterization is at the heart of fiction; it is a large part of the means by which we distinguish "literary" fiction from popular fiction intended for one quick read. In the popular fiction, often all the characters are stereotypes. The interest lies in the plot. The reader is swept along by suspense and doesn't much care that the characters are flat, the setting is standard, and the dialogue could have been written by a computer.

But a well-written story often provides the delight of a multifaceted, true-to-life person, and allows the reader's understanding of the person's culture to be enriched by the acquaintance of a fictional individual. And in a sense, the created individual is "more real than real"—think, for instance, of Dostoyevsky's Prince Myshkin or Salinger's Holden Caulfield. The fictional character may have a purity and an intensity that are rarely seen in real life but that are still believable, still possible. How does the writer achieve this depth and verisimilitude?

If you were to walk into a roomful of real and fictional people, let's say well-known writers and their most famous creations—Holden Caulfield and J. D. Salinger, Jay Gatsby and F. Scott Fitzgerald, Ántonia and Willa Cather, Sethe and Toni Morrison—who do you think would appear more real? There would be the characters, dressed as they were in the novel, saying the sort of thing they always said, and there would be the writers, blundering about with no script.

A movie was made at Princeton one summer, when classes were not in session, and one of the professors was heard to comment on how much more like students the actors looked than did the few real students who were hanging around finishing their projects.

So what is the secret to creating characters that live? How do you characterize? Of course, writers preparing potboilers in a series characterize one way, creating "types" with a few deft strokes, whereas serious writers use a variety of other methods. But basically, there are a few means by which you can communicate information about your characters to the reader. Subtlety and economy are important; you cannot go into extended explanations of motive or belief.

You might start by asking, How do you know what real people, your friends and neighbors and enemies, are like? What brings you to conclude, "Joe is willing to be helpful but stingy with money," or "Patricia always knows what you are thinking"? You will come up with specific acts, comments, and images that characterize this person for you. You can then use these to represent the person to others.

1. *You can describe the person directly.* Physical appearance and clothing help to define character. Just for fun, you might even make out a data sheet for your character. Start at the bottom: would your character be wearing Nikes, Chuck Taylors, Tony Lama boots, flip-flops? Work your way up. What kind of hair does your character have? If he's bald, is he proudly bald? Or does he comb the few remaining strands carefully over the shining scalp?

   You would not, of course, provide all the details on your data sheet in the short story, but your sheet might help you to visualize the character and allow you to find the right details as they become relevant. And physical description is often very important as an interest-raising device as well as for characterization. With physical description as with every other method, you are going to have to leave most of the story untold. If you want the person to be very stylish, one or two details will do. You don't have to identify every garment down to the socks.

You may be directly describing your character's psychology as well; that is, you may find a reason to state directly something about her character. Perhaps the reason is only to emphasize a contrast between what would be expected and what the character does in this case. Usually, though, you will not discuss the character's psychology so much as you will show it.

2. *Another major way of characterizing is through your description of what your character says and does.* Dialogue gives much information about age, education level, degree of social awareness, and so on. And of course action speaks too—if not "louder than words," at least distinctly.

3. *A third way of characterizing is through the way that other characters react to your character.* Is he liked, feared, respected, tolerated, hated? Sometimes an apparent discrepancy between the character's behavior and the reaction she provokes may be telling. An old woman, for instance, may seem genteel and polite, but if other characters respond to her with fear, the reader gets a telegraph message: not all is what it seems, because there is an underside to this person's character that will surface later and no doubt play an important part in the story.

You will probably need to use all these methods of characterizing, direct description, dialogue and action, and others' responses, to create a believable fictional person. Moreover, you will have to make character and plot work smoothly together. Often, if you begin with a plot, you may find yourself making your protagonist behave out of character so that you can tie things up smoothly and keep to your original plotline. On the other hand, if you begin with a character, you may wind up with a nice evocative character sketch but no real plot.

It hard to do, the best approach is to conceive of the two together—both character and plot. It is also best to be flexible about both, but especially about plot. Then you may be willing to alter the ending if it seems to you and to others that "she just wouldn't do that."

Although it is often easiest to base a character on a real person, doing this still does not mean that it will be easy. Let's say your character is based on yourself. First, of course, there is a lot about ourselves we don't know, but let's agree that you know more about yourself than you do about anyone else. You won't have any trouble with a basic physical description, you know what you like to do, and you may even be able to give a reasonable representation of your speech in writing. But can you describe yourself from an observer's viewpoint, for example, your way of getting up from a chair or of answering the phone? Can you see the defects in your character, and balance them against your virtues, so that the person you are describing seems whole and real?

Moreover, basing a character on someone you know well has its own problems, because you may find that you feel disloyal to a friend or relative if the person in your story has negative characteristics. Yet, it is true that real people have flaws, and often it is necessary even to exaggerate them in fiction.

Frequently you will create a main character, at least for your first story, who is somewhat like you, but you will concentrate on those elements of personality that surface in response to a particular situation. You can't create a character that is fully complete, but you can make someone who appears realistic within the confines of your fictional world.

The best practice for characterization is analysis of well-drawn characters. A method for doing this kind of analysis is to take a favorite short story—preferably a very short one, five to eight pages—and photocopy it. Now take two highlighters, and first, in one color, highlight all the passages that directly characterize the main character. In the other color, highlight those passages that indirectly characterize the main character. (Yes, in some stories, this method will cause most of the story to be highlighted.) Now describe the techniques that the author has used to characterize indirectly. Are there any techniques that you had not thought of or had not noticed before? Consider the methods used to characterize directly. For example, indirectly, the author might have naive people cuddle up to the main character while the more sophisticated people shun him; directly, the character might be described as "cold, emotionless." What kind of person does the speaker seem to be in "Some of Us Had Been Threatening Our Friend Colby"? How do you know?

The following short story by Chuck Taylor attempts to get inside the mind of a boy who has been imprisoned, to show the boy's confused sense of injustice. What does the story say about the boy's growing up? Do you think the writer agrees with the boy in how the blame is placed? This is indeed a story of character—plot and other elements are secondary. How does Taylor characterize the boy through his unwritten letter?

·· **Chuck Taylor**

*You Owe Me**

These are the words I'd write you, dad, if I were the writing kind. Sitting in this cell at the county jail, I got plenty of time to think.

I'm remembering what happened fifteen years ago when I was ten and Mack was five. We'd just moved from Fort Worth into this new Las Cruces apartment. You know how we were always moving back then? You and mom were always getting laid off. Before Fort Worth we lived in Shreveport, and before that Tyler, and before that San Angelo, where Mack was born.

Anyway, you put Mack in this day care a block up from the apartment, and me in this elementary school farther up closer to downtown. You and mom were excited cause you both had found better paying jobs.

*Chuck Taylor, "You Owe Me" is reprinted by permission of the author.

You were building frames for houses, and she was doing secretary work for the same construction company.

The second day we were there you drove down to El Paso and took us across the international bridge. We walked around the crowded plaza of downtown Juarez and heard Spanish spoken everywhere. It was amazing. The Mexicans were all dressed up, the men in black suits, the women if frilly dresses, and just getting out of church.

But things settled soon enough into the old routine. I got out of school at three-thirty. This yellow van loaded with kids picked me up in front of my school and took me over to Mack's day care around four. Either you or mom picked Mack and me up there around five-thirty.

We got to the apartment around six and mom started cooking in that narrow little kitchen we had. You sat down with us on this mattress we slept on the floor of the living room, and we watched "X-Men" on that little portable TV.

Then we ate supper, squeezed around the card table near the front door. After that you'd take a beer and go for a walk in the desert behind the apartment while mom gathered up the dishes and cleaned the kitchen.

Mack and I went to play with neighbor kids till it got dark. There was this Wes kid Mack liked. The two of them would take pieces of cardboard and slide down this rocky dirt incline next to the apartment. I don't remember who I played with—maybe I just watched Mack and Wes do their thing.

On the weekends, a couple of hours after lunch, you'd take us swimming at this park up high in the foothills of the Oregon mountains. I remember you telling us about how precious water was in the desert. They had this big blue circular slide Mack and I went down. You'd be at the bottom smiling to catch us and make sure we didn't drown.

You also started teaching me how to play pool at the apartment clubhouse. Mack would watch cartoons on the big screen TV they had there.

Life was OK—not easy—but OK, just like it's always been. Then one night after supper you had to go back to work. No big deal. You'd done it lots of times on your other jobs. Mack and I sat on the mattress and watched TV. Later Mom had us take our baths and put us to bed.

Very late that night I woke up. I went to the door and peered down the hallway into the living room. All the lights were on and I could hear Mom talking to different people on the phone, apologizing for waking them up. Between calls she cried a little and wiped her tears on a napkin.

When we got up the next morning, you still weren't there. Mom said you were staying at a friend's in Albuquerque, helping on a job up there for more money. She said you'd be coming back soon. I asked mom when and she said "I don't know, hon, but soon." We got dressed and mom fed us cereal and juice and took Mack to day care and me to school.

But that job lasted a long time, and you never came back. I remember finally you did come and get some clothes and fishing equipment. Then I remember you came for Mack's birthday. Mom got mad about how you hung the piñata on this tree in the back. Later I remember you taking us to Burger King and how the shakes were bad because the milk was spoiled.

One night Mom got drunk and went into the back room and dumped over all your boxes of tools and stuff. It was the first time I had seen anyone drunk. I didn't understand what was going on, and it scared me to death. We were supposed to be asleep but Mom was playing the Eagles so loud it hurt my ears. Mack and I put our fingers in our ears and got out of our bunks and peered out a crack in the bedroom door.

When I woke up in the morning the place was a total mess. It looked like somebody'd gone through all the closets and drawers and pulled out everything and ripped it all up. Sharp pieces of broken dishes were on the kitchen floor.

Then I remember, after a month or so, Mom calling up this guy at work and talking all the time, and later this guy coming for dinner and staying the night. David ended up being around for several years, even after we'd left Las Cruces and moved to Waco. He was into running, and for a while I'd go running with him. From then on all the rooms smelled of marijuana.

A good while before we moved to Waco, we all went out to eat at a Mexican restaurant and met your girlfriend Betty. Later Mack and I'd come over weekends and play with Betty's kids. The oldest liked to do the things I did. I suppose Stacie's the best friend I ever had. I hear she is in Austin working at a gas station.

So that's the story. If I worked at it I could remember more—but why bother? This is why I don't write to you in Austin, and why I don't call. It's also why I've had problems. If you don't believe, you can call the counselor at the drug treatment center I was in before ending up in jail.

This is also why, if I do call, or if I do come by to see you and your new third wife—what's her name?–you need to be nice. You owe me. I'm your son.

When I get out of here, you need to come and pick me up. It ain't far from Austin to Waco. After you pick me up, you need to take me out for a steak dinner, and then drive me back to Austin and let me stay in one of those extra bedrooms in that fancy new house on the lake they tell me you got since you became a contractor.

Then, you should give me money. A lot of money. That way, I won't break in your house and steal your things—like I did to mom and at brother Mack's.

What does the son believe that the father "owes" him?

Here are some considerations:

1. Your character must act consistently, or there must be reasons behind apparent inconsistent behavior that suggest a coherence of character. Your character may be timid, for instance, but may be tricked into courage in a particular situation. This courageous behavior might then change the character's attitude toward himself—not drastically, but significantly—and give him more courage generally for the future. You can't, however, expect complete character reversals in the course of a short story.

2. Your character must seem real. To provide realism, be as detailed as you can in presenting your character, but make sure that the details you present are relevant to the character. All the physical details you present should be precise and telling. Consider clothing, for instance: What might it mean if a young woman wore old-fashioned clothing, perhaps clothing of her mother's generation? What might it mean if an old man dresses like his son? And if your characters are trendy, make sure that your own knowledge of what's in is up-to-date. Everything about your character must cohere. If your peer-group readers think something is inconsistent, probably it is.

3. Names are important. Think of what comes to mind when you hear these women's names: Karen, Paige, Cybelle, Barbara, Shelley. Imagine a room filled with these men: Kent, Buford, Mickey, Hunter, and Giles. Even one given name, Katherine, can change into Katie, Kate, Kitty, Kathy, Kathie— and can change connotations with each nickname. Let your character's name reflect him or her. When you add last names, you are going to need to consider family derivation: Anderson, Perrin, Donelli, McKay, and Jones all suggest various ethnicities. Your character's full name should be a statement. Look at how writers like Henry James use names. Read his story "Daisy Miller," for instance, and ask what is communicated by each name. If the main character were named "Daffodil Carpenter," the story would not have the same effect at all.

4. Your minor characters are important too, but unfortunately you cannot take the space to characterize them fully. Therefore, you need to suggest personality with a few deft strokes. The party bore, the obsessive housewife, and other stereotypes can be easily sketched in if they are needed to advance the plot. You don't want to rely on stereotypes, but occasionally you have to. The problem with, and advantage of, stereotypes of this sort is that the reader thinks immediately, "Oh, I know someone just like that," and grants your character the reality that the characterization may not have earned. You might want to take a close look at the minor characters in your favorite stories to see how much has been done to create them. Consider the minor characters in Philip Roth's stories, for instance. How much space does he devote to characterizing them? How does he do so? You might read "Goodbye, Columbus" to examine the minor characters.

5. The farther you go from your own direct knowledge and experience, the harder it will be to create characters, but you aren't limited to your own experience for the plot and setting. You can, for instance, write a fantasy or science fiction story using characters based on yourself and people you know. Just set down the basic premise of your story: it is the year 2050, for instance, and all reproduction is done in the lab—and then import your characters.

6. Avoid trouble by changing the physical appearance and other details of characters who are based on people you know. It is true that often people don't recognize fictional versions of themselves, but they might. Also, inventing details like size and occupation gives you more freedom to form your character—he may be based on Mike Logan, but he has turned into Mark Allaman, and he doesn't have to do what Mike always does if you don't want him to.

EXERCISES

1. Think up full names for each of the following characters:
   a. Middle-aged English teacher, strict grammarian
   b. Small child, brought to adult party, getting underfoot and being a pest
   c. New York police officer
   d. College student—hyperstudious
   e. College student—full-time party goer
   f. Rude individual in parking lot, who cuts you off and then shakes a fist at you
   g. Dull professor who always lectures from twenty-year-old notes
   h. Charismatic student leader
   i. Televangelist
   j. Rodeo star

   Note that none of these characters is identified by sex. You have probably done so in your naming of them. Now, from your list, take the character that you like best and can imagine most completely. For this character, do the following:
   a. Create a plot, and outline it in a paragraph.
   b. Describe the character, giving information about appearance and psychology.
   c. Have your character engage in a brief dialogue with a second character that you choose from the list.

   Now, let the class break up into groups of three. You could also form pairs, if that would be more convenient. In your group or pair, you should each share the description that you have written about your favorite character. Now, create a dialogue with the other or others. It doesn't matter whether the characters all turn out to be the same type; a chat among three hyperstudious computer science majors—who also engage in role-playing games—might be even more interesting than a chat among a grammarian, a New York police officer, and a small pest.

   Note that this exercise will involve collaboration on a plot. You have to create some kind of situation in which the three characters might actually meet to get involved in a conversation, which should reflect some of the circumstances of that meeting. This exercise will also allow you to see how other people react to your imagined character. Does the character seem to evoke respect? affection? contempt? Is this reaction what you expected?

Type up your dialogue so that you each have a copy, remembering that you have the right to the parts you have written for use in other circumstances.

2. Write a sketch involving two characters, one based on you ten years ago and another based on you ten years from now. Name your characters. Then create a situation in which they interact, having them talk a bit.

3. Make up a data sheet for a character. What is important to know about a person to get a sense of what he or she is like: age, hair color, habits, place of origin, education, fantasies? Prepare a list of what you consider the most important considerations. Then share these lists with other class members, to see to what extent you agree on what is important. Now, exchange data sheets, and fill out someone else's data sheet with information about the main character in a story you are working on. Form groups of four or five class members, and produce a composite data sheet for your group.

4. Following is the beginning of a story by fiction writer Jill Patterson. Analyze how she characterizes through dialogue and action. Write down what you know of each character that you encounter in this brief excerpt. What is the speaker like? What indication of tension do you see in the narrative?

.... **Jill Patterson**

From *Strawberry Fields**

I watched Grandmother yank the weeds in the small garden as our blue Chevy rumbled up the hill. Her plump body stooped close to the dirt, and her grey hair shook with her jerky movements. I could imagine the curses she spat at the thick grass that choked her strawberries. Mom was sleeping heavily in the porch swing. One pink arm slipped and dangled toward the wooden floor. Her age didn't bother her looks or the men who took her home. Anyone could see the fleshy curves rise and fall under her blouse. Unbuttoned too far for modesty, I thought. Her blond hair disappeared in sponge curlers, and a bottle of nail polish rested beneath the slight motion of the swing.

Nodding to her, I told Grady, "Looks like Mom expects company tonight."

*Jill Patterson, paragraphs from "Strawberry Fields" are reprinted by permission of the author.

He glanced at the rag-doll figure paralyzed in the shade. "Lay on the horn, will you? I want some attention." He leaned across the cab and slammed his palm on the horn.

"God, Grady. Grandmother will have a stroke."

"No real harm done. Nothing to get all hung up about."

Grandmother continued her gardening. Every day for the last ten years, I had watched Grandmother struggle to control her garden. Her farm was the only home I could remember since Mom had moved us there when I was six. My memories of Dad didn't come too clearly or too often. Any images of his physical appearance which might be stored in my head surfaced only for a couple of seconds before they blurred with the one photo of him Mom kept in her nightstand drawer. Sometimes I would hold that photo and wonder if his eyes were always as stiff as Grady's seemed—or if it was just that one photo, that one moment when his picture was taken.

I parked the truck beside the house. The rusty sun flashed through the mimosa leaves and peppered the blue hood. Fella crept out from under the house, and I stroked only his clean brown fur to be safe. The grass had grown too high. I quit petting him to scratch my own legs. Fella turned to Grady.

"Damn mangy dog. Should just shoot him. Stop his misery." He pushed Fella away with his shin, and the dog crawled back to the cool earth.

I ignored Grady and his attempts to prove how tough he could be. He was small for seventeen. Mom always joked about his baby-face. But I thought his jaw had grown tighter, and I'd seen his blue eyes glare like a rabid dog's.

Grandmother left her garden and struggled toward us with a full bucket of berries. "Michelle, did you get the embroidery thread like I told you?"

"Give me that bucket, Grandmother. That's too heavy for you."

"Did you hear me, Mickie?" She handed me the bucket. "The thread. Did you remember?"

Point of View

> Literature is the one place in any society where, within the secrecy of our own heads, we can hear voices talking about everything in every possible way.
>
> —Salman Rushdie

What you see depends on where you're looking from. Point of view refers to the perspective from which the reader gets the story. The point of view is the answer to the question: through whose consciousness are the events slanted? Sometimes there is one point of view clearly maintained throughout the story. In other cases, the point of view changes. Often the reader of a straightforward short story doesn't question or analyze point of view, although this element of fiction provides the narrative with much of its life or interest.

Point of view allows us to "know" fictional characters. We associate Holden Caulfield's language, his exaggerations and repetitions and cussings, with something that we think of as the essential Holden. He may be more real to us than people we know. When a point of view is successfully represented, we tend to feel that the story is "realistic," that the character is "real."

We don't think about point of view as such, any more than we think of terms like *metaphor* while we are enjoying a poem. Later, we may invoke the terminology to answer the question of why the poem or story was so successful. However, it tends to register if there is anything untoward about the point of view. If there is a sudden shift from "she" to "I," for instance, or if we are being shown the world through one man's mind and this focus abruptly changes—or if the "I" speaker dies—the reader may feel disconcerted and dissatisfied. In experimental fiction, shifts, disconnections, and other disruptions of point of view may occur. Sometimes this technique is used largely to violate expectations, while often a special effect is intended that cannot be achieved through ordinary means. Before experimenting, though, the writer usually needs to become familiar with the traditional points of view and to be comfortable using them.

Creating a unified point of view can be a way to pull your story together and to give it meaning. If you are going to use multiple points of view, the changes should have thematic significance. For example, Tolstoy's long, segmented story "The Death of Ivan Ilych" begins with the perceptions of someone who is attending his own funeral, and then shifts around among other perspectives as the story flashes back to the events before the beginning of Ivan's long, painful dying. As Ivan comes closer to his death, the consciousness through which events are perceived becomes more exclusively his, intensifying the way that mortal illness separates one person from the others and also forcing the reader to share Ivan's experiences.

Although some contemporary stories with multiple or shifting viewpoints seem at first to have no reason for the changes, often a close reading will disclose one. Toni Morrison's *Beloved*, for instance, uses a shifting point of view to show

how one character blurs into another and an individual merges with history. At a key point in the novel, Morrison has placed three short sections providing the fragmented thoughts of each of her three major women characters, Denver, Sethe, and Beloved; and then Morrison has a section in which all their thoughts run together, showing how in one sense the three women are one person. She also entwines Beloved's thoughts with images of the slave trade, locating her in history as well as in present time.

Several points of view are available to the writer. There is, of course, the first person singular. Telling the story in this way allows the writer to give the main character real depth; few characters "come alive" for the reader like J. D. Salinger's Holden Caulfield in *The Catcher in the Rye* or Sylvia Plath's Esther Greenwood in *The Bell Jar*. It is true that both of these examples are from novels, but short stories can produce the same kind of rounded characters through first person narration.

The disadvantages of first person singular must be considered, however. First, and probably most obvious, is the problem that the writer is limited to the chosen character's observations. J. D. Salinger can't decide to add to the reader's understanding of events and of character by stepping outside his narrative and editorializing. (OK, so maybe he can, but most readers wouldn't like it.) It is very tricky to get a message through to the reader that the narrator doesn't see or understand; if that technique is used, the writer is creating an "unreliable narrator" whose observations are based on misunderstanding, like Benjy, the three-year-old "idiot" who records a part of the action in William Faulkner's novel *The Sound and the Fury*. This "unreliable narrator" device can be effective, but it is difficult; most writers in most situations content themselves with simply presenting the events as the narrator sees them, without trying to undermine the narrator's report.

More common than first person are third person omniscient and third person limited omniscient. In third person omniscient, the writer gets into everyone's mind in turn. The owner of the voice reporting the events—whom we may call the speaker of the story—knows everything. The benefit of the third person omniscient is that all responses can be described directly. The writer doesn't have to figure out how a character might indirectly show embarrassment, or fear, or anger—the writer can describe what the character feels. A disadvantage is that often a short story told in this way seems to lack focus, because it doesn't center clearly on a single character. Another problem is that often a novice writer has trouble realistically inventing a group of characters in depth. It is hard enough to create one believable character and to sketch in the others as types.

More common in short story writing is third person limited omniscient, which not only tells the story in the third person but also allows the reader to look into the mind of only one character. Usually this is the main character, although occasionally the story will be slanted through the consciousness of someone close to the main character for a particular reason (for instance, because the main character gets killed and someone is therefore needed to describe the subsequent events).

Many writers find that the third person limited omniscient point of view provides the most freedom. The focus is maintained by centering the story on the perceptions of the main character, but the writer is not forced to use the main character's diction consistently. Moreover, this point of view is often most successful in pulling the reader into the story. The reader comes to identify with the main character, learning things with him or her, beginning to see the world with his or her eyes. Occasionally the reader is deliberately misled in some way, as is the case in John Cheever's wonderful story "The Swimmer." We are given the perceptions of a middle-aged alcoholic who has decided to swim his way home from a pool party by crossing all the pools between his host's house and his own. At the end of the story, we learn that the main character's perceptions are actually misperceptions, caused by alcohol and denial, and that his life is very different from what he (and we) thought it was.

A less frequently adopted point of view is that of the objective speaker, who gets into no one's mind and appears to report only that which could be perceived by an outsider. This reporter's eye view gives a hard surface to the story, but it requires a high level of interpretive subtlety. The writer can't ever say, "Sarah was shocked." Instead, the writer must say something like, "Sarah's eyebrows went up" or "Sarah dropped her cup of coffee, slumped forward, and fell at the stranger's feet."

To become aware of how various writers use point of view, look at a book containing short stories that are familiar to you—a collection that you have read, for instance, or an anthology that you have used in another class. In the book, find several different points of view. Ask yourself how the point of view affects the narrative. This can be an especially useful exercise if you are looking at a collection of stories by a versatile writer. Look at James Hannah's short-story collection *Desperate Measures*, for instance, and note how the different points of view contribute to characterization and plot.

EXAMPLES OF TYPES OF NARRATION

Objective Narration.   The objective point of view is seldom used, although Hemingway sometimes used it. In an objective narration, no one's mind is explored, but events are reported as though seen objectively, from the outside. This kind of writing creates the effect of an emotional minimalism, because any information given about the characters' inner lives has to be implied by what they say and do. Unless the writer is extremely skilled, the effect of an objective narration is likely to be an emotional flatness without reverberations. Following is part of the tale of Red Ridinghood told objectively, with no attempt at subtlety.

"What big teeth you have, Grandma!" Red Ridinghood said.
"The better to EAT you with!" the wolf responded, throwing the quilt off the bed and leaping at Red, teeth bared. But at that moment a woodcutter who had been

passing by the cottage rushed through the open door, hatchet waving, and with one slashing blow he killed the wolf before it had a chance to touch Red.

Third Person Limited Omniscient Narration.   The third-person limited omniscient point of view provides more flexibility in description and allows the author to enter the mind of only one character. All other characters are described externally.

Red was terrified; even without her glasses she knew her grandmother from a wolf. She smiled encouragingly. I have to keep the wolf talking, she thought. If we get into a long chat, perhaps he won't get to thinking about food. Besides, where's Grandma? He just ate. Perhaps I can get him to talk about himself.

"Wh-what big eyes you have, Grandma," she stammered. Now, that was dumb, she thought. I should have asked him a question about his hobbies or something.

"The better to see you, my dear," said the wolf.

Third Person Omniscient Narration.   Like the third person limited, there is more flexibility in description. Also, the third person omniscient allows the writer to get inside everyone's mind.

Red Ridinghood struggled with the latch, At last, thought the wolf. The old lady was as tough as that poodle I had for breakfast. But I will have to rest a bit to work up my appetite. "How kind of you to visit your sick old grandmother, my dear," he called out in a high, wavering voice.

Omigosh that's a wolf! Red thought. She glanced back at the door, but she'd shut it. She raised her basket as though to ward off the attack. "Grandmother, I've brought you some neat's-foot-jelly," she said, making a strong effort to speak firmly and brightly.

First Person Narration.   First person, of course, gives one speaking voice, usually but not always that of the main character. The point of view limits the narrative to what that person can see, understand, and report.

I was very hungry indeed. The old poodle I had snatched in the park from behind the azalea bush while its owners were discussing the tax increase had been very tough and unsatisfying. Besides, that was over six hours ago. I craved tender meat. I was trying to picture a delightful dinner of spring lamb from the Hopper farm, my imaginings unfortunately punctured by the thought of Ms. Hopper's shotgun, when there on the public footpath approached a most-delicious looking example of young humanity. I poised to leap, but then I noticed a woodcutter nearby, and I thought, alas, this is too public a place for dinner. I will have to delay my dining and use my brain . . .

Student writers used to be instructed never to change the point of view. If you begin with a limited omniscient perspective, you were not to change ever to the vision of another character, or to omniscient perspective. But many pre-modernist, modernist, and postmodernist writers do use multiple points of view and shifting points of view. Leo Tolstoy's "The Death of Ivan Ilych," for instance, begins with the viewpoint of a casual acquaintance at Ilych's funeral, but as the narrative retreats to Ilych's whole career and his long, painful death, the reader enters more and more intensely into the center of Ilych's consciousness. The shift is purposeful—Tolstoy wants the reader to "be the onlooker, to whom Ilych's death is a chance for promotion and the annoying obligation to attend a funeral, and then to "be" Ilych, who learns by dying what it means to live. It is a story that once read is not forgotten. About changing perspectives, it should be enough to say that the beginning writer is wise to maintain one point of view but that once experience has been gained, the writer may want to shift points of view to achieve specific effects.

Changing the point of view is often the first and most serious revision of a story—you may decide, for instance, that the third person point of view that you were using was confused and awkward and that the story should have been told in first person. Changing the point of view may enliven the story, but the change involves every level of the story—you are also changing the method of characterization, because now you are using the voice of the main character, and you are changing the way you get across information to the reader.

The elements of fiction are all interconnected, and when you tweak one, you change the others. There exists no formula for good fiction. The "scene and consequences" method is helpful sometimes, but it does not cover all the patterns you might want to use to structure your events. The main requirement for good writing is constant analytical reading. Whenever you read a fine piece of fiction, ask yourself what made it good and how its parts fit together. Notice how long the scenes are, by what means the reader is brought smoothly from one scene to the next, and how the background material necessary to understanding the plot is communicated to the reader. In other words, read stories as would a fiction writer, as discussed earlier. When devices work for others, borrow them. Your style will develop, and the awkwardness that plagues every new fiction writer will diminish as you continue to read and write.

EXERCISES

1. Form groups of four, and assign a point of view to each member. Then choose a fairy tale. Each group member should tell the tale in her or his assigned point of view—first person, limited omniscient, omniscient, and objective. If the class doesn't break up easily into groups of four, include five members in some groups, and give two of them limited omniscient viewpoints and assign them characters in the tale from whose perspective the story will be told. Here are some tales to use: Three Little Pigs, Cinderella, Snow White and the Seven Dwarves, Rumplestiltskin, Puss in Boots, Jack and the Beanstalk.

2. From the local paper, take some simple narrative report. If you can, find one with some humor or pathos in it. Now tell this story from two different points of view. Then look at the results. How do the two narratives differ? Which one do you find more successful, and why? Does this narrative have the promise of turning into any

kind of short story? What point of view would you use to tell the story if you do find some potential in it?

3. Tell a well-known story—fact or fable, history or literature—from the point of view of some minor character, using the first person. You might want to use a Bible story for this exercise, or a Greek myth.

4. From the objective point of view, describe something that happened to you. Make it a simple, ordinary event: getting a traffic ticket, or opening a bank account, or buying shoes. Now look at your objective account. Does it imply anything about the event that had not previously struck you? Is there anything in this ordinary event, for example, that might give it a place in fiction?

5. This collaborative exercise can be used for poetry as well as fiction. Your instructor will put on the computer a story from Greek myth, such as the tale of Circe and the way she changed Odysseus' men into swine. You will be asked to read the text and choose a part, which might in this case be Circe, Odysseus, or any one of Odysseus' men either before or after the change. When you come to the part of the tale where the character is named or alluded to, then insert a paragraph in the character's voice—or a poem in the paragraph's voice. Thus you will have the chance to enter the Circe text and take part in it, and the "new" text will include a number of fresh voices. If there are twenty-five of you, there might be five machines that each contain the text, and five groups to create new texts.

Creative Nonfiction

You may not want to fiction-alize your experiences but prefer to present them much as they happened. Or you wish to write about others' lives or current events, without fictionaliz-ing. You want to write creative nonfiction.

> There is no life that can be recaptured wholly, as it was, which is to say that all biography is ultimately fiction. What does that tell you about the nature of life, and does one really want to know?
>
> —Bernard Malamud, *Dubin's Lives*

Creative nonfiction is a rapidly growing field, with new courses and workshops springing up all over the country. Providing a generally accepted definition is not easy, nor is it always simple to distinguish fiction from nonfiction. "Novels" such as Maxine Hong Kingston's *Woman Warrior* and Sylvia Plath's *The Bell Jar* might more accurately be described as creative nonfiction. This slippery genre is variously defined and understood, and it may range from the friendly personal experience essay—the "familiar essay" of earlier times, and often of freshman English courses—to tough, realistic journalistic feature stories told in the third person. You can see that since a lot of personal experience goes into fiction, the essay may blur into the short story.

Creative nonfiction requires as much careful rearrangement of experience as does fiction, and in many of the same ways. Elements of creative nonfiction that are similar to those of fiction include dialogue, description, and characterization. Many of the same methods are used, although there is usually less dialogue in nonfiction (there usually are no extended conversations that carry the plot), and there is less likely the need to characterize several people fully. Point of view and plot are different. Autobiographical narrative is in the first person, and character sketch is also often in the first person (telling how the character appeared to, or interacted with, a narrator.) And you don't need to figure out whether Angie would have dropped Bill at a particular point, because the plot is more or less what actually happened. This treatment does not mean that it won't be hard to pace your narrative, making things seem as if they happen naturally and bringing the reader along smoothly without apparent leaps or gaps.

Point of view: Even in the first person, characterization is necessary. For instance, the first draft of a student's essay begins, "Before I took my first job, I did not know what 'work' meant." He then begins the tale of his first job, but he hasn't recreated his earlier self, the one who was easygoing and unfocused and goalless. So the beginning of the story doesn't seem quite right somehow: the person he is representing doesn't seem like the type of worker to be having the difficulties that he has. The writer of a personal narrative doesn't have the complicated point of view problem that the fiction writer has, but the writer must keep the persona consistent, and if there are two personae—representing, perhaps, a younger and an older self—these must be developed in such a way as to make the change seem logical.

Plot: The main plotting problem for the creator of personal narrative involves framing. The writer must decide just how much to include in the essay and to draw an imaginary line around it. Thus, minor characters who were there may be left out, and conversation remembered perfectly well as part of the scene may also be omitted. You fictionalize somewhat when you write a personal essay. You decide what your overall goal for the piece is, and you select details that fit it, omitting anything that is not directly relevant to your objectives. For example, if you are describing a scene at a dance that ended in a fist fight, you might want to focus on those details that led to the confrontation. You may remember a lot of other details and bits of conversations, but you might include only enough of these to indicate the size of the crowd and the nature of the gathering—they would, in fact, become background. You might leave out people, conversations, and events that you remember as part of the scene, because they were not relevant to the growing tension between the two main characters and might even distract from the narrative.

Consider both plot and point of view in the following passage from Ann Loux's unpublished memoir of growing up in Mississippi. Note how the child's point of view is caught by the sentence structure as well as the details. Consider how the details add up to give a picture of a way of life. If in fact on the front porch atop a card table, there was a stack of copies of *Photoplay*, Loux doesn't (and wouldn't) mention it.

.... **Ann Loux**

*[Untitled Memoir]**

Auntie K lived all her life in the house her father built. Great grandfather Clarke was a contractor and he set out to prove he could make a cellar that wouldn't fill with water in Greenville, Mississippi, where the water table is a few inches below ground. His cellar was dry a few years, according to Auntie K; then it filled up with water when the river rose way high and never did drain. Nobody built another cellar in town.

*Ann Loux, paragraphs from unpublished memoir are reprinted by permission of the author.

We could see water down there beneath the house if we knelt beside the broken lattice and peered in. My brother and I used to dare the visiting cousins to rescue the treasures we could spot in the shadows—a half-submerged commode, a rocking chair, three floating baskets. They all seemed within easy reach of the long-handled rake, but they never were. No telling how deep that water went. None of us ever got up the nerve to lower ourselves down in there. It smelled like old, old earth.

The front porch leaned a full foot on the right side where the adults sat and rocked under the ceiling fan. The screens were rusty, mashed out and pulled loose around the edges, especially on the kids' side. Only the left side fence next to Miss Lelia's property still stood, not really separating her sweet heart roses from Auntie K's roses and azaleas. The ornate wrought iron was all twisted up from where they'd tried to dig it out but couldn't. The fence around front had gone for the war effort. The third floor garret went up in the 1927 fire.

The kitchen floor sloped so low at the yard end that we could roll marbles downhill from the stove to the back door. The white metal table had chipped cups full of water around its feet so ants couldn't crawl into Auntie K's food.

Loux's memoir catches many details, but the specifics have been chosen to produce the impression of the decay of the older generation's South and of the younger generation's curiosity and resilience.

The student beginning to write creative nonfiction should reread the suggestions in the fiction section before beginning. Also, the student should read several creative nonfiction essays from well-known writers such as Annie Dillard and Virginia Woolf. As a reader, getting used to a form is the first step in attempting to exploit the form as a writer.

With nonfiction as well as fiction, you need a plan. Like the fiction writer, you have something to say through the experiences you present; you are not merely describing them as interesting anecdotes from a life. Several major writers have described their mental difficulties in creative nonfiction pieces; see F. Scott Fitzgerald's *The Crack-Up* or William Styron's *Darkness Visible,* for instance. Others have shown the effects of ethnicity and cultural crossings on childhood development; a good example is Maxine Hong Kingston's *Woman Warrior,* considered by some a novel but described on the cover as a "memoir." You will see that the line between fiction and nonfiction is thin, especially as there is always an element of imagination (as well as misperception) in our reporting and as there is a lot of fact in fiction.

To consider the genre as it will be discussed here, a general definition is useful. Creative nonfiction, generally, is the nontechnical essay. There are a number of overlapping categories of creative nonfiction that you might want to consider. *Autobiographical narratives* tell some experience from the writer's past. *Creative argumentation* presents a position in a relaxed, discursive way. *Character sketches* and other biographical essays (sometimes combined with interviews) introduce a public person, or sometimes a private one, to the reader. Other kinds of creative exposition may involve the sharing of a hobby or of a perspective. You might describe how to make soap in the way your elderly relatives make it, and although the reader will learn how to make soap, what you want most is to share the feel of the lives of the soap-makers. You might describe bird-watching in such a way as to raise environmental awareness. The only key to this somewhat ill-defined genre is the word "creative." These are not essays that explain how to install a water heater or that show the steps of photosynthesis. Instead they involve the personality of the writer in some way.

We are going to look more closely at two kinds of creative nonfiction: the autobiographical narrative and the character sketch/interview. These two kinds of creative nonfiction are sometimes grouped together as "life writing."

In each case, the writer needs to begin by determining audience: who is intended as the reader of this piece? We think about audience in writing fiction and poetry, too, but here we often assume simply that the story is for those who read literary fiction, and that the poem is for poetry-readers; maybe we dream of getting something into the *New Yorker* someday and so define our audience in that way. It is harder for creative nonfiction, because the realities are more pressing. An interview for *People Magazine* will differ from a character sketch encountered in the *Atlantic Monthly*. We will concentrate more on the somewhat "literary" creative nonfiction in defining principles and practice, but much of what we say will be applicable to the essay for any audience.

The autobiographical narrative is much like what used to be called the personal essay, which frequently turned out to be the friendly nostalgic piece that cozied you up as you read it and scratched the back of your neck. The appropriate topics were your grandmother's kitchen and your uncle's magic tricks, and the essays, when successful, left you with a warm glow. (When unsuccessful, they left you with the feeling that you had eaten a two-pound marshmallow.) The interview/character sketch was similar, often focusing on a favorite teacher or local "character." A frequently consulted source for examples of both types was the *Reader's Digest*.

The updated version of the familiar essay may have the detail of its predecessor but not the comfort. There are no appropriate, or inappropriate, topics: the essay may be about an experience that is painful or embarrassing or enlightening, or even all three. Its purpose may be to represent a significant event that played a major part in framing your perspective. You may wish to describe the experience so vividly that the reader feels that he or she has "been there" and understands what generalization you drew from your experience.

The contemporary character essay is less likely to be a one-sided caricature. The idea now is less to eulogize someone indiscriminately but instead to make an individual come alive for the reader. You will want to focus on the elements of appearance, speech, and manner that set this person apart. For both the character sketch and the familiar essay, you will want to have a thesis—a point you are making through the event or the person described.

Autobiographical Narrative _____

The method of choosing a topic and framing your essay is different for creative nonfiction from that for fiction. In fiction, you often begin with a plot. In creative nonfiction, particularly of the autobiographical narrative sort, you are likely to begin with a significant experience: going back to a place you hadn't seen since childhood; learning a new skill, after numerous false starts; having a "first" experience that struck you as memorable; going through a parting; attending reunions. For consideration, here is a list of the topics of major essays, which ranged from fifteen to twenty typewritten pages, that were submitted in one class:

1. Going back to the small town of her childhood after ten years in the city
2. His first experience in a foreign school
3. Recovering from injuries sustained in a serious auto crash
4. Learning aikido (a karatelike discipline)
5. What it is like to come from two cultures
6. Working for a congressman
7. Single motherhood
8. Resigning from the police force
9. Having cosmetic surgery
10. Volunteer work for the Literacy Guild
11. Working for the university police as a dispatcher
12. Breaking off a destructive relationship
13. Experiencing subtle forms of discrimination
14. Learning to appreciate a difficult relative
15. Being a nonnative English speaker

All these essays initially came from each writer's own personal experience. Of course, one could write noncreative, that is, research, essays on many of these topics. And research is frequently done to add another dimension to a personal narrative. However, the basic material in the personal narrative comes from your own life. The essay on cosmetic surgery, for instance, begins with the writer's experience of himself as not attractive. He then saved money for cosmetic surgery and underwent the process, which did correct the facial flaws. His initial joy at the success was followed by depression as he realized that not everything that made him unhappy was related to these correctable problems. His own conclusions about his experience are supported by some research he did into whether expectations of cosmetic surgery are usually met. The essay on resigning from the police force contains no research. The speaker briefly narrates three events in which he was involved, each illustrating what he found to be a flaw in the system. His decision to resign seems naturally to be warranted by the events. The student who wrote about subtle forms of discrimination also described three events, each of which demonstrated prejudice of a sort that not everyone is aware of. She supported her conclusions with a little primary research that took the form of interviews with other students who had experienced similar problems.

Usually, then, you have two purposes for your creative nonfiction essay. First, you want to describe an experience or a set of similar experiences so vividly that the reader can share them. You want to give him or her a taste of what it is like to arrest someone or to bring up children alone or to be unable to understand fully the language in which you are being educated. To do this, you think of all the concrete details, the sounds and sights and smells, that will make the scene real. Second, you usually want to make some kind of point about this experience—and you want to do so subtly, so that the reader is drawn toward your perception and does not feel clubbed over the head.

To begin, then, revisualize your experience. Review it again in your head, jotting down everything you can remember about it. A helpful exercise at this point would be to get together with a classmate, listen to her story, and tug at the corners of her experience to see whether you can draw more out of it. Then invite her to do the same for you. When you are listening to her account, write down questions you might have about it. Ask the questions, and ask more questions in response to the answers. Sooner or later it is likely that your responses may show her something new about this experience or may even prod more memories awake. This interaction may also help you both get a handle on how you want to present the experience and what conclusions you want to draw—and want the reader to draw—from it.

When you are ready to begin your essay, you may want to frame it. That is, you may want to define its limits: where the narrative begins and ends, from what perspective the events are reported, who is included. You may find that you are fictionalizing somewhat to get the essay into manageable limits. For example, you might leave out people or even part of the event. If you are writing about a wedding reception, for instance, you won't be able to include all of it. Your account will not be a recording like that of a camcorder set up in a corner focused on the center of the room. You will choose those details, and even those participants, that represent the experience in the light in which you want to display it.

RESEARCHING YOURSELF

To understand your experience more fully, you may want to do some personal research. *How strange a concept, you might think—I am the expert on me. No need to look me up, or to consult others. After all, if someone wanted to know about my life, the person would ask me.*

Although this view is true, your perspective on the events of your life is not a bird's-eye view. Depending on what you want to write about and what you want the reader to learn about, "personal research" may be useful. If you participated in a historic event, for instance, you need some of the details of that event that you have forgotten and other details that you never knew. I was on the Selma, Alabama march, for instance, but I remember mostly little physical details—the faces of my fellow marchers, the words of the songs we sang. The march was in March of 1965 to protest treatment of African Americans—even the specific incidents that generated it are blurred in my mind. But I can't remember the dates. I don't know much about the organization of the march: someone suggested that we go, and we went. I would have to do a lot of research about the event before I could write meaningfully about it. Moreover, I would learn more about my experience by reading about the broader issues. So, the first thing I would do would be to consult a reference source, and then I would look for contemporary news accounts. I would try both to bring back the feelings and beliefs of the time, and to get a perspective on them. With some facts and discussion to structure my memories, I would be on my way.

Writing about family history will definitely profit from research. Your parents immigrated? When? How? What were their initial experiences upon arrival? What were they expecting? Were their expectations met? You will ask them, of course, but you will also want to read some accounts of immigration from many points of view—those of the immigrants, those of the sociologists, those of the creators of immigration policies.

Genealogical research may be useful to life writing. You may find photos and documents concerning your relatives, and a close examination of these may reveal family traits that help you characterize family and self. As genealogy is a bit tangential to our work, we won't discuss how to do it, but there are many web sources for those who want to try (including Ancestors.com and the genealogy options on AOL and many search engines). Be careful, though—genealogy can become a consuming passion, with the acquisition of more facts and documents becoming far more important than the desire to write about family.

But even casual little essays may benefit from an infusion of found fact. Perhaps you would like to share a treasured family recipe that always marked a special holiday for you. Maybe it is a stew of meat, peanuts, and spices, and just the scent of it brings back all the previous family holidays and good times. Maybe it is Turkish delight, that famous Eastern candy that the witch uses to lure the child in *The Lion, the Witch, and the Wardrobe*, by C. S. Lewis. Where does the recipe come from? Is it just your family's, or is there a wider group who enjoy it?

"Personal research" sources either may be regular research materials such as reference books or may be primary sources such as letters, interviews, family documents, or local archives. A lot of speedy personal research can be done on the web, using the standard search engines such as Google, Yahoo, Go, Alta Vista, and Webcrawler. Google is particularly helpful because it allows you to limit searches very easily and because it is quick. You will soon be able to compare your great-grandmother's candle-making methods with those of others or find out whether the home cures she practiced were her own specialties or were in general use.

Doing research into the event you want to narrate may help you to set up the frame. To frame your event, you need to have decided what you want to do with that material—what you are going to narrate, and to what end. Let us imagine that you have a frightening experience you want to narrate: you took a late-night taxi back to the dorm room from the airport, and you got a cabbie whose wife had just left him and who drove you through the deserted streets of Pittsburgh for an hour at breakneck speed, talking about how he was going to drive his cab off a cliff. You were so alarmed that you didn't think about anything except whether he was going to finish off both of you. When he finally dumped you out in front of the dormitory, refusing to accept the fare, you were too shaken to note his identity or his license number.

When you got back to your room, you thought about what to do: Call the police? Call the cab company? You finally decided that they probably wouldn't believe you, and since it was 3 A.M. and you were tired, you went to bed. The next morning the event seemed like a dream. For the next couple of weeks you looked warily and guiltily at the newspaper for a news story about a taxi driver taking himself, and possibly a fare, over a cliff. But there wasn't one.

First, you might have someone ask you questions about the experience, and you take notes on any new details that occurred to you: details of the driver's appearance, things he said that you had forgotten, things that you saw through the window. This is not the sort of event that lends itself to personal research, although you might want to look up some information about the place where it happened, to make sure your details were accurate and precise. Then, you might frame the experience. What do you want to convey, in addition to what happened? Perhaps you always thought that you would be prepared for something like this and capable of decisive action, but found that you were not. Therefore, this becomes a personal-revelation story that represents a stage in growing up. Perhaps you want to suggest also that fear, when it is over, often seems illusory.

Knowing these goals helps you frame the narrative. Do you want to start it before the taxi ride, with the landing of the airplane? Perhaps you might, if your reaction to the landing shows the naive self-confidence that will soon be tested. Or you might for the same reason simply begin with the departure from the airport. Because of your focus, you will not try to develop any characters except you and the cabbie. Others will be mentioned only briefly as part of the setting. You might want to contrast the relative safety of the crowded airport with the frightening isolation you felt when alone with the troubled driver.

Once the narrative has been framed—which is your way of outlining it—you begin to write. Let the first draft be as complete as possible; worry about the editing process later. Describe the event in all its detail from beginning to end. Present the dialogue just like fictional dialogue (you might want to look at that section of the text). Remember that every new speaker will begin a new paragraph, even if the speech is only a single word.

"You comfy back there?" He looked back at me over his shoulder, making me even more nervous. I wanted to tell him to keep his eyes on the road. The dark waters of the Allegheny whizzed past on the left.

"Yes. I'm fine."
"Because I don't want you to feel uncomfortable. See, we're not going right straight home."

Put in all the detail you can think of. If some of it seems irrelevant or over-done later, you can cut it out. For the first draft, though, be inclusive. You may want to end the first draft with the conclusion of the event, not with whatever speculation or interpretation you wish to finish with. The first draft, then, will give you a chance to examine the event as narrative and to determine what you want to do with this narrative.

One way of taking the next step is to let someone else look at the draft now: your instructor, or another student whose judgment you trust. Let the person read the essay without your commenting on it. The reader can then tell you what your experience as narrated seems to be saying, and what ideas and atti-tudes are embedded in your work. Have you narrated the tale in such a manner as to present it the way you wanted? Your expert reader may then ask you more questions about the experience. Answering these may help you sort out any-thing that appears muddled or unclear in your description.

Now read the essay carefully, taking notes. Ask yourself these questions:

1. What does the first paragraph do? Does it set the scene, introduce the char-acters, provide enough drama to hook the reader? Perhaps you need to cut out some of the beginning to enhance the sense of excitement.

2. Does the action seem normally paced, that is, do you get the sense that things are happening normally; or are there jerks, or do things seem to hap-pen too quickly or too slowly? If the story drags, try leaving out transitions. Instead of describing how the cabbie opened the trunk and put your suitcase in it, then opened the cab door for you, and so on, just get to the ride: "As the cab pulled away from the airport, I noticed how quiet and isolated the outskirts of the city were at that hour . . ." If the story seems jerky, you may need to add some transitions. A common transition technique is just to leave a gap in the essay to indicate a lapse of time or to put a few asterisks in the middle of a blank line. But this technique may not work—the sense of some-thing missing may still be present. To sustain the reader's subjective sense of time passing appropriately is not easy. You may have to try several ap-proaches before you get the right effect.

3. Does the dialogue sound normal and natural? (See the dialogue section in Chapter 2.) It is hard to make a correct distinction between conversation, which has false starts and repetitions and boring irrelevancies, and dialogue, which is conversation that has been streamlined and made to fit the goals of the essay or story without losing its natural sound.

4. Is all the description relevant to the points you wish to make about the char-acters and their encounter? If not, cut it, even if it is good description. (Save the excised bits in a file—they may come in useful later.)

5. How well does the ending work? If you have concluded the first draft with the end of the event, you now need to write your real ending—a closure that emphasizes, without preaching, the points you want to make about what happened. Read the endings to some creative nonfiction essays to see how professional writers have handled this problem.

Those are some of the big issues. There are also, of course, the issues that are part of all composition review. Check spelling, sentence structure, use of active verbs, paragraphing, punctuation, word usage—everything you would check if this were a critical essay. Remember that elements such as paragraphing are affected by both subject and style. To describe a very active scene, you will most likely use shorter paragraphs, lots of action verbs, and shorter sentences. If the tone is relaxed and meditative, you will use longer paragraphs and sentences. Sentence fragments are appropriate in some kinds of creative nonfiction but not in others. After you've answered the big questions, fine-tune the small elements. When you are ready with your final draft, you should have a unified, coherent essay and a great feeling of accomplishment.

Character Essay

The character essay is a different problem. For one thing, the boundary between the feature story and the character essay is hazy. In this book we want to emphasize the "creative" element in creative nonfiction, so we are setting as a goal the kind of character essay in which an individual is not merely described but also understood. We are considering the interview as one way of approaching the essay, but we are not attempting to outline the kind of essay in which the interview is simply reported as it happened: "An Interview with Hillary Clinton"—and for which the entire success lies in the reporter's skills at interviewing.

Often personal narrative and character essay, or sketch, overlap. You want to write about someone because you know the person, because his or her life touches yours. Maybe this is someone well-known, at least locally, with whom you have worked, and you have encountered a different side of his personality from the public image. You can, of course, write an essay about a relative, but this is a hazardous undertaking. You are unlikely to have the kind of distance needed to write an account that seems to have some sort of objectivity. For the same reason, it also frequently doesn't work to write about someone you loathe. Best subjects are often teachers who influenced you, bosses and coworkers, maybe someone you found you were wrong about. The finest essays usually depict people whom the writers know well enough to describe, but not so well that they can't detach from them to get a clear view.

The character sketch, too, generally has some point other than simply remembering Aunt Sally. You want the essay to warn, to inspire, to suggest solutions to problems. Even the character sketches that used to be found in the *Reader's Digest* under the heading of "The Most Unforgettable Person I Ever Met" had these kinds of goals. The Most Unforgettable Person was often unforgettable because she or he taught the narrator that persistence was necessary to success, that you should not judge people by appearances, and so on. You might have more complex motives for your sketch, but you still have something that you want to communicate through it.

Who are you writing about, and for what purpose? You may be writing an essay about a famous person who does a lot of good for the community. You might be writing about a rock star, a relative, or your boss. You want to introduce this person, the subtleties of character that make up her or his individuality, to the reader. Also, you want to express an attitude about your subject and what she or he represents. The most successful character essays usually communicate the attitude or thesis idea through the details of the individual and her or his life.

A consideration of your readership would help you outline the scope of the essay. You always, of course, take into consideration that you are writing for an audience, but with a character sketch, you might want to be more specific than usual in the analysis. Are you, in fact, writing for the readership of the *Reader's Digest? Atlantic Monthly? New Yorker?* What values does your readership share? What education? How are you placed with respect to your readership? One of the exercises on pp. 89–90 involves audience analysis; you might fill out an audience analysis sheet for your essay.

A procedure for preparing a first character sketch might involve the following steps. Select someone who is vivid in your mind—often this will not be someone you are extremely close to, such as a parent. If you are very close to someone, you probably can't represent that person objectively. Consider a coach, a grade school teacher who influenced you, your first real friend, or a boss. Now think of this person's main characteristics, and write them down the center of the page, in a list form. Now freewrite for about ten minutes. Using your list, scribble down incidents, comments, and so on, associated with each characteristic. If this is a sarcastic, snide coworker, for example, note every put-down you can remember that the person made.

Now, write a physical description of the person. Physical descriptions are hard at first—but you can learn to sketch them quickly. Think of the details that make this individual unique—about hairstyle, glasses, facial shape, complexion, clothing, walk. Does the person not care about clothing particularly, usually appearing in a pair of jeans and a sweatshirt with a faded logo? What is the logo? Is she, instead, very fashionable, wearing whatever is the latest style? Or is she an idiosyncratic dresser, wearing unusual clothing that somehow comments on her character?

Is it possible to interview the person, or if not, to interview someone who shared your experience? Character sketches often derive their vitality from interviews, and of course the reported interview in itself is a form of creative nonfiction.

INTERVIEWING SKILLS

For creative nonfiction of all kinds, it is useful to be a good interviewer. You may be interviewing your own elderly relatives or the family members of a well-known writer, and although some aspects of the interview are different if you know the interviewee, others are not. The following suggestions are directed toward those who are interviewing people not known to them, but many of the suggestions apply in all cases.

First, you need to find addresses and phone numbers for your intended interviewee. From biographies and news articles you will find places of residence; you may look up exact addresses and numbers on the web, using Yahoo Peoplefinder, Anywho, or any similar service. If you are looking for a writer, you may find him or her through the Poets' and Writers' Directory, which is accessible from pw.org on the net.

Then you must contact the individual. A polite letter may be the best way, but e-mail works well too, and in a pinch, you may try phoning. Explain your area of interest. It helps if you are looking at your project as a future publication rather than as a class project, but avoid saying anything untrue. Respond to the individual's questions, and set up the interview time. If you are phoning, it helps to know what you want to ask before the call—I have been told twice, "Well, I really can't spare the time for an interview, but I will answer any questions you happen to have right now."

If the interview is to be a scheduled, formal one, be sure to be on time rather than early or late, and be dressed professionally. Bring both writing materials and a tape recorder; some people do not wish to be recorded. I always prefer to record but will tell interviewees that if they wish, they can listen to the recording and excise off the record anything that they want.

Of course, you will have prepared questions to ask, but don't stick too closely to them. It is all right if the person interviewed wishes to digress; often you will get more passionate and more interesting responses in that way. Respond yourself to what is said—avoid just going on to the next question. It is important to engage with the speaker, so that he or she feels part of an interesting conversation. You may want to relate his or her experiences to your own; if so, do this briefly. You don't want to take over the conversation but gently to steer it in the direction you want it to go.

Be aware of the tension inherent in the interview situation. The interviewee has agreed to speak with you because the person has an image to maintain, a position to defend, a justification to make. But as a writer, you are interested in the truth—even if the truth does not do as much honor to the interviewee as he or she would like. But ordinarily you don't want (we hope) to "bash" the interviewee, either. Notice when the interviewee becomes uneasy with the questions and attempts to be disarming by taking the interview in another direction, at least temporarily.

Ask whether you may meet with your interviewee again; if you both enjoyed the interview, you may have made a friend.

It is best to go over notes or tapes and to write down all useful information—dress, impressions, mannerisms, general appearance, data about the location of the interview—immediately, because these memories fly away fast. Then you can begin to assess the value of the interview to your project (if the project is not simply the interview itself) and to plan how you will use it.

After you have collected all available materials, it's time to shape your paper. What is your overall thesis? Is this someone who behaved in a negative way superficially, but underneath—when it counted—was supportive? Or was it someone whose refusal to respond to friendship limited his or her life? After you decide what statement you want to make indirectly through your characterization, use your freewriting list to find details to support your thesis. Use the physical description where it seems best to fit into the essay. Often the person's appearance is described in the beginning, but it need not be. And you may want to break up the description and slip parts of it throughout the sketch.

When you have the first draft of your creative nonfiction essay, then set up a workshop for it. Your class members may break up into groups for the workshop, or they may all focus on one story at a time. However you do it, you may want to consider the following issues.

1. Is the voice consistent throughout the essay, that is, does the same person seem to be speaking throughout all of it?

2. Does the speaker's motivation seem clear and consistent?

3. Is the speaker sympathetic, or has the writer made him or her seem offkey somehow—smug, perhaps, or condescending? This is a hard issue to discuss, but it is important. It is easy to miss a cue—a phrase that has bad resonances and reflects discredit on the character. Workshop participants should be constructive and diplomatic—although it is hard to be both.

4. How is the essay divided into scenes? Does the pacing work? You might mark off the scenes so that you can discuss how many there are, whether they are all necessary, and whether they are well-linked together.

5. How does the dialogue sound? Is it realistic? Is any of it obviously intended just to get information across to the reader? Can such dialogue be made to sound more natural?

6. Is the description vivid, relevant, accurate?

7. Is the theme of the essay clear without being overdone, that is, without making the essay sound preachy?

8. If the essay is a character sketch, do you feel that you have a real sense of this person's individuality, and do you believe that this individual was worth knowing and writing about?

9. Can you make at least three specific suggestions to the writer about possible changes—minor or major—that you think would improve the work?

10. Often a well-written essay makes you want to write—causes you to think about parallel experiences or people in your own life. Does this essay do that? How?

CREATIVE NONFICTION ASSIGNMENT AND SAMPLE RESPONSE

Describe a very familiar street or neighborhood. It can be a present or past address, or somewhere you often visit. Try to include as many concrete details as you can. Avoid making a judgmental generalization, like "Mill Street was a peaceful, beautiful place to live." Instead, show, don't tell. Most of us are ambivalent about our neighborhoods, finding some elements that are attractive and some that are not. If your attitude is mixed about the place you are describing, let this ambivalence show in your description. In the following description, which is a sample answer to this assignment, what details show that the writer has mixed feelings about the place she is discussing?

The Neighborhood

All the lawns are mowed here, and each front yard has a mildly innovative garden, a small rock garden or a colorful patch of hydrangeas, baby's breath, perhaps a few larger hibiscus and peonies. Most of the homes have little herb gardens in back, lemon verbena, mint, oregano, thyme.

The back yards are hidden, though, behind wooden privacy fences; you must be invited to admire the herb and vegetable gardens, to sit in the wrought iron chairs, hammocks, swings. The grass is soft Kentucky bluegrass, it feels like a carpet under bare feet. I sit in a swing and write this. Invisible neighbors in gardens surround me; I hear them talking about going out to the nursery to pick up plant food and flowerpots, arguing mildly about who has to pick up Robin and Kirsten from their soccer game.

I have been in other neighborhoods where the back fences were chain-link and you could watch rottweilers pace and children swing for hours unhappily on old rope swings. Sidewalks are swept and clean here, there are no broken places with grass growing through. Dogs are walked, but always on leashes, accompanied by a stout woman with a bag and scoop. No cats roam. The speed limit signs say 25 miles an hour and mean it. One sees no police, but knows that a police car would materialize, doubtless telephoned, should someone cruise through at 40 or toss a McDonald's bag out on a lawn.

It is very quiet here. In the distance, outside, you hear cars on the highway. This place seems far from the highway, far from going anywhere or coming from anywhere. There are birdbaths and sundials in the garden. The homes are stucco or stone, not too large, but just the right size for families. People work in their gardens. They grow old. The seasons change. The leaves fall.*

*Paragraphs from student story by Janie Grace, "The Neighborhood" are reprinted by permission of the author.

This is a quiet essay about a quiet place—perhaps you have a noisier neigborhood in mind, a street rich with color and life. Write your response to this prompt.

EXERCISES

The exercises here are a very mixed group because of the nature of the genre. Instructors will choose those that fit individual approaches to creative nonfiction.

1. Interview an elderly person who is not a member of your family to get a glimpse of a different time period. You may need several visits to get the specifics you want. Write up the interview as if you were writing an essay for the *Reader's Digest.*

2. Write a process essay in which the procedure being described has some value beyond the surface value, for instance, you may describe how to prepare a dish that is a favorite with your family or ethnic group. As you describe the preparation, allow the reader to see the shared assumptions that underlie the creation and consumption. Another possibility would be to describe some traditional activity like fly fishing that was done with a parent. Let the description of the process throw light on the relationship.

3. Describe a scene that was for you the threshold of a different world—a different social group, a different generation, a different religious practice. Did you cross the threshold, or did you go back to your more familiar environment? Did you learn from the experience? Let the answers to these questions shape what you put into the description.

4. Take a survey and write up the results as if for your student newspaper; in your essay, interpret the results. You may wish to do this with your class as the sample group; in this way, although a creative writing class isn't exactly a random sample of the population, you will have willing participants. Formulate the questions carefully to avoid ambiguous or indefinite replies. You may choose a controversial question: Would you call yourself pro-choice, pro-life, or neither? Or you may include related questions, so that you have more room to analyze the outcome: Are you in favor of legalizing marijuana use? Have you ever smoked marijuana? If you like, create a whimsical survey. Be sure to make responses anonymous. Without knowing anything about statistical analysis (and you aren't going to learn anything about it here), you are not going to be able to supply weighty evidence for a thesis, but you will get a bit of practice in writing about informal survey results, and such surveys are often convenient shortcuts in journalism.

5. Take a popular journal that you frequently read, like *Newsweek* or *Reader's Digest* or *Cosmopolitan*—whatever happens to be on your coffee table. Now do a brief audience analysis of it. Considering the audience that this journal usually has, answer the following questions:

    a. What is the approximate age range of its readers?

    b. What range of education do they represent?

    c. What shared interests make the readers choose this journal?

    d. Is the magazine intended mostly for one sex?

    e. What biases would you expect these readers to share?

    f.   Where are these readers on the ladder of expertise in the subjects discussed? (For *Scientific American,* they are likely to be high up—the writers can expect to write for fellow scientists and a few others with a science-based college-level education. In *Newsweek,* the same subject may be covered for a much more heterogeneous audience.)

    g.   What kinds of rhetorical appeals would be likely to work for this audience? What kinds would be likely to alienate these readers?

Analyze the essays in the journal to consider how they reflect this readership. How long are they? How long are the paragraphs? The sentences? What kind of topics does this journal discuss? When the writer uses materials from sources, such as information about medical treatments, how specific is the writer about where those materials came from? Now write a feature essay specifically designed for this journal.

6.   Following is a passage from Ted Estess's long essay on parenting, which was written as a kind of letter-journal addressed to a friend. Read it carefully, noting what kind of person the speaker/writer appears to be, what indications he gives of what the relationship with his son is like, and how he uses dialogue to characterize. Note how he uses concrete detail. Analyze how the discussion of music and of different kinds of music discloses character.

                                          Ted Estess

*Parental Limits**

It was bound to happen: Barrett has caught the yen to try something new. He wants to add that most graceful of all ways to hook a fish and that, of course, is fly fishing.

He has thought about it for a couple of years. His grandparents even gave him a fly rod for his birthday two years ago, but he was not ready for it. The rod sat at the house until last week when we were packing to come up here. He said he'd like to take it along just in case. I called myself being careful, but I broke the tip getting the rod in the trunk. Barrett was magnanimous, but magnanimity comes cheap to him. "That's OK, Dad," he said. "We can get another one."

So yesterday after lunch, we went down to Granby, fifteen miles south, to get set up for fly fishing. Driving down, I thought how strange it is for me to spend this much time on fishing. I never fished at all before Barrett, except for a few days in Colorado in 1962 and a half dozen days in Montana in 1975. And here I am spending the best part of Barrett's youth helping him catch a fish. Yesterday I spent another Colorado after-

*Passage from Ted Estess' essay, "Parental Limits," is reprinted with his permission.

noon driving fifteen miles to get a fly rod in which I have little or no interest.

"Dad," Barrett interrupted to say, "where should we try first with the fly rod?"

"Let's go to Shadow Lake where we were the other night. You'll need plenty of room getting started."

Driving along Granby Lake, my mind drifted to the complexities of being a parent. For years, parents have been told that they are the determinative influence on the way their children turn out. All the books on parenting tell you that. Read books to the child, and the child will be a reader. Introduce good music into the child's environment, and the child will be musical and like good music. Promote neatness and order in the house, and the child will be neat and orderly. A place for everything and everything in its place. Even the Good Book promotes this notion: Bring up a child in the way that he should go and he will not depart from it. It sounds simple enough. Something like climbing a mountain.

Yesterday as we passed Shadow Lake, it was clear to me: I don't believe it, not any more. Often these days I don't see a connection between how parents parent and the way their children turn out. Take Harriet and Chris Benson, the two children of my friends Malcolm and Susan Benson. Harriet is in The Hague, the chief assistant to some justice at the World Court. She's helping to run Western Europe, two years out of college, for goodness sake. After quitting high school and running away from home, Chris is a cook in a Burger King in Jacksonville, Florida. Malcolm and Susan did the same thing, or close to it, with both kids. Should they take credit for one kid who is helping run the world and blame for the other who is as lost as a rabbit in Grand Central Station? I don't know about other parents, but I will forego taking credit for what my son does in this world if I don't have to take the blame. He can credit and blame himself.

Of late, I've begun to think that being a parent is not like climbing a mountain. It's not like that at all. It's like getting to know a face. When you climb a mountain, you go in one direction—up. And you know when you get to the top. But you are never finished and done with a face. A face is always changing. Your knowledge of a face is always incomplete, unfinished. You're not traveling up all the time either.

"Dad, I can't stand that music. Who is that? Beethoven?"

We've come to the end of Granby Reservoir, and I know I'm right. Who my son is has little to do with me. There is positive discontinuity between my parenting and the way he's turning out. When I was his age, I loved Beethoven. I wanted to study piano so I could play the Pathetique Sonata. My good friend who is a Holocaust survivor once told me that some days he doesn't recognize his son Nathan. Not long ago they went to the beach together, just the two of them, father and son alone for the first time in a month, and all Nathan wanted to do was play video games. From Buchenwald to video games. There is no connection, none.

But as we pull into Granby, it's clear what I'm going to do: I'm going to keep fishing with my son. Without him I would never wet a line. With him I'll even buy the rod. I'll sit beside him at the lake and read a book to him. We can even take a cassette player along and listen to Brahms as I read. I want him to love the Brahms Intermezzos, hear the yearning and feel the ache of those melodies. Maybe he'll get hooked on David Copperfield, not the magician but the novel, like I did when I was in the 8th grade. I couldn't get enough of David Copperfield.

But he'll have none of it, I know. I might as well give it up. Let go. Get unhooked. I'll just have to release myself from credit and blame, get unhooked from all that.

We listen to Guns and Roses on the way back from Granby. In Bill's Bargain Fishing Store, we found a great fly rod, a real beauty made by a man who lives twelve miles out of town, but not a bargain. He drove in to bring us the rod as we waited in the store. He said, "I tell you about fly fishing. It's a great way to catch fish. But don't look down on people who don't fly fish. That's the worst thing fly fishermen do. They think fly fishing is the only way to fish. It's not." He told me that he'll put a tip on that rod I broke if I bring it to him. "Won't cost but two or three dollars," he said.

On the way north to our place Barrett and I stop at Shadow Lake to try out the new rod. It is a beautiful rod. I think I'll take the rod I broke down to Granby next week. Get a new tip put on it and maybe give it a try.

When you have finished examining the Estess passage, write a letter to a friend in which you narrate an event that shows something about one of your own relationships and that uses an event to reveal this conflict, concord, or mixture of the two.

Here is another creative nonfiction essay to study and discuss; this is Texas writer Palmer Hall's account of boating off Matagorda Island.

Boatmen's Dreams*

> As for our memories,
> The Sea takes from us and gives to us,
> And Love, also, sharpens our focus.
> What remains, though, that is from the poet.
>
> —Holderlin
>
> Boatmen and waterbirds dream the same dream
> —Su Tung-p'o, tr. by Burton Watson

When I was very young, my family and I visited my grandmother in what has since become the St. Mark's Wildlife Refuge along the northern Gulf Coast of Florida each summer. Every day when we were there, I would walk down a sandy path from her house to the beach and stare out across Wakulla Bay at a tiny island we all called Patty's Island. One day when my father took me fishing way out past the island into the deeper waters of Appalachicola Bay, a sudden storm blew up, dark gray clouds, repeated jagged bolts of lightning, wind that whipped the normally smooth surface of the bay into large swells with foaming white caps. The outboard motor on the small boat wouldn't start and we drifted in towards land several miles from my grandmother's house.

I was not frightened. "Don't worry," my father said. "We don't have to do a damned thing except ride it out. If necessary we can put ashore on Patty's Island." I remember enjoying the storm. Out on the water, tossing up and down in that little twelve-foot boat, I yelled and laughed. The whole time we drifted, rain stinging my bare back and chest, my father disassembled the motor, greased all the parts, and put it back together. When he pulled on the rope, the engine coughed back to life and he told me to take us back home.

This morning I have driven to a different coast with a different kind of vessel, a 17½ foot Mohawk canoe, tied to the top of my Jeep. I am going to Matagorda Island in the Coastal Bend of Texas to remember, to build links between the me who is well into middle age and the me who, at

---

*Palmer Hall, "Boatmen's Dreams" is reprinted by permision of the author.

nine years old, took the handle of the outboard motor and steered be-tween Patty's Island and the East Goose Creek oyster bars to bring a small boat through driving rain and beach it on the sand of the tidal flats at Wakulla Beach.

I am, once again, worrying about the weather. The wind is picking up and, if it strengthens, I will be unable to put my canoe into Espiritu Santo Bay and paddle the four miles out to Matagorda Island. I can drift back, the wind always blows to shore along the Gulf Coast of Texas midway through the Coastal Bend, but fighting strong headwinds in a small canoe is rarely worth the effort. What I want to do is get the canoe into the water and paddle out before the heat builds and the wind picks up.

I stop first at the Coast Guard Station at Port O'Connor and look out at the bay. I cannot see Matagorda Island because of an intervening is-land made when the Intracoastal Canal was cut through the coast line. Barges move from Florida through Alabama, Mississippi, Louisiana and Texas on that canal and, along the way, pass the habitat of the Whooping Cranes at the Aransas Wildlife Refuge across Espiritu Santo from Matagorda Island.

I am relieved to find the winds mild, after all, and only a few fishing boats on the bay. I am able to paddle away from shore without too much worry about being run over by power boats and shrimpers, a constant problem for people who put out from shore in quiet transports, without motors, without sails. No thick layer of clouds covers the sky, only the normal bank of cumulus clouds out over the Gulf and it has grown hot. By the time I have paddled across the bay and approached the tidal flats of Matagorda Island I am sticky with the salty air and sweat. Moving slowly along the western shore of the barrier island, the lee side, I can hear, only a mile to the west across the narrow sandy island, the Gulf of Mexico send waves crashing onto the beaches, waves that would easily flip my canoe.

The water here in the bay is shallow, only about two to five feet deep for miles and miles though it is broken into deeper channels from time to time. I stop paddling and drift over sea weeds. What wind there is pushes the canoe to the north, away from shore a little, but tracking the coast. After a short rest, I tie the ends of my small seining net, the bottom lined with small weights, to the last strut at the stern of the canoe and feel the whole thing shudder to a stop as I throw the net behind me. The canoe lurches as if I had dropped a heavy sea anchor overboard to drag it along the bottom.

If I were a shrimper, I would rev up the two diesel engines in my boat and try to make two to three knots in the bay waters. Behind me, my net would stretch back 78 feet with two wooden "doors" keeping the front open, and, flying above the scoop, dozens of sea gulls and other water birds would dive down to capture the small fish and shrimp that escape through the opening, frequently wounded, unable to swim easily. The gulls would wait as I culled the "trash" fish, fingerling speckled trout and red fish, jelly fish, sting rays, crabs, trash, all but the shrimp, from the net and threw it overboard. Then they would shriek and dive into the water.

My father had always wanted that life, the life of a professional shrimper, but it is not a life that appeals to me. I have met shrimpers, have been out as a volunteer deckhand on a shrimp boat that lumbered along the beaches of the Gulf of Mexico, sometimes ten or twelve miles out from shore, and it is hot, sweaty, debilitating work. The men and, now, women who trawl for shrimp in Gulf waters have a difficult life. They labor at a business with low profits and one that is absolutely dependent, as is the life of a farmer, on the whims of nature and upon man's apparent desire to ruin the environment that provides the crop. Shrimpers, though, are like so many of the rest of us. When they finish a beer they heave it over the side with the rest of their trash and help foul the waters even more.

The canoe moves erratically, if at all, as I paddle with the wind and manage to drag the very small net forward only about thirty feet before throwing the paddle down and pulling the net back into the canoe. The brown mesh of strings is a muddy mess, coated with seaweed, its basket brimming with the same kind of trash the shrimpers haul in. I separate a dozen or so white shrimp (*penaeus setiferus*) and a half dozen brown shrimp (*penaeus aztecas*) and put them quickly into the bucket that I had earlier filled with seawater and drape the net over the prow of the canoe to dry.

The white shrimp I will have for lunch later, boiled over an open fire on the island or back on the mainland if I can find enough driftwood to make a fire. The brown shrimp are for bait. The drought in South Texas has affected the shrimp breeding grounds of Espiritu Santo Bay and the other bays that depend on fresh water runoff from the rivers to reduce salinity. The shrimp I catch are much smaller than the shrimp I would have caught only a few years ago. It is a delicate balance, this relationship between the rivers, the bays and the ocean. The largest shrimp swim in the Gulf of Mexico, and breed there, but the bays and estuaries are the major hatcheries and the shrimp that start life there swim in the bays until they are large and ready to breed. Then they migrate through the openings in the islands to get to deeper water.

When I have the better shrimp culled, enough to eat and enough to use for bait, I paddle the canoe to shore and take a quick swim to get the slime from the net off my hands and arms and let the net finish drying in the hot sun before folding it and heading back out into the bay.

High tide today is at 11 A.M. and I am back on the bay as the water be-gins to race out through the cuts in Pass Cavallo or around the southwest end of the island at Cedar Bayou. It's a hot, lazy day and I let the eight pound test line drift out behind me as the canoe moves on its own above the weedy bottom of the bay. What I hope to catch today are two or three speckled trout, enough for dinner, before I load the canoe back onto the Jeep and drive back home. It is lovely lying down in a canoe and drifting, a line strung out behind you, baited with a live shrimp, not paying atten-tion to much of anything, just drifting and thinking, falling half asleep.

The last time I came here, I had taken the ferry from Port O'Connor. It is restricted to pedestrians only. The only motorized traffic on the island is used by the U.S. Park and Wildlife Service. I walked through the state park and along old roads that took me to the Matagorda Lighthouse and across the eroding runways placed there in the 1940s when the Army Air Corps used the island for bombing practice. Matagorda Island, though owned mostly by the Texas Conservancy, is not a "pure" wilderness area. The scars that we put on it in the past will remain for years to come, probably even surviving a storm surge from all but the most powerful hurricane.

When shrimpers gather, they talk about shrimp and shrimping, just as the rest of us talk about our own work when we get together. At Port O'Connor, the shrimpers complain much as the farmers to the north complain, about the drought, about the need for long, soaking rains, per-haps even wish for one of the tropical storms now brewing on the east coast of South America and heading for landfall in Central America to make the cut past Yucatan and enter the Gulf, blowing westerly, miles out from Galveston Island and then turn north across Matagorda Island and Espiritu Santo Bay and on up to San Antonio and the Hill Country to wash back down through flooding rivers until the water sucked up from the oceans pours back down into the bays to bolster the next crop of shrimp.

In the 1970s, the average shrimp boat caught 600–700 pounds of shrimp each day, by the late 1980s that average catch had dropped to 400–500 pounds per day. In the 1990s, though there are fewer shrimpers, the per boat catch has dropped even more. The shrimpers blame the weather more than anything else, this current cycle of drought, though there is a healthy share of blame dumped upon foreign, meaning Mexi-can, shrimpers fishing in U.S. coastal waters and there remains an un-easy state of peaceful coexistence between the Vietnamese and "American" shrimpers. That state of grudging truce is far preferable to the armed warfare of the late 70s and early 80s when several Vietnamese boats were shot at and burned.

My father wanted to live the kind of life these men and women live. He was brought up on coastal waters and fished almost every summer day of his life when he was a young boy. Each year of his life was, somehow, measured by the sea: WWII in the Merchant Marine, pleasure fishing even when he was at home in Florida and in Texas, and afterwards as a member of the Masters, Mates and Pilots Union, until that life ended when his ship vanished at sea. His dream was natural, the dream of an entrepreneur who knows his field and wants independence from the bosses. Still, it would have been a hard life.

I am awakened when a sharp strike moves the rod in my hand and, for a few minutes play at fisherman with what turns out to be a twelve-inch speckled trout, much too small to keep. Over the next half hour, I pull in six more, letting all of them off the hook without taking them out of the water. I have caught enough—enough fish, enough shrimp, enough sun—though I have caught no fish to keep. It's three o'clock and I paddle back to shore, pushed by the now strong wind from the Gulf. When I reach shore, I walk along the tide line pulling the canoe to get the kinks out of my shoulders and back. I do not feel like fighting the wind with paddles. By five o'clock I am back where I had parked the Jeep.

I start a small fire on the beach and boil the remaining white shrimp in fresh water with a shrimp broil mix of spices before throwing them into a small baggie and placing them in the cooler. I let them grow cold as I pull the canoe out of the water and tie it down again on top of the Jeep and stow the other gear in the back.

With two more hours of daylight, I sit down in shallow salt water and eat the cold shrimp and drink a Lone Star beer. I watch a small shrimp boat out in the bay, trundling through the water, and drink to the captain and the deckhands. From a distance, watching the boat plow through the water, almost seeming not to move, dozens of sea gulls following behind, I can almost buy into my father's and the captain's dream. But it is only the long day, the feeling of contentment in eating the shrimp I have caught, drinking an ice cold beer. These are boatmen's dreams and dreams almost reinforced by the cries of waterbirds. They are not for me.

Compare the different tones and implications of the Estess and the Hall essays as you plan your own essay.

Poetry

4

Sources

> Poetry begins in delight and ends in wisdom.
>
> —Robert Frost

Today's poems can be about any subject at all. Readers once thought that the type of literature called *poetry* should be about such topics as love or spring. In the nineteenth century, sweet, decorative poetry was tremendously popular; many topics were considered taboo. But this limitation does not hold in the twenty-first century. Poetry—just as dramas and stories have done since ancient times—can now concern itself with anything.

Even so, a poem must not merely state its concerns. Rather, good poetry must be grounded not only in experience but also in observation and detail. It should disclose itself through the description of specific objects.

To write poetry in the modern (or postmodern) world, the poet not only must observe well and ground personal experiences in detail but also must "think small." That is, writers of poems should strive to write about particulars rather than generalities. Often larger realities or truths can be alluded to by way of the "smallness" of particularities. Rather than writing a poem stating that "apples are delicious," the poet must write about a particular apple. The poet must *show* rather than *tell* the apple's appealing qualities. Thus the poet who writes about apples can show the "truth" about the marvelous nature of this specific fruit. And of course truth has layers—sensory, metaphysical, symbolic. The apple is a geometric sphere; it is a crunchy fruit; it is the temptation in the garden of Eden. A good poet will move at ease among the various levels of meaning.

In *A Poetry Handbook,* contemporary poet Mary Oliver claims that poets must be serious, not merely flirtatious, with and about their work. She says that in order to do so, poets should literally make and keep appointments with their "writer" or "poet" selves. Both of these hints are invaluable admonitions to new, young, or student writers.

Poetry was once thought to be a form of literature that was either lengthy and narrative (telling a story) or short and lyric, having to do only with somewhat romantic subjects: death, love, lost love, or spring. Contemporary poetry, however, can be and is about any kind of topic: war, marital harmony or discord, pollution, sexuality, child rearing, even child abuse—or more traditional subjects such as loneliness, joy, and love. Even the latter subjects, however, now tend to be "shown," not "told." Essentially, poems must be grounded in some specifically observed details—something about our real world—its objects, properties, or conditions.

Poetry (especially short, lyrical poems) has been traditionally thought to be about emotions, and indeed, it still is. Yet in modern times more than ever, good poems are also about experience of every kind. Contemporary experience is filled with all kinds of emotions, positive and negative; moreover, today—especially with the advent of modern psychology, psychoanalysis, and the common varieties of psychological therapy—all kinds of emotions are allowed to surface, to be spoken of, and to be dealt with.

Current poetry, then, like modern and contemporary fiction, must reflect our actual lives. This is not to say that people do not fall in love anymore or experience the joys of spring or the sadnesses of death. These realities still exist, of course—and the better poets also write good poems about them. Yet because these are timeless subjects, they are often worn. One must find original and captivating metaphors to show readers these experiences.

Moreover, we are now free to write about myriad kinds of experiences and emotions that are not positive. Suppose that you want to write a poem about the O. J. Simpson murder trial; a mother who has killed her offspring; a man who has raped small children; or the wars in Rwanda or Bosnia. Is this risk allowed?

The answer is yes. These events, even if experienced only vicariously constitute a large part of our lives. Such tragedies have existed in some form since the beginning of history. Yet today, in our current global-village world, we are constantly made aware of such distressing events. We deal with them in various ways—choosing to ignore, block out, deny, or grieve. Some of us even participate in some kind of social action. Why should we not be willing to write about events that are already looming in our mind's eye?

We cannot write a poem, however, that merely says in its conclusion, "War is bad, bloody. It kills, and I hate it." Such a direct statement that is not freshly or imaginatively conveyed merely "tells" our feelings, rather than "shows" them. Today writers tend to *show*. A poet needs to capture his or her experience, even the emotive experiences of her or his hearts, in an observation that includes details. Poems must portray specific objects or events, which may mirror, metamorphose, or symbolize, what our feelings are—our griefs or our joys.

To write a poem today, one still listens to one's heart or observes one's soul. But poets also are challenged to *see* the outside, objective world—not just the subjective interior of themselves. The poet must cause or allow the readers to see the world as well. As the novelist Joseph Conrad wrote, "My task . . . is to make you see."

Finally, today we are also challenged to "think small." What do those words mean, and why should we do so? To think small is to think not about circumscribed topics but in limited units. A poet may not be able to write a poem, however, about "how to end war." Yet she can, for example, construct a poem about one war experience that the poet has seen, read, or heard about, which characterizes the horrors or the violent atrocities of war. In this way, a poet can at least show one unit of reality that he or she has witnessed.

Poetry has no real "purpose"—short of "telling tales," as it were, concerning what resides in the human heart. Yet a heartfelt expression that is grounded in vivid and realistic images can more likely affect another person, the reader, who may be moved enough to change a political viewpoint or to take some action.

Fiction writer Donald Barthelme claimed in his creative writing classes that the worst sin of any writer is to bore one's audience. Barthelme maintained that if a reader is not seriously and curiously interested in a story by the first paragraph, preferably the first line, then the "ballgame" is already over: the writer has lost her or his reader. The same is true of poems and poets.

Although all writers write first to deal with their own feelings or discoveries, professional writers, even professional student writers, must have as a goal to try to interest some reader—even if only one's classmate or teacher. And if no one is interested enough to read a work, then the writer has already failed. All writers, including poets, indeed must catch someone's attention. Therefore a writer's, and a poet's, first responsibility is to interest another person. To do this, the writer must choose fresh subjects or choose new and cutting ways to enter old, tried, or traditional ones—such as love, sex, death, or spring.

Again, Mary Oliver maintains that any writer, and any poet, must first of all be serious—not glum nor morbid, but serious. Anything less, she claims, constitutes the writer as a mere flirt, not a serious lover of what one is trying to do. To be serious, Oliver claims, is to be committed. And to be committed is to do our work in a systematic manner. Oliver goes on to say that nothing happens in any job, in any work, and certainly not in any art, unless the doer—the artist—is first of all "there."

But then, what does Oliver mean? It seems that what she intends is that we must be in places that cause or allow us to be attentive to life—our own and that of others. But beyond this, we must be there in time and space with our work. In other words, we must be at some table, desk, or comparable writing space, doing our writing.

A question that we could ask ourselves as we begin to learn how to become poets is, What kind of lover of my work do I really want to be? Awkward? Fickle? Inattentive? Unfaithful? Or trustworthy? To be attentive means to be there—in our hearts, with our eyes, and also, with our dictionary, thesaurus, papers, and pencils or pens—keeping our appointments with our intended poet self, at certain times, at our writing places.

E X E R C I S E S   ....

Try to avoid rhyme in all of the following assignments. You will have a chance to work with rhyme and meter later; for now, concentrate on image and thought.

1. Write a poem, not over ten lines long, about a boating or other accident on or near a lake that you have witnessed—or that you can imagine. Consider (a) what you saw; (b) what you felt as you witnessed the action; (c) what you feel about that event even now; and (d) how that event is like anything else in your own or someone else's life in which there was nearly a great loss. (*Suggestion:* Do not use rhyme.)

2. Write a poem not over one page in length, perhaps a bit of narrative (telling a story), about a time when you yourself nearly had a bad accident. Or write about an accident that you can imagine that you might have had: (a) you almost got your finger cut in a garbage disposal at the sink; (b) you stepped backward off of a platform at a baseball game; (c) you did not use goggles while mowing the lawn, and a rock flew up and hit you, nearly grazing your eye; (d) you missed the lift seat at the ski slope while trying to get on; and fell down; and (e) you were trying to listen to the radio while driving your car, and becoming distracted, by the news, you banged into another car.

3. Write a poem about the following: You became so angry at your mother, father, brother, sister, friend, child, husband, or wife that you were tempted to strike out in physical violence. What would have happened if you had done so?

4. Write a poem about the following: You are disappointed that you did not get the job, the certain vacation time, the promotion, or the affection of a beloved person that you wanted. You thus begin to think that your life is always like this, that good things do not happen to you, that you are not rewarded, that it has always been this way for you. Therefore, you are no good.

5. Write a poem dealing with one of following: (1) You watch a news story about violence, perhaps in a part of the world that is unfamiliar to you. You are tempted to dismiss the knowledge of the tragic event. But then, you find that you can't escape images of the event: chaos in the streets, interviews with survivors. (2) Or you listen to or read a news report about a place in the world, far away, that you *have* visited. For example, consider the case of Sybil, who just today heard about two Jewish deaths, at the hands of angry Palestinians, in a place called the "Wadi Qilt," near Jericho, in modern-day Israel. This place is a large gorge, often attracting tourists or hikers. She herself was in that very place several years ago, as both a tourist and a hiker. At the time she felt fairly safe—and was only harassed by some tiny beggar children along the way, asking for coins. Now she remembers the beggar kids, and how she felt when she gave them money, how hot she was, how she observed the scenery, and how she wanted to leave. What else was near this place? What else had she seen and done that very day, the day she was there? But today she reads in a Denver newspaper that yesterday two youths were killed in the very spot where she had hiked. What does she feel? What does she vicariously experience because she has been there? What does she remember? What can she write about that place now? At this point, how can the poet include this latest news about the place in her description of the gorge?

Details and Images _____

> Nuns and mothers worship images . . .
>   —William Butler Yeats, "Among School Children"

What does it mean to use detail in poetry? How do we learn to do it? It is reasonable to assume that poetry needs to be grounded in the concrete and therefore must be full of detail. We must not merely tell about our or others' emotion. Rather, we have to show it. We must reveal feeling through some particular details about something other than the feeling itself—some particular element or object of the world. Emotions by themselves are not usually valid subject matter in literature. Remember Donald Barthelme's observations about boring our reader, and ask yourself, "Who will want to listen to my statement, complaint, or whining, if I merely say, "Oh Geez, I feel sad"?

Rather than fall into this trap, we need to communicate to our reader what the circumstances of our emotions are. Sometimes contemporary poets seem merely to give us "facts" about a situation, and then they trust that these factual details will elicit emotion—or the "resonance" (echoed emotion or thought) from the facts. The poem serves as an artifact that reminds the writer of a set of circumstances and evokes parallel sentiments in the reader. The first part is easy enough: recollecting events or experiences that occasioned the writing. The second part is the real task of poetry, and it is difficult to accomplish. As Wallace Stevens wrote in "The Poem That Took the Place of the Mountain," "There it was, word for word, / The poem that took the place of a mountain."

A poem for a time must "take the place of the mountain." But a paradox remains: the mountain—or, the specific detail—must be in the poem. The speaker in a poem must not just talk about facts concerning mountains. Rather, by the use of details, the poet brings the mountain to the poem.

To accomplish this, we must first use the correct factual information. We can't call a trout or an alligator a mammal, since it is not. We can't comment that, in Maine, the daffodils were brightly blooming in December. The point is, be absolutely accurate in your details. Also, use correct terminology. It is said that Homer knew Greek medicine so well when he wrote the *Iliad* and the *Odyssey* that some modern readers have mistaken him for a Greek doctor. How could they have done so? Apparently because of the fact that if Homer, the great epic writer, did not already know facts about medical issues, he apparently made the effort to learn—not just generally but specifically.

We must engage in the same process. Often getting these details involves some research. If necessary, go to the library, to the supermarket, or the forestry department; or call the language department of a nearby college or university, or the particular embassy that houses the information that you need. Much casual information is available on-line—sometimes all you need to do is to go to www.infoseek.com or www.altavista.com and type in the name of the plant or animal you want identified, or the historical battle you seek information about, and hit "send."

Several times, when using a foreign word or writing about a distant place, I have telephoned an embassy and asked for a specific location, a spelling, or some other information concerning my writing. "How do you spell Nijmegen in Holland?" I once asked the Dutch embassy. "What is the name of the town in Crete, the largest one of the northwestern shore?" I inquired of the Greek embassy. Although I had been once been to both these places, I had forgotten some details—and I now wanted to write about the places and needed to be absolutely accurate.

Next, we want to be specific. Usually it is best not to call an oak or a birch or a larch just a "tree." We don't want to be overly abstract, but rather to deal directly with the exact subject. For example, consider the following contemporary poem.

.... **William Stafford**

*Traveling Through the Dark**

Traveling through the dark I found a deer
dead on the edge of the Wilson River road.
It is usually best to roll them into the canyon:
that road is narrow; to swerve might make more dead.

By the glow of the tail-light I stumbled back of the car
and stood by the heap, a doe, a recent killing;
she had stiffened already, almost cold.
I dragged her off; she was large in the belly.

My fingers touching her side brought me the reason—
her side was warm; her fawn lay there waiting,
alive, still, never to be born.
Beside that mountain road I hesitated.

The car aimed ahead its lowered parking lights;
under the hood purred the steady engine.
I stood in the glare of the warm exhaust turning red;
around our group I could hear the wilderness listen.

I thought hard for us all—my only swerving—
then pushed her over the edge into the river.

Notice how Stafford uses particulars. The speaker in the poem is traveling not on just any road but on the Wilson River road. We learn that this particular road is narrow—therefore potentially dangerous. He finds a dead wild animal, a specific species of wilderness life—a deer. Deer are usually thought to be graceful, lovely, and harmless. The speaker stands in the dark, above this dead animal, which he learns is pregnant with a live fawn in her belly. His way is illuminated only by the parking lights and by the red tail-light of his car. He finds the animal cold, yet warm from the fawn in her belly—not unlike the car engine, which "purred" under the car hood.

In the end, the speaker must make a moral decision. He chooses the safety of human beings over the possible life of an unborn fawn. The river into which he throws both dead mother and live fawn becomes symbolic—not merely the literal river but also the river of life and of time.

The title of the poem also uses symbol: the "dark" through which the poet travels is not only the physical darkness but also the darkness of a moral ambivalence. Though in making the decision the speaker was ambivalent, the poem is not. The setting and action of the poem are extremely clear, precisely by the choice of the poet's very specific details.

We should realize, moreover, that the choice of details reveals the tone, or the speaker's attitude, toward the material, the subject matter, and ultimately the theme of the poem. Here are some other poems that talk about specific situations. See if you can determine the writer's tone toward each.

Sharon Olds

35/10*

Brushing out my daughter's dark
silken hair before the mirror
I see the grey gleaming on my head,
the silver-haired servant behind her. Why is it
just as we begin to go
they begin to arrive, the fold in my neck
clarifying as the fine bones of her
hips sharpen? As my skin shows
its dry pitting, she opens like a small
pale flower on the tip of a cactus;
as my last chances to bear a child
are falling through my body, the duds among them,

her full purse of eggs, round and
firm as hard-boiled yolks, is about
to snap its clasp. I brush her tangled
fragrant hair at bedtime. It's an old
story—the oldest we have on our planet—
the story of replacement.

.... **Maxine Kumin**

The Envelope*

It is true, Martin Heidegger, as you have written,
I fear to cease, even knowing that at the hour
of my death my daughters will absorb me, even
knowing they will carry me about forever
inside them, an arrested fetus, even as I carry
the ghost of my mother under my navel, a nervy
little androgynous person, a miracle
folded in lotus position.
Like these old pear-shaped Russian dolls that open
at the middle to reveal another and another, down
to the pea-sized, irreducible minim,
may we carry our mothers forth in our bellies.
May we, borne onward by our daughters, ride
in the envelope of Almost-Infinity,
that chain letter good for the next twenty-five
thousand days of their lives.

.... **Sharon Olds**

The Moment**

When I saw the dark Egyptian stain,
I went down into the house to find you, Mother—

*"The Envelope." Copyright © 1978 by Maxine Kumin, from *Selected Poems* 1960–1990 by Maxine Kumin. Used by permission of W. W. Norton & Company, Inc.

**"The Moment" from *The Dead and the Living* by Sharon Olds, copyright © 1987 by Sharon Olds. Used by permission of Alfred A. Knopf, a division of Random House, Inc.

past the grandfather clock, with its huge
ochre moon, past the burnt
sienna woodwork, rubbed and glazed.
I went deeper and deeper down into the
body of the house, down below the
level of the earth. It must have been
the maid's day off, for I found you there
where I had never found you, by the wash tubs,
your hands thrust deep in soapy water,
and above your head, the blazing windows
at the surface of the ground.
You looked up from the iron sink,
a small haggard pretty woman
of 40, one week divorced.
"I've got my period, Mom," I said,
and saw your face abruptly break open and
glow with joy. "Baby," you said,
coming toward me, hands out and
covered with tiny delicate bubbles like seeds.

Obviously, all these poems are about mother-daughter relationships. More specifically, they concern daughters growing up and therefore replacing the mothers—or at least filling the female progenitors' roles.

In each poem, it is the mother, not the daughter, who speaks. Each mother looks, from a certain perspective, at the passing of time and at her own replacement. Therefore, in each poem the attitude of the speaker toward the subject matter, and therefore the tone, is all-important. Can we ascertain what tone pervades each poem? Is it apparent? How do we figure it out? What adjectives could we use to describe it?

Besides creating attitude or tone, the choice of details communicates ideas. William Carlos Williams made an observation that is now famous: "No ideas but in things . . ." Williams, who was a noted doctor, a famous poet, and an outstanding fiction writer, as well as a husband and father, was a brilliant man. Surely he had ideas. So what did Williams mean by that statement?

Probably he meant that in modern writing, ideas have to be embedded in specific details. "Go in fear of abstractions," said Ezra Pound, who was another modern poet and influenced Williams. (Another belief of Pound—and a bit of good advice—was that poetry must be at least as well written as prose!)

Here is another poem that tells a story almost entirely in images and that leaves itself open for interpretation.

*Seeing a Medusa**

Only that tinge of crimson-pink
like cyclamen flashing
drew me down, made me see you

in the heave of the wake, all
pale-jelly innard
on your side, resisting nothing

in the wash of green glass, clear gray, the waves
calm today, steady, as you slap
up and down in their hands: a nest

of tentacles rolling with the foam,
then hanging, white with poison. You collapse
an inbreath of water, shudder. Glide.

Gone, before I grew faint
leaning over the boat; gone,
before I even knew

it was you—alive! Not knowing. Reliving
the blow, remembering: you, torn out, despised,
and flung dripping to the waves.

To understand this poem we need to know what a medusa is. In Greek mythology, Medusa was a gorgon—a female monster with snakes for hair, who turned anyone who looked at her to stone. But she was mortal and was beheaded by Perseus. A medusa is also a kind of jellyfish. Which is this medusa, and what happens to it/her? What do you think the poem is "really" about? There may not be agreement about the interpretation, but the images themselves are clear, distinct, and memorable.

What both Pound and Williams seem to mean is that in poetry, universals must be communicated through particulars—a very old, even Platonic, idea. But today the details of specific images are crucial in poetry. Consider Marianne Moore's statement in her poem entitled "Poetry," that in poems we must create "real toads in imaginary gardens." Moore, considered to be one of the "god-mothers"—or "grandmothers," if you will, of contemporary poetry—stressed the need for vivid images. She also said, "I would rather be told too little than too much."

E X E R C I S E S

1. Write a poem of not more than ten lines that (a) is full of visual images; (b) includes a detail in practically every line; (c) has no image or reference that any reader would need to have explained; and (d) suggests an abstract idea but does not state it.

2. Study a rock, a piece of wood, or other small natural object for about twenty minutes. Then, write a short poem (one-half page) about the object, in which the poem is loaded with particular description—details—of what you observe.

3. Watch carefully some process that if it is not downright boring, is at least not normally a matter of note. Some examples are eggs frying in a pan, a bug climbing up a pile of books, and laundry going around and around in the dryer. Now describe the process as precisely as possible in a free-verse poem.

4. Write a poem in which you yourself have dealt with the death of an animal—either physically or emotionally or both. Be specific. Describe the animal. Rather than telling of your emotions about the death, embody your emotions in the description.

5. Write a poem about something that your parents did when you were small, as well as the details of doing it. Try not to tell how this (possibly recurrent) action made you feel, but communicate through the details the feeling it gave you.

Some Poetic Devices

> In science one tries to tell people, in such a way as to be understood by everyone, something that no one ever knew before. But in poetry, it's the exact opposite.
>
> —Paul Dirac

SIMILES

One way to construct details is to create an image in which one thing is compared to another. *Simile* is one device that does just that. Most of us learned about similes in high school. When Robert Burns wrote, "My luve is like a red, red rose," he created one. Perhaps today we might think of that comparison as worn-out—but when Burns first imagined the line, it was no doubt original and inventive. The line is also extremely imagistic and descriptive. In what ways?

First, love, like roses, is pleasing. Love is also as intense as the beauty of a rose. Love is fresh and often appears flawless—at least at first. In the case of red roses, their color is immensely passionate—like the "color" of heat. The color red, moreover, is thought to be "hot," like love (blue love is, of course, cold, absent, worn-out, abandoned, or the like).

Although we may not consciously consider the issue of brevity when a rose or love is in first bloom, the loveliness of both rose and love is actually fleeting. Flowers will very soon grow out of their first bud into their full maturity and then wane, shed their petals, and die. Love, too, cannot last indefinitely. Either the persons in love will age and ultimately die, or, perhaps sooner, love will somehow fail—as we know by the statistics of our current divorce rate and by our frequently broken and abandoned homes.

So then, *similes* are a figure of speech that begin with "like" or "as"—comparing one thing to another in an openly stated manner. We can compare noun to noun, adjective to adjective, adverb to adverb, and the like. "My luve is like a red, red rose" is comparing noun to noun.

The following is a poem that uses similes in a variety of ways. See whether you can find them, and ask yourself whether the comparisons are logical, imagistic, and original. Determine whether the similes help the subject matter and the theme of the poem to become more apparent, immediate, dramatic, and alive to you. Try to decide whether the similes please you, and why—or if they are somehow arbitrary, contrived, or even ridiculous.

William Shakespeare

Sonnet 130

My mistress' eyes are nothing like the sun;
Coral is far more red than her lips' red;
If snow be white, why then her breasts are dun;
If hairs be wires, black wires grow on her head.
I have seen roses damasked, red and white,
But no such roses see I in her cheeks;
And in some perfumes is there more delight
Than in the breath that from my mistress reeks.
I love to hear her speak, yet well I know
That music hath a far more pleasing sound;
I grant I never saw a goddess go;
My mistress, when she walks, treads on the ground:
    And yet, by heaven, I think my love as rare
    As any she belied with false compare.

How many (reversed) similes do you find here? Are they effective? Which are the most dramatic? Do the similes help us grasp what the poem is trying to be about? Was Shakespeare original or hackneyed in his use of simile here? What is he actually saying about worn-out similes? Does he really like his mistress? How do we know? Would he compare her with anything at all? Or is she compared with specific things for very logical reasons?

Note how contemporary poet Rachel Loden uses a sequence of similes and metaphors to get across a state of being, a mood, and a plea to an unknown "you." This is an "open" poem, with a variety of ways of reading it. Does this poem pull you in through its sequence of comparisons? How does it make you feel?

.... **Rachel Loden**

*The Castle**

If I come to you as some bitter herb,
if I come to you cold and wrinkled as the moon,
if I call to you, not even knowing that I call,
like a she-cat lost and yowling in the rain,

if I immolate before you,
if my head is filled with water,
if you are stone when you look on me,
and yet you stay to be my mirror,

then my lap is filled with golden apples
and I am seven daughters dancing
in the all-night place beneath the fathers,
I am seven pairs of threadbare slippers in the morning.

Here is an old poem of mine in which I use simile. Analyze the poem, and evaluate my success or lack of it in employing this device. Similes do not come easily for me—I am more comfortable, and perhaps more of a natural, with metaphor. As I remember the construction of this poem, I worked on these similes a long time. The poem is about a trip I once took to the Mediterranean Greek island of Crete. I actually began writing the poem in a tavern in the town that the poem names, by the edge of the lapping sea. But later I tried to show what some of the images of the place were "like." Was I at all successful? Do my similes help you to picture the scenes?

*Rachel Loden, "The Castle" was first published in Southern Poetry Review. Reprinted by permission of the author.

*Agía Galíni**

(Southern Crete: 1983)

Like vultures bending over bones,
old women in black hover, squat, pick
dry greens shriveled by July heat—
light so bright that we veil
with umbrellas, sunglasses, shawls.
Pines and cypress once shadowed this
island. Now bent olive trees rattle in
wind-gusts that won't stop. At noon in Vorízia,
I watch an old man, cursing, wash parts
of an olive press. "Some people leave home
to see what they can become," I imagine
he says. He does not. But Kazantzákis left,
and Theotokopolis—unlike this mother
who leads an ass bearing her baby,
waterjugs, dust . . . .

I've crossed oceans for the town
Agía Galína (Holy Serenity) to see
one cat stalk trash pails behind
a cafe where John Denver sings songs
(cut in L.A.) about Colorado. Here
bare-breasted British, Norwegian, German
girls sun themselves as if Apollo can't
go as far north as their misty seas.

Then at Knossós,
we tramp on the continent's
oldest road, while Anna, from Oxford,
tired of med school, cleans rooms,
then picks field tomatoes when
the restless settle after the seasons
these waiters hate. Like blonde,
pregnant Helena from Copenhagen,

*Sybil Pittman Estess, "Agía Galíni" is reprinted by permission of the author. Published in *Seeing the Desert Green,* Latitudes Press, 1987.

who owns our cheap pension, Anna is
hooked by her dark, Greek fisherman.

For twenty-one nights, I imagine Aphrodite
rising in starry air over these ancient
waters. But even Zeus, born in the cave on
Mt. Dikti, fled long ago with Europa
who had said *adió* to Phoenícia.

Like many of us, deities
seldom sit quietly at home.

"Return soon," the telegram at the one-
room P.O. says. So those contented friends,
back by the fires, call and call to ask
what we find when we go so far away
from them—just as we would ask
the old gods. All they could say is
what we must know: "We can't
answer, can't come back."

METAPHORS

Metaphors, like similes, make comparisons. However, in a metaphor, "like" or "as" are not used, so that the reader of the poem must figure out the comparisons that are implied. Much of a metaphor's effectiveness depends on nuance, tone, inference, and innuendo. Metaphors are sometimes obvious, but often they are subtle. They always directly or indirectly compare one thing to another in order to enlarge the image of the basic subject, to help us picture it or to make it more dramatic.

Here is a contemporary poem based on metaphors. What are the implied comparisons? Are they appropriate, original, picturesque, imaginative, understandable, and good?

Naomi Replansky

*Housing Shortage**

I tried to live small.
I took a narrow bed.
I held my elbows to my sides.
I tried to step carefully

*Replansky, Naomi, "Housing Shortage" is from *The Dangerous World: New and Selected Poems,* 1934–1994, Another Chicago Press, 1994. Reprinted by permission of the author.

And to think softly
And to breathe shallowly
In my portion of air
And to disturb no one.

But see how I spread out and I cannot help it.
I take to myself more and more, and I take nothing
That I do not need, but my needs grow like weeds,
All over and invading; I clutter this place
With all the apparatus of living.
You stumble over it daily.

And then my lungs take their fill.
And then you gasp for air.

Excuse me for living,
But, since I am living,
Given inches, I take yards,
Taking yards, dream of miles,
And a landscape, unbounded
And vast in abandon.

And you dreaming the same.

.... **Ruth Stone**

*Advice**

My hazard wouldn't be yours, not ever;
But every doom, like a hazelnut, comes down
To its own worm. So I am rocking here
Like any granny with her apron over her head
Saying, lordy me. It's my trouble.
There's nothing to be learned this way.
If I heard a girl crying help
I would go to save her;
But you hardly ever hear those words.
Dear children, you must try to say
Something when you are in need.
Don't confuse hunger with greed;
And don't wait until you are dead.

*Ruth Stone, "Advice" is reprinted by permission of the author.

What are the basic metaphors of this poem? Are they obscure? Do they work, even though we may have to think about or evaluate the implied comparisons for quite a while? What, for example, is being given as "advice," in the poem by Stone? How does that relate to the theme of the poem? What is the basic "hazard" that she warns against? What is the "hunger" to which the poem refers and which the poet claims should not be denied and should not be confused "with greed"?

SYMBOLS

Symbols are pervasive and large metaphors. They may be seen as metaphors extended into some image of a force or reality that is primal, perhaps, or universal, or even unconscious. They can be experienced or related to by most people from most places and cultures. They include aspects of the weather—sunshine, storms, wind—or natural features such as rivers, streams, or the ocean. Rainbows, for example, are symbols—to us in the Western world usually associated with promise or hope. They are images of beauty, as well. But rainbows usually mean much more, whether we witness them in reality, or see paintings or photographs of them—or whether we encounter them in literature.

Storms are a negative kind of symbol. They are destructive, potentially life-threatening forces. In literature they symbolize discord or destruction as well. They always mean something foreboding. Rain, too, is used as a symbol—usually of sadness. In movies, rain often symbolizes melancholy. (Someone will have lost a loved one or be about to experience a tragedy, and the scene will be shot in the rain.) Another word for this technique in literature is "pathetic fallacy"—as when it seems as if nature itself sympathizes with human pain.

The ocean is a natural element that symbolizes a universal force, and often an engulfing one. (Thus for something to be "oceanic" is for it to be of huge magnitude.) Other natural symbols that we use frequently and even unconsciously include seasons or elements—spring, summer, fall, and winter; water, wind, earth, and fire.

Can you think of some symbols? One would be snakes. Serpents have been a symbol since ancient times, as we see in the myth of Adam and Eve in the Bible. In our culture they usually represent, or symbolize, evil or temptation or destruction. In other cultures, particularly in parts of Asia—snakes often suggest the opposite: wholeness or healing. We must understand how a symbol is used within its culture in order to determine its meaning.

Here are two poems about serpents. The first poem is set in the Pacific Northwest of the United States—the Olympic Peninsula. The second one is about a rattlesnake in the Midwest, which appeared in a dream. In both poems, snakes symbolize the ominous.

.... **Sybil Pittman Estess**

*Olympic Coast**

Here where they looked out for enemies
from 1904 till 1953,
a white-and-green sloop glides, glides
going its easy direction.
One man paddles a small boat, slowly
as a snail crawls. Indigo waves splash
the white coastguard lighthouse, a placid
guide, beaming bright red, red, red.
Oh look! Clouds break on slumbering
Mt. Baker, always shrouded in white.
See how today we believe
northwestern volcanoes and rain
will stay in abeyance.
This crystalline, trusty air calms all
July. No 1942-type December snipers
will take us. Or serpents lull and
then coil in mid-summer grass.

*The Rattlesnake Dream**

The dream you had about the six-foot rattler
springing up at you past your head. . . . Image

came from the scene in Cather's *My Ántonia,*
the text you just taught. Luckily, you woke

before it bit—the fangs being on their way
down. It didn't destroy you—old black serpent

who took even Eve for her ride. Did it really
disappear when you woke? Where did it hide?

They say serpents can heal. See it a symbol.
It stood straight up on its legs. It had eyes,

*Sybil Pittman Estess, "Olympic Coast" in *Seeing the Desert Green* and "The Rattlesnake Dream" are reprinted by permission of the author. "The Rattlesnake Dream" was published in *Mid-Western Quarterly,* 1999.

an expression so terrible and maliciously human.
It would have struck you dead without your own

craftiness: you woke, spoke your mind to timeless
snake. Then you went about your actual day

carrying on your usual, good evil way, choosing
the better one as much as you consciously could.

Two other of my poems, which follow, use a storm, in this case a terrible, deadly hurricane that occurred in 1969 on the gulf coast of Mississippi. The storm in the poem "Hurricane Camille" symbolizes the awful forces of nature. Such deadliness cannot be contained, the speaker seems to imply in the poem. The forces of nature often take lives. Human action against such forces—such as mothers' tying their babies in trees—is sometimes ineffectual and meaningless.

.... **Sybil Pittman Estess**

*Hurricane Camille**

Sixty miles inland, winds clock 200.
In the eye of it, stillness.
Before, after, we shut our ears
all night. My mother grips a Bible
as trees fall, breaking like sticks.

At 7:00 A.M. skies are El Greco
green, then bright blue as August dawns.
Our homes without light or water.
Everything hot. But by the bay,
the tidal wave rises fifty feet.

They find babies tied high to
trees—by mothers who had hoped.

The final poem is about a real experience on the coast of Texas, when the poet was shown the remains of a prehistoric beast that a man had gathered along the shoreline. Those remains, specifically mastodon teeth, became a symbol in the poem of something mysterious and terrifying.

*Sybil Pittman Estess, "Hurrican Camille" reprinted by permission of the author. It first was published in *Seeing the Desert Green.*

*Mastodon Teeth**

Orange coral, tan sea-cork, fishnets
hang in curves over the formica bar
of his hermit hut, the man from Racine,
a curator who's lived for seven years
on this beach-cliff in south Texas.
He scavenges the coral from the Caribbean,
perhaps Cancún. He shows us petrified wood,
as we fight off troops of mosquitos,
the fields of Texas expanding beyond us,
the "Danger"-marked sea below. . . .
Three pieces he holds off until the end—
two five-inch mastodon teeth, one mammoth's bones.

The teeth are encrusted with nipple-like
cusps that make them bumpy and ugly and odd.
They aren't at all like teeth of a toy elephant,
or glassed, dated relics in some museum.
No, real mastodon teeth simply lie
in my quaking hands—casual remains of a monster
near Brazoria. The man keeps them with
a foot-long piece of the old pachyderm's bone.

Dear old beachcomber, you loosed fear
in me on that hot and itchy night
under an August moon. Fangs gnawed in
my kneading nightmares, and I waked knowing
this: of all there was of these beasts,
only their teeth remain.

How does each of the four poems employ symbol? Are the symbols universal or local? Do they suggest some timeless and cosmic reality (Destruction in the case of the hurricane, or prehistoric mystery unable to be comprehended or assimilated by moderns, in the case of the mastodon teeth)?

*Sybil Pittman Estess, "Mastodon Teeth" is reprinted by permission of the author. Published in Seeing the Desert Green.

ALLUSIONS

An *allusion* is a reference—usually to some source from one's culture, either in art, literature, music, mythology, or popular knowledge. When Lady Macbeth in Shakespeare's play *Macbeth* is trying, by candlelight, to rub the imaginary bloodstains off her hands, she speaks the words, "Out, Out, damned spot. . . ." Much later, in the twentieth century, the American poet Robert Frost wrote a poem in which he employs an allusion from the same Shakespearean tragedy to title a poem about someone's early death. Frost's poem "Out, Out—" is about a young boy who accidentally cuts his hand off in a powerful saw at a lumbermill and bleeds to death. Frost uses "Out, Out—" to refer to the brief "candlelight" of our lives. He constructs an allusion to this brief "candlelight" when he shows us the actual candle and its light that Lady Macbeth holds.

A reader must be familiar with *Macbeth* in order to understand the reference in Frost's title "Out, Out—," which is an overt allusion. The more educated we are, the more we have read and studied, and the more we have lived and experienced life and our own culture and that of others, the better able we will be to "catch" or grasp allusions that we encounter. For that reason, it is important to read a great deal, to become as educated as possible—and to be acquainted with as much art, religion, philosophy, music, and history—and even science—as we can.

In the culture of the Western hemisphere, at least, it is crucial to read and know both the Jewish Bible and the Christian Bible. These religious texts have influenced and shaped much of Western thought, in theology, philosophy, music, art, and literature. Without knowing something about these books, one is virtually lost in much Western literature. We should know the basic dramatic stories of the Old Testament, as Christians refer to the first part of their Bible. (Jewish people refer to the initial books of the Old Testament as the Torah.) Without a background in these basic texts of our culture, we will miss many references in literature and in poetry.

Other sources are important to read and to have in one's educational repertoire as well: Greek mythology and mythologies from other cultures. Also valuable are the great Greek and Roman writers—Homer, Sophocles, Horace, and Cicero, for example. And on down through the history of Western literature and philosophy lie indispensable texts for writers to possess in their intellectual reserve. The more we read, the more we know, and also the more we understand and participate in the common culture of our heritage.

Following are poems that use specific allusions. Can you find them?

.... **Denise Levertov**

*O Taste and See**

> The world is
> not with us enough.
> **O taste and see**

*"O Taste and See" by Denise Levertov, from *Poems* 1960–1967, copyright © 1964 by Denise Levertov. Reprinted by permission of New Directions Publishing Corp.

the subway Bible poster said,
meaning **The Lord,** meaning
if anything all that lives
to the imagination's tongue,

grief, mercy, language,
tangerine, weather, to
breathe them, bite,
savor, chew, swallow, transform

into our fresh our
deaths, crossing the street, plum, quince,
living in the orchard and being

hungry, and plucking
the fruit.

This Levertov poem alludes to several things. The first two lines are an allusion to a romantic poem by William Wordsworth that begins, "The world is too much with us . . ." Then, the third line of the poem is a direct quotation from Psalms in the Bible. In the ending of the poem, Levertov has included an allusion to the story of the Garden of Eden.

How does this poet use these allusions in this poem? To what effect? For what meaning? What does it take for us to be able to understand and recognize these references?

Here is another poem with allusions to Christian religion and to the traditional sacramental worship that for centuries has been central to its liturgy, especially in the Roman Catholic, Eastern Orthodox, and Anglican (English) church.

·· **Lynn Ungar**

*Common Prayer**

Sunday morning at the marina
Barely enough wind to keep the kites aloft
and so we drifted to the ground
to nibble bagels, chocolate,
giant loose-skinned oranges,
random poetry, blades of grass

*Lynn Ungar, "Common Prayer" from *Cries of the Spirit,* Beacon Press.

Sacraments and indulgences
for the first of Spring.

And in the moment before sleep
my breast against your arm
sang *Gloria*
and the soles of my feet
cried *Sanctus* to the sun
Placing the last chocolate
in your mouth I whispered
"This is my body, take and eat"
and we melted   very slowly
on the earth's tongue

A reader does not have to be a Christian or to participate in Christian religious services in order to understand or even appreciate this poem. But one does have to be literate about services in the traditional Christian liturgy. Why? Because without that literate acquaintance with the religion, one cannot grasp the allusions in the poem: to the Sacraments; to the singing of *Gloria*; to the crying of *Sanctus* (meaning "holy"); to the quotation from Jesus' words at the last supper with his disciples (always a part of the eucharist celebration in the church): "This is my body, take and eat." The poem itself has as its explicit subject sensuality and sexuality. The allusions of the poem only aid the reader toward the poem's real subject and theme.

We should note that to read this poem, to understand and appreciate it, is not the same as treating it as a devotional piece. Rather, to like this poem may be merely to engage in an act of appreciation of how the poet has appropriated the culture of her heritage in a fresh way. For example, traditionally on Sunday morning, a Christian would be in a church service, not out on a sporting expedition "at the marina." A traditional Christian person probably would not consider such things as "bagels, chocolate, / giant loose-skinned oranges, random poetry, blades of grass" to be "Sacraments and indulgences. . . ." (Indulgences were pardons from punishment that priests granted, in the past, for forgiven sins—but note the double meaning with the ordinary understanding of *indulgence*.)

And who would imagine that *a breast* against someone's (presumably a lover's) arm could sing *Gloria?* Or that the soles of *her feet* could cry *Sanctus*—who except some artist, in this case a poet, who is attempting to imagine praise to God in a new, fresh, and personally meaningful way? At the end of this poem, the poet imagines even that the entire world, not just one person, is in the process of taking holy eucharist—that is, of taking the entire earth into one's self, as sacrament. Moreover, the things of the world are themselves the elements of communion. The poet implies this thought when she writes, "we melted very slowly / on the earth's tongue."

Some people might say that such an imagination, such a poem, is sacrilegious. However, others might disagree, seeing the poem as implying that one can praise in many ways. Someone might imagine seeing a wonderful Sunday morning in the beautiful outdoors with a loved one as a "liturgy." But a reader could not have appreciated the poem without understanding its allusions. The same would have been the case if the poem had made comparable references to other religions—say Buddhism, Hinduism, Islam, or Judaism. The specific religious allusions here are mere vehicles to the real tenor, or meaning, of these poems—which, it turns out, is not about traditional religion at all.

Yet if a reader does not understand the references, given that the poet has not made the allusions too obscure, the reason is that the reader is not educated, well-read, or experienced enough. If the latter is the case, the reader needs to use reference books and study the sources of the allusions.

If in fact the poet uses obscure allusions, sometimes the poet provides footnotes to explain the material. The famous modern poets Ezra Pound and T. S. Eliot often used this technique, and the contemporary poet Edward Hirsch has done so. Most contemporary poets, however, tend not to use obscure allusions.

MYTH

Myth is used in much the same way as allusion—to enhance, magnify, and give larger meaning to a poem's content and theme. We may use the word *myth* to mean a master narrative—a story told again and again that acquires an importance beyond ordinary fact. Much Western literature employs mythology, from James Joyce's *Ulysses* to William Butler's Yeats' poem "Leda and the Swan" to Gerard Manley Hopkins's poem "To Christ Our Lord." Jewish or Christian stories might be employed, or any Greek, Nordic, or Germanic myth. American Indians of course have their own myths, and some writers from the American West use these frequently.

Here is a poem that titles itself after the Greek myth about Paris and Helen. Try to determine how and why the poet used this story for this particular poem. How does the myth function in the poem? Is it successful in enhancing the meaning of the poem?

.... **Judy Grahn**

*Paris and Helen**

> He called her: golden dawn
> She called him: the wind whistles
>
> He called her: heart of the sky
> She called him: message bringer

*Judy Grahn, "Paris and Helen" from *The Queen of Wands,* Crossing Press. Reprinted by permission of the author.

He called her: mother of pearl,
   barley woman, rice provider,
   millet basket, corn maid,
   flax princess, all-maker, weef

She called him: fawn, roebuck,
   stag, courage, thunderman,
   all-in-green, mountain strider,
   keeper of forests, my-love-rides

He called her: the tree is
She called him: bird dancing

He called her: who stands,
   has stood, will always stand
She called him: arriver

He called her: the heart and the womb
   are similar
She called him: arrow in my heart.

One might not like or agree with how Paris and Helen are compared with this couple, who are somewhere in a very different setting from ancient Greece. First, however, one has to know about the myth-story of the Greek pair before being able to evaluate how the contemporary poet has used this tale. One interpretation is that the Greek myth is used merely as an image of classical and timeless lovers. The poet interprets her love (including the final pain that the woman feels) as being like that of Helen and interprets her lover as Paris. The myth, as suggested in the title, enhances her poem.

EXERCISES ....

1. Try writing a short poem in which you use at least three similes. State the comparisons directly, using "like" or "as."

2. Build a poem upon one metaphor. The poem should be no longer than one page. Imply that something is like something else, but do not state the comparison directly. Let the reader figure it out.

3. Using either a storm, an ocean, a river, a stream, or a rainbow, build a short poem around a symbol. Avoid clichés and things commonly said or thought about these natural elements.

4. Create a free verse poem around an allusion, either from literature, art, popular culture, or music. (For example, you could use Superman, or Elvis Presley, or the

Beatles, or some more contemporary star or public figure. Or use the Bible or other well-known religious text.) Be sure that the allusion is appropriate and makes sense. Consider using it in your title.

5. Using a Bible story or Greek or Roman literature as a basis, write a poem. Try to make both the subject and the theme of the poem contemporary and relevant to our time. Avoid using rhyme.

6. Medieval people used animals to portray character traits; see whether you can explore the symbolism of an animal in a poem. Try to give enough details about the actual animal so that the reader continues to find the animal itself believable.

Lyric and Narrative Poems _____

> Poetry is boned with ideas, nerved and blooded with emotions, all held together by the delicate, tough skin of words.
>
> —Paul Engle

Two types of traditional poetry are *lyric* and *narrative.* Much literature is concerned with emotion, and traditionally, emotion has been the basis of many pieces of good literature—such as feelings of joy, sadness, or love. Lyric poetry is primarily expressive. And an intelligent and a sensitive reader will experience the same emotion as in the writing. Often, as in the case of tragedy, the reader experiences a catharsis; that is, one can often feel a purging or a cleansing by the end of the work. It is a feeling of having participated in someone else'e pain, an identification with the sorrow or tragedy. Part of catharsis within a tragedy is, according to Aristotle in his *Poetics,* a feeling of "pity" for the tragic figure and of "fear," lest the same tragedy befall oneself. In other words, "There but for the grace of God go I."

In their book *A Handbook for the Study of Poetry,* Lynn Altenbernd and Leslie L. Lewis define lyric poetry in this way:

One of the characteristics that distinguishes literature from nonliterary writing is its concern with conveying the emotion that accompanies an experience, and of all the literary forms poetry deals with emotion most ably. The very large body of poetry concerned primarily with expressing emotion is called *lyric poetry.*

Emotion can be conveyed in many ways: the connotations of the diction, the lilt or drag of the rhythms, the associations surrounding the images, the significance of the events narrated—all these elements cooperate to establish the feeling. Hence, the reader's experience, learning, and sensitivity are all necessary to help detect the emotional quality of a poem. Sometimes a poet will declare his or her emotion by naming it, by saying that he or she experiences it. But modern literary critics are inclined to distrust the efficacy of this method of communicating emotion. Indeed, the poet T. S. Eliot, who was one of the most influential twentieth-century literary theorists, insisted that art can convey emotion only by presenting what he calls an "objective correlative":

> An objective correlative is *an object, an action, a situation which is the "formula" of that particular emotion and which, when presented to the reader, produces a sense impression that elicits the emotion.*

T. S. Eliot's theory of the "objective correlative" is now famous, and you have already met it indirectly in the discussion of precision and detail. It means that the skilled writer embodies the emotion in an object or external situation that suggests the emotion, rather than describing the feeling directly. As an example of a poem that begins with a statement of emotion and continues with imagery that justifies the emotional claim, a sort of precursor of Eliot's objective correlative, Altenbernd and Lewis quote this sonnet by William Wordsworth:

William Wordsworth

Composed upon Westminster Bridge, Sept. 3, 1802

Earth has not anything to show more fair:
Dull would he be of soul who could pass by
A sight so touching in its majesty:
This city now doth, like a garment, wear
The beauty of the morning; silent, bare
Ships, towers, domes, theatres, and temples lie
Open unto the fields, and to the sky;
All bright and glittering in the smokeless air.
Never did sun more beautifully steep
In his first splendour, valley, rock, or hill;
Ne'er saw I, never felt, a calm so deep!
The river glideth at his own sweet will:
Dear God! the very houses seem asleep;
And all that mighty heart is lying still!

What is the objective correlative for the emotion of the speaker in this poem? How do the images of the city in early morning become an analogue for the emotions of the speaker? Is this analogue, or objective correlative, appropriate? How does it affect you as reader?

We should notice that often tone creates emotion in the lyric poem. Good readers will listen and look and search carefully for the tone, or attitude, of lyric poems. Here is another lyric poem on a similar theme as that of Wordworth's natural beauty—which has a particular tone. See whether you can ascertain what the tone of the poem is, what the speaker of the poem is saying about beauty, and what the speaker is attempting to communicate about the loveliness of this particular scene. How does she equate beauty with "the soul" (actually a very traditionally romantic idea!)?

.... **Sybil Pittman Estess**

*Coffee in Cazenovia**

I sip coffee in Cazenovia
from a gold-daisied, Syracuse China cup.
I ask myself, What makes the soul grip?
Does it stick by taste? This thickly-brewed bean—

the hot, sweet caffeine steaming. Or by smell?
Sniffs of French wine, mint tea, cheese, roses, oil?
This lake gleams in mid-August light; those boats
bask in late summer's ease. . . . Are we bound tight

by sound? Your silence. The gift of one voice
from childhood. Our own boy baby's cry
that long night. Does touch determine spirit?
Yours; ours; theirs; its; God's; pain's. Everything

in sight kisses, then shifts. So dearly missed
after death.

Which is the one sentence that actually gives away the idea of this poem? How is this theme then embodied in the objective correlative of the details?

Lyric poetry is considered to be melodic, to capture emotions, and to be subjective. How do both "Composed upon Westminster Bridge" and "Coffee in Cazenovia" fit these categories? Thrall, Hibbard, and Holman in their *Handbook to Literature* maintain that "The lyric is perhaps the most broadly inclusive of all the various types of verse. In a sense it could be argued, perhaps, to be not so much a form as a manner of writing." Indeed, most of the world's great short poems fit into the lyrical category. Probably most of the ones you have already written do so, too.

*Sybil Pittman Estess, "Coffee in Cazenovia" is reprinted by permission of the author. Published in *New Texas: 1991*.

Narrative poetry, unlike lyric, creates a story or tells a tale. Great poems have been written in narrative form for centuries—from such book-length works as Homer's *Iliad* and *Odyssey,* to Virgil's *Aeneid,* to Dante's *The Divine Comedy,* to Milton's *Paradise Lost.* Thrall, Hibbard, and Holman define narrative verse as: "a nondramatic poem which tells a story or presents a narrative, whether simple or complex, long or short." *Epics* and *Ballads* are among the many kinds of narrative poems.

An epic is a long poem, usually about a heroic adventure or episode, often having to do with the legends of a particular country or locale. Although you are unlikely to take on the writing of an epic, you may want to use the epic conventions for some other purpose. A ballad is a type of songlike poem—defined by Thrall, Hibbard, and Holman as "a form of verse adapted for singing or recitation and primarily characterized by its presentation in simple form of a dramatic or exciting episode."

In ballads, the supernatural often plays a part in events, and physical courage and love are frequent subjects. The incidents usually happen to common or local persons, not to elevated or royal ones. Ballads minimize characterization and description, and tend to present tragic situations. Often they are built upon the repetition of refrains, and they are episodic in that they stress an episode of high drama or pathos. Usually they are written in some kind of ballad rhyme stanza, such as abcb. The rhyme is often "approximate rhyme" rather than "true rhyme." A folk ballad is actually designed to be sung and is traditionally composed by an anonymous author, transmitted orally for years or generations before being written down. It usually goes through modification through the processes of oral transmission. Of course, poets have deliberately written ballads in imitation of the folk ballads, and these are often called "art ballads."

Here are a few stanzas not of a folk ballad but rather of a poem written in a traditional ballad form by an English Romantic poet.

John Keats

La Belle Dame Sans Merci

O, what can ail thee, knight-at-arms,
    Alone and palely loitering?
The sedge has withered from the lake,
    And no birds sing.

O, what can ail thee, knight-at-arms,
    So haggard and so woe-begone?
The squirrel's granary is full,
    And the harvest's done.

I see a lily on thy brow,
    With anguish moist and fever dew;
And on thy cheeks a fading rose
    Fast withereth too.

I met a lady in the means,
    Full beautiful—a faery's child
Her hair was long, her foot was light,
    And her eyes were wild.

I made a garland for her head,
    And bracelets too, and fragrant zone;
She looked at me as she did love,
    And made sweet moan.

I set her on my pacing steed,
    And nothing else saw all day long;
For sidelong would she bend, and sing
    A faery's song.

The ballad goes on for six more stanzas, telling a traditional story of enchantment and desertion, and finally returns to the present:

And this is why I sojourn here
    Alone and palely loitering,
though the sedge has withered from the lake,
    And no birds sing.

You may want to create a ballad with the typical romantic trappings or may want to play with the form—put a silly tale into a ballad, or recount some local incident as though it were mythic.

Dramatic monologues are often also narrative poems. The dramatic monologue is a single speech in which the reader assumes that a listener, and often the speaker, is telling the story—the most famous dramatic monologue being perhaps Robert Browning's "My Last Duchess," which tells in the duke's voice of how he had his last young wife killed for her innocent enthusiasms and was now in the market for another wife. Dramatic monologues may be fun to write, because they contain many of the elements of fiction—the reader wants to know "what happened"—but they are densely packed with poetic devices as well.

Other kinds of narrative poems may be written in traditional forms or more contemporary free verse forms. Many, perhaps most, poems have some narrative elements—that is, they are based on some story elements, even if these are drastically abbreviated. Many narrative poems tell a story in a rather straightforward manner—as in the case of ballads. In other narrative poems, the story is more veiled, made vivid by the drama of the action of the characters, and perhaps by their dialogue. Following are two short narrative poems by the American poet Edwin Arlington Robinson. In the first, the tale is out front and is clear. The second contains an embedded story that is more obscure or hidden or covert. Can we figure out anything about the second one? Ask yourself such questions as the following about the second: Why is the story in quotation marks? What does the title mean? Why can this be said to be a narrative poem?

Edwin Arlington Robinson

Richard Cory

Whenever Richard Cory went down town,
We people on the pavement loked at him:
He was a gentleman from sole to crown,
Clean favored, and imperially slim.

And he was always quietly arrayed,
And he was always human when he talked;
But still he fluttered pulses when he said,
"Good-morning," and he glittered when he walked.

And he was rich—yes, richer than a king—
And admirably schooled in every grace:
In fine, we thought that he was everything
To make us wish that we were in his place.

So on we worked, and waited for the light,
And went without the meat, and cursed the bread;
And Richard Cory, one calm summer night,
Went home and put a bullet through his head.

How Annandale Went Out

"They called in Annandale—and I was there
To flourish, to find words, and to attend:
Liar, physician, hypocrite, and friend,
I watched him; and the sight was not so fair
As one or two that I had seen elsewhere:
An apparatus not for me to mend—

A wreck, with hell between him and the end,
Remained of Annandale; and I was there.
I knew the ruin as I knew the man;
So put the two together, if you can,
Remembering the worse you know of me.
Now view yourself as I was, on the spot—
With a slight kind of engine. Do you see?
Like this. . . . You wouldn't hang me? I thought not."

These and other Robinson poems contain the element of suspense; the reader wants to know what happened and how it all turned out. You may wish to tell a historical story in poetry; if so, look up some of Robert Browning's work in the library or on the Internet and study his narrative forms.

But narrative and lyric are not completely separate: most lyrics contain some narration, and most narrative poems contain some element of expression. Sometimes there is so much of both that the poem is hard to classify. Such poems are sometimes referred to as "lyrical narratives." An example of this type of poem is the contemporary poet Elizabeth Bishop's narrative-lyrical poem "The Fish," which is found in many anthologies. This poem is essentially lyric, yet without the implied story that the poem tells—that a woman went fishing, caught a fish, and ultimately let it go—there would be no factual basis for the lyricism of the poem. Another example, a recent poem that both tells a story and reflects lyrically upon the narrative, follows.

·· **Kelly Cherry**

*Lt. Col. Valentina Vladimirovna Tereshkova**

first woman to orbit the earth,
June 16–June 19, 1963

It looked like an apple
or a Christmas orange:
I wanted to eat it.
I could taste the juice
trickling down my throat,
my tongue smarted,
my teeth were chilled.

*Kelly Cherry, "Lt. Col. Valentina Vladimirovna Tereshkova" reprinted by permission of the author.

How sweet those mountains seemed,
how cool and tangy, the Daugava!

What scrawl of history
had sent me so far from home? . . .

When I was a girl in school, comrades,
seemingly lazy as a lizard
sprawled on a rock in Tashkent,
I dreamed of conquest.
My hands tugged at my arms,
I caught flies on my tongue.

Now my soul's as hushed as the Steppes on a winter night;
snow drifts in my brain, something
shifts, sinks, subsides inside,

and some undying pulse hoists my body
like a flag, and sends me up,
like Nureyev.
From my samovar I fill my cup with air,
and it overflows.
Who knows who scatters the bright cloud?

Two days and almost twenty-three hours
I looked at light,
scanning its lines like a book.
My conclusions:

At last I saw the way
time turns,
like a key in a lock,
and night becomes day,
and sun burns away the primeval mist,
and day is, and is not.

Listen, earthmen,
comrades of the soil,
I saw the Black Sea shrink to a drop
of dew and disappear;
I could blot out Mother Russia with my thumb in thin air;
the whole world was nearly not there.

It looked like an apple
or a Christmas orange:
I wanted to eat it.
I thought, It is pleasant to the eyes,
good for food,
and eating it would make men and women wise.

I could taste the juice
trickling down my throat,
my tongue smarted,
my teeth were chilled.
How sweet those mountains seemed,
how cool and tangy, the Dangava!

Which parts of the poem are narrative? Where do you find lyrical elements?

EXERCISES ....

1. Write a lyrical poem that expresses emotions without stating the theme directly, using what Eliot calls an "objective correlative."

2. Write a narrative poem, one that tells a story and is about one page long.

3. Write a lyrical narrative that tells a short vignette story.

4. Write a dramatic monologue in which you give voice to a literary underdog—someone who is heartily disliked in his or her story. Let the character tell his or her side of the tale. Some examples are Grendel from *Beowulf,* or the Duke and the Dauphin from Mark Twain's *The Adventures of Huckleberry Finn.*

Language as Music _____

> The essentials of poetry are rhythm, dance, and the human voice.
>
> —Earle Birney

Not only do poets choose words in their poetry very consciously and for specific reasons, but also they select carefully the sounds of those words. Language is not music; it denotes meaning as well as connotes meaning. Yet a poet, who is an artist of words, is doing more than merely transferring information. The poet is choosing partly for the sake of sound, often to reinforce denotative meanings of words. Some people who write about poetry refer to its "verbal music." Such "music" may be pursued for its own sake. In the very best poetry, the music of the poem helps to communicate the nature of the experience that the poem describes. Often the sounds express the very meaning of the poem.

Good poets either consciously or unconsciously arrange patterns of words by sound. Anyone who studies music learns that we receive pleasure by two contrasting musical patterns: repetition and its opposite, variation. People who have spent time near the sea know that the ocean is endlessly repetitious yet constantly changing—according to wind patterns, the tides, storms, and even the seasons. Sports are other examples of action that is repeated yet is ultimately quite various. Each game, therefore, provides its own interests. Human beings tend to love the familiar yet also the new and exciting. So it is with the sounds within poems.

Rhymes are a repetitious sound. "True" rhymes consist of the repeated sounds coming at the ends of lines. Here is a short poem with repeated sounds at the ends of lines:

.... **Ogden Nash**

*The Turtle**

> The turtle lives 'twixt plated decks
> Which practically conceal its sex.
> I think it clever of the turtle
> In such a fix to be so fertile.

Quickly we can see that the words "decks" and "sex" are not spelled alike. Yet these words sound alike, with the exception of their initial consonant sounds. The same principle is true for the words "turtle" and "fertile." Note that these two words have what we term "perfect rhyme," even though they begin with different consonants and are spelled quite differently. Nash is having fun with words, using perfect but nevertheless eccentric rhyme, alliteration, and an emphatic rhythm to entertain us.

Poets often repeat single sounds, units of sound, initial consonant sounds, whole syllables, entire words, phrases, lines, or even a series of lines. In good poems, the repetition itself will be pleasing to the ear and will give one dimension of structure to the poem.

Some people who write about poetry—commentators, who are usually referred to as "critics"—discuss "hard" and "soft" sounds, or "hard" and "soft" diction. In his book *Writing Poems*, Wallace Boisseau claims that words and word sounds contain overtones and nuances. He writes that sound "connotations are the feelings, the approval or disapproval, that go along with essentially the same denotative information in different words." When we as poets choose the words

---

*Ogden Nash, "The Turtle" from *Verses from 1929 On*. Copyright © 1930 by Odgen Nash. Reprinted by permission of Curtis Brown, Ltd.

of our poems, we should consider not only the meanings and the nuances but also the sounds of the words. We might ask ourselves: Does this word have a happy sound? Is it light and lyrical? Or is the word gloomy, dark, heavy? With these decisions comes the emotional tone of our poem.

In his book *Three Genres,* Stephen Minot reminds us of the following:

> It is hard to imagine a musical composer who doesn't spend a good deal of time listening to music. Yet some beginning poets are reluctant to read too much published poetry for fear of being influenced . . . [but] only by reading—preferably aloud—can one begin to appreciate the ways in which poetry is written for the ear.

In their book *Reading Poetry,* Fred Millett, Arthur Hoffman, and David Clark claim the following:

> [T]he good poet, even at his most serious, is having fun with words, and at his most playful is saying things worth listening to. . . . The element of sound-pattern in poetry is of inestimable importance, because it is one of the most reliable means—perhaps only slightly less reliable than the element of rhythm—by which the poet casts his spell over us and persuades us to attend to a subject that seems important to him and to feel toward it as he wishes us to feel.

Like music, then, poetry appeals to the ear. When the sound is pleasing and the sounds tend to work well together, we call that effect *euphony.* When the opposite results, with dissonant or grating or harsh sounds, we refer to that effect as *cacophony.*

Sometimes sounds actually convey certain ideas, as in these words: "slick," "slimy," "slippery," or "slushy." These words, all beginning with the letters "sl," seem to suggest or convey the concept of wetness and smoothness. Yet other words beginning with the same consonants could have the opposite effect. Consider "slave," "slow," or "sledgehammer." These words surely do not convey the concept of wetness, and their very "sl" sounds tend to suggest a hardness, slowness, or sluggishness. Here is an example of a little poem full of repeated sounds. Can you analyze the sounds and their apparent effect?

·· **Janie Grace**

*Snake**

    Can I not sleeping slip
    This sticky sloth of self-loath
    Waking worth
    And fleet slide forth?

*Janie Grace; "Snake" reprinted by permission of the author.

This is yet another snake poem, but with a positive connotation. What is this poem about? How does the title of the poem represent a metaphor? What is the metaphor of the title doing in the rest of the poem? Where are repeated sounds? For what purpose are these sounds repeated?

Now consider the possibility of a poem in which sound alone was the determining factor—where meaning was overruled by sound. The closest we might come to such a poem might be the following from Lewis Carroll's *Through the Looking-Glass and What Alice Found There.*

Lewis Carroll

Jabberwocky

'Twas brillig, and the slithy toves
Did gyre and gimble in the wabe:
All mimsy were the borogoves,
And the mome raths outgrabe.

"Beware the Jabberwock, my son!
The jaws that bite, the claws that catch!
Beware the Jubjub bird, and shun
The frumious Bandersnatch!"

He took his vorpal sword in hand:
Long time the manxome foe he sought—
So rested he by the Tumtum tree,
And stood awhile in thought.

And, as in uffish thought he stood,
The Jabberwock, with eyes of flame,
Came whiffling through the tulgey wood,
And burbled as it came!

One, two! One, two! And through and through
The vorpal blade went snicker-snack!
He left it dead, and with its head
He went galumphing back.

"And, has thou slain the Jabberwock?
Come to my arms, my beamish boy!
O frabjous day! Callooh! Callay!"
He chortled in his joy.

'Twas brillig, and the slithy toves
Did gyre and gimble in the wabe;
All mimsy were the borogoves,
And the mome raths outgrabe.

Lewis Carroll was playful with words and made up a lot of them in this poem—but can you summarize the poem's plot, despite its invented words? To experiment on your own, write a short rhymed poem in which you invent a lot of words. (It certainly is easier to rhyme this way.)

ALLITERATION, ASSONANCE, AND CONSONANCE

Alliteration is the repetition of beginning sounds, as in the line "I picked a peck of pickled peppers." My father used to joke with his two daughters and ask them how fast we could repeat the lines "If Peter Piper picked a peck of pickled peppers, / so how many pickled peppers did Peter Piper pick?"

Assonance is defined as repeated vowel sounds, whether the vowels are at the beginning, the middle, or the end of words. "These pink walls wink but don't look like ink" has alliteration in the words "walls" and "wink" and the words "look" and "like." But the line also has assonance, which in this case is assonance used as perfect rhyme in the words "wink" and "ink."

But what about the line "The wax has too much acid for the back of the cat"? Here there are repeated short *a,* or *ah* sounds in the words "wax," "acid," "back," and "cat"—though none of these words are perfectly rhymed. (My own son's names are "Benjamin" and "Barrett." Do these names used in succession have alliteration, assonance, or both?)

Consonance is repeated consonant sounds that are not at the beginning of words. The line "The cat and the bat are battering and swatting the flies" uses all of the following devices: perfect rhyme, assonance, and also consonance. The latter device is heard in the *t*s of "cat" and "bat" and also "battering" and "swatting," since all of these words have the (explosive) consonant *t* within them. (Consonants are said to be "explosive" if your lips have to "explode," as it were, while speaking the words. Consonants such as *t, b, c,* and the like are explosive. *M*s and *n*s are the opposite kinds of consonant sounds, which we might label nonexplosive or harmonious sounds.)

Where is the *consonance* in the following line "Why so pale and wan fond lover?" from "Song," by Sir John Suckling? What other devices—alliteration and assonance— do you also hear in the line? Note that in this line, "wan" and "fond" provide assonance sounds, even though the vowels are not identical. In the case of "wan" and "fond," the vowels are not alike, yet the vowels sounds are very similar.

Now take this beginning stanza of a well-known poem by a famous poet, and analyze it thoroughly for all three of these devices: alliteration, assonance, and consonance. You might circle the alliterative sounds, put squares around the assonance, and put hearts around the consonance.

Now try these lines. Again, find alliteration, assonance, or consonance:

.... **Henry Vaughan**

from *The Retreat*

> Happy those early days! when I
> Shin'd in my angel-infancy.
> Before I understood this place
> Appointed for my second race,
> Or taught my soul to fancy aught
> But a white, celestial thought,
> When yet I had not walked above
> A mile, or two, from my first love,
> And looking back (at that short space)
> Could see a glimpse of His bright face.

Now ask yourself what overall effect all these sounds have on you. Perhaps the perfect rhymes here at the end of lines give form and order to the poem, although the poem is really not written around "rhyme for rhyme's sake." And do the repetitions of the *Is* have a particular result in effect and even in meaning? What about the other long *i* sounds that reinforce the effect of the *Is*? Where are those sounds? Why are they there? Are there particular consonant sounds that you can point out? If so, where? And how does assonance play a role in the total effect of sound patterns here in this carefully controlled and constructed poem?

E X E R C I S E S   ....

1. In the textbook *Reading Poetry*, the authors state that "alliterative linkages serve basically to call attention to the items linked." Write a poem of four lines in which you use alliteration to link items.

2. Write a line that you consider particularly beautiful because of the manner in which you use assonance.

3. Write a short poem of six to eight lines in which you use consonants that explode and are therefore heard as grating, threatening, dangerous, or angry sounds.

4. Write two or three lines with vowels that sound harmonious and soothing, and repeat a certain vowel sound.

5. Underline the exploding consonant sounds in this poem title: "The Rape of the Lock." Which beginning consonant sounds in the two nouns in this title are not explosive?

6. Explain why one group of consonants is explosive and the other is not.

KINDS OF RHYME

Rhyme has both like sounds and different sounds. The unlike sounds are mostly at the first of the word. The similar sounds are usually at the word's end.

Repeated sounds may be simply vowels (I/my) or vowels with additional consonant sounds (*ear/beer; like/mike*). This kind of very-close rhyme is referred to as "exact" or "true" rhyme.

When vowel sounds are similar but not exactly alike, the rhyme is called "slant" or "off" rhyme. Examples of slant or off-rhyme are *love/groove; bait/bit; lit/light.* We can see that both true and slant (or off) rhyme involve both sameness and dissimilarity. What types of rhyme are the following pairs of words: *line/wine; divine/sign; tame/lane; despair/my hair?*

The textbook *Reading Poetry* claims that "the pattern made by the rhyme words . . . is one . . . means by which the poet may give his poem the formal element [known as] stanza." A rhymed *stanza* is a group of lines in which the last words of each line rhyme or form some pattern of rhyme.

Later, when we discuss formal poetry and types of forms, we will examine such rhyme patterns as those appearing in sonnets, villanelles, limericks, and other forms. But here are two examples of poems that have rhymes and rhyme patterns. For now, simply concentrate on finding the rhymes at the end of lines. Before you conclude your examination of these poems, determine whether each of the rhymes is true or slant rhyme. Analyze these two examples:

.... **Robert Burns**

A Red, Red Rose

> O, my Luve's like a red, red rose
>   That's newly sprung in June.
> O, my Luve's like the melodie
>   That's sweetly play'd in tune.
>
> As fair art thou, my bonnie lass,
>   So deep in luve am I;
> And I will love thee still, my Dear,
>   Till a' the seas gang dry.
>
> Till a' the seas gang dry, my Dear,
>   And the rocks melt wi' the sun;
> And I will love thee still, my Dear,
>   While the sands o' life shall run.

And fare thee weel, my only Luve,
  And fare thee weel a while!
And I will come again, my Luve,
  Tho' it were ten thousand mile!

.... **Robert Phillips**

*Here & There**

There was that winter a freezing of fire
and in tumbled nights the enlightening
of a pair, side by side, who were not there.
Though they shared a common bed, one flew out
west to San Diego, the other dreamed
a plaid figure on a New Hampshire mare.
From habit they slept spoon-fashion: Yin, Yang.
A transcontinental cold divided.

Their future seemed all of Manhattan's sky-
line, blacked out. Their match could not brighten that.
When spring came, oozing its thaw and its thud,
together they alone walked flowered fields,
stealing a blossom here, a blossom there,
and seeing nothing living, anywhere.

Although other terminology applied to rhyme that poets and poetry critics employ may seem complicated, it is merely a means of distinguishing various possibilities of how rhyme may be employed. "Strong rhymes" are true rhymes of one-syllable words: *may/lay; tea/see; lewd/mood*. "Weak rhymes" appear in words of two or more syllables (usually at least two of the syllables are perfectly rhymed): *highly/shyly; mightily/frightfully; gayly/daily*. *Internal rhyme* refers to rhymed words within the line, whereas end rhyme refers to rhymed words at ends of lines.

E X E R C I S E S   ....

1. Which of these pairs are true rhymes: bear/pare; through/rough; rue/through; Jew/threw; folly/lolly; licks/ticks; tight/light; bite/bit.

*"Here and There" by Robert Phillips. Published in *Personal Accounts,* Ontario Review Press, 1986. Reprinted by permission.

2.   Which of the pairs in item 1 are weak and which are strong rhymes?

3.   Write two sets of rhymed couplets (two lines) that end in true rhyme.

4.   Do the same as in #3, but end the lines in slant rhyme.

The Line

> Poetry is the opening and closing of a door, leaving those who look through to guess what is seen during a moment.
> —Carl Sandburg

The following poem is not rhymed. Try to determine, then, what basic poetry elements—words, connotations, simile, metaphors, or line breaks—essentially constitute this poem as a poem. In other words, find what this poem cannot do without.

William Carlos Williams

The Red Wheelbarrow*

so much depends
upon

a red wheel
barrow

glazed with rain
water

beside the white
chickens

This poem does not use end rhyme, yet there is an order and a form in the poem. It is written in what is now commonly called *free verse*—with no set number of syllables in the lines and no set rhythm to a line. The line itself is the unit of verse here. When the poem is set in print, the lines are consciously broken at specific points that are determined solely by the poet.

In the glossary of the textbook *Three Genres*, by Stephen Minot, the author writes of this line: "The inclusion of the line as a part of the art form rather than merely a printer's concern is one of the fundamental distinctions between verse and prose." Denise Levertov maintained that a break in a line is a pause that is like a punctuation mark—equal, she claimed, to half a comma. She thought that the pause of a line break is necessarily present, since it takes the reader several seconds to adjust one's eyes from the end of one line to the beginning of the next. The reader of a poem necessarily has to pause for this momentary process. In contemporary poetry, in which the poet often has taken much liberty not to include end rhymes nor to write in traditional forms, the line break is the primary element of the poem. Consequently, it is essential for the poet to employ line breaks purposely. A reader of contemporary poems must consider why lines are "enjambed" where they are. (*Enjambment* means breaking a line but not ending the sentence, that is, carrying over a sentence from one line to the other.)

Consider the following poem:

.... **J. Pittman McGehee**

*Drumright, OK., 1952**

Crouched on porch steps counting cars.
Waiting. Mother smokes on the
crushed velvet sofa rubbing her
legs. Cellophane, clear and stretched
tight on the empty package: Camels.
Brother builds a model plane. Match
sticks, toothpicks, balsa. Tedious,
tentative. Focused, furrowed brow
step by step. Patience. Unaware
of time. Tissue paper taut.
The dust feels moist on the cracked
concrete. Sheba rolls in the mud by
the sunflowers: dog days. Cat-eyed car
lights come on slowly then fade fast.
Sidewalk stone tossing, pacing up and
down. Fireflies fight for dark in the
street light and time is a night train.

A reader of contemporary poems must consider why lines were broken where they were. Why, in the second line of the poem, does the line break fall

*J. Pittman McGehee, "Drumright, OK., 1952," reprinted by permission of the author.

between the article "the" and the adjective with its following phrase "crushed velvet sofa"? Why are the fourth and fifth lines broken where they are, between "stretched" and "tight"? Note that all of these lines are about the same length. Why did the poet apparently follow this method of form? How would it have changed the poem if in the ninth line, the word "of" had been included after "Unaware" rather than on the following line? In the last two lines, again, the poet chooses to separate "the" from the noun that the article describes: "street light." Why? How is the rhythm of the poem affected by this procedure? How is the meaning of the last line changed?

In Williams's poem "The Red Wheelbarrow," everything in this short, imagistic poem depends on where the lines are broken. What if the poem had been written in the following way?

> so much depends upon a
> red wheel barrow glazed
> with rain water beside
> the
> white
> chickens

How would the rhythm of the poem be different? How would the stress of the emphases of the poem change? How would the poem be a different poem from the one that Williams wrote?

Now try the same process on this longer and slightly more difficult poem:

.... **Janet McCann**

*Julian of Norwich**

> locked in, permitted a cat
> "to catch the mice," fed reasonably,
> allowed to walk in the garden,
>
> (it would have been, I should think, an herbal garden
> with tiny flowers, distinct, austere scents)
>
> seeing others only through the window,
> narrow, called a "squint,"
> locked in, locked out, locked,

*Janet McCann, "Julian of Norwich" published in *Windhover*, 1999. Reprinted by permission of the author.

with the key, though, in her heart,
with the book of the key in her hand.

(I can see her hand, small, freckled, white,
a breviary in it)

less locked than I am
though enclosed, through choice
in the room, in the occasional garden
with the clean medicinal scents,
the rows of purslane,
comfrey, arnica,

(Her clothing, the habit
heavy, just right for the weather, and not
suffocating)

(The full office in its entirety,
every day, beginning before dawn)

And Grace coming, through the window,
not strangely, and also into the garden,

not strangely, invited, through habit
and the mind's true and proper direction,

a sudden sweetness,

a plenty, a tangle of wild roses.

Ask yourself why the first three lines in this poem are broken where they are. Why does the poet choose to make the fourth line (the first line in parentheses) slightly longer than the first three lines? Does her decision matter? Why is the second line in the fourth strophe (division part) so brief? Does the brevity of this line correspond to what is being described in the subject matter of the line? Is this correspondence significant? Explain what you see as the reasons for the particular line breaks of the last lines that are presented singly, that is, not contained in a couplet (a two-line group) or a strophe (a group of unrhymed lines). Finally, determine why once in the poem the poet breaks a line after just one word: "suffocating." Does this line break also fit the content of the line?

Here is a poem by Robert Phillips that is not written in rhyme or any other form except three-line stanzas, which are called tercets. Prepare a detailed explanation of why you think Phillips broke each line exactly where he did. (A good class exercise might be to break the class into seven groups, the same number of groups as the number of stanzas in the poem. Let each group give an explanation of one stanza's line breaks, or three lines.)

*In August**

Slow as the rhetoric of Warren G. Harding,
summer staggers to its knees, stunned
as a poleaxed steer at slaughter.

Beside the highway, vegetable stands groan,
sweet corn, peaches lolling like Rubens' nudes,
tomatoes red as Red Cross plasma.

In the fields, scarecrows are empty-headed
uncles. Ponds shadow green as Canada
geese fly by. Sand congregates in swimsuit crotches.

Day lilies trumpet the garden's four corners,
black-eyed susans meet the day's eye,
loosestrife floods the marshes with fire.

Chipmunks assume the shape of pears,
snakes snooze and dream of shrews,
robins bob for worms like apples in a barrel.

Air-conditioners sigh, captive dolphins;
dust-pussies lie under country beds;
crickets, domesticated Vivaldis.

Night drops, a lady's chemise, not too clean.
Insects, both sexes, dive-bomb the porch light.
The planet like love slowly turns to ice.

Other exercises to try with this poem may include the following topics that we have already discussed: Find alliteration, assonance, consonance, or internal rhyme. Find similes or metaphors. Explain what is being compared to what, and comment on whether the comparison is imaginative and effective.

*"In August" by Robert Phillips. Published in *Personal Accounts,* Ontario Review Press, 1986. Reprinted by permission.

EXERCISES ....

1. Try to explain why poet Paul Christensen broke the lines of the following three poems where he did.

.... **Paul Christensen**

A Haven from the Storm*

It's Christmas at the liquor store;
the paper Santas are hanging
in the flocked window, with bells
and green holly. It is cold out,
and the drunks are counting their money
in the parking lot. Someone
is moving in a mist of seasonal memory
inside, growing gold from the lights.
She is beautiful and innocent,
part of the heaven that beckons
in a rack of whiskey bottles.

One by one the drunks line up
asking in sheepish voices
for a pint of Vodka, or a quart
of the cheapest bourbon.
The air swirls with snowflakes and traffic lights.
In a cramped apartment, a child
prays for Nike running shoes
to the click of ice cubes from the livingroom.

Be patient says the lamb
in the butchershop, hanging
from a shiny hook. The grinder
is idle by the bench, and the knives
are laid to rest against the wall.
Have mercy says the dog
chained to the ouside faucet,
shivering on its boney legs.
Given the world's unyielding principles,
a liquor store is haven from the storm.

*Paul Christensen, "A Haven from the Storm," reprinted by permission of the author.

Texas in the Middle of the Nineteenth Century*

We are faced with a small god
wrapped in bible paper,
newly torn from the earth.
It wears a swaddling of roots
and mud, the red of a goat's blood
tingeing its muscles.

The Indians concede its capture
and leave, vowing a return.
But under these fierce
heavens of an August noon,
we are the conquerors, and this
brown god of thorns and snake teeth

grows tame with our milk,
and sleeps in the crook
of our long sleeves. We move
in a procession of land-grabbing
and slaughter, driving the wildness
into heaven, easing the rivers
down a shallow grave of cotton fields.

Soon enough will rise our churches,
and a steeple to scrape
the stars and pierce the dark
with our ambitions. Already
the coyote weeps on a hill,
and hears the creep of human shoes.

With this lord of snaggle teeth
and profit, this god of double
chin, a belly full of gold,
this ikon of oil gluts,
old demon-haunted plastic doll,
we shall not want for rage.

*Paul Christensen, "Texas in the Middle of the Nineteenth Century," reprinted by permission of the author.

The Mist Over Lake Somerville*

Morning comes over the roofs
in a flood of gold paint
and old suitcases full of shirts.
The whores are sleeping until noon
and will not know the gaudy
splendor of a new Sunday.

They roll in dreams of money
and a beige Cadillac
heading south; they hear
the music of tuxedo players
sliding their trombones
into a cloud of silk.

The Christians are eating breakfast
to the mumble of radios,
carving a brick of margarine
to soften their toast.
Their shoes are hard, the soap
smells of troubled memories.

What the preacher does
is private knowledge; only
a certain devotee of holiness
can know the truth. He putters
at his mirror in a naked trance,
touching the hairs of his mole.

Meanwhile, at the water's edge,
an egret shakes its feathers
and spreads out in its notch
of cypress. It is a soul
caught in the clutches
of the flesh, white and unused.

2. Ask yourself these questions about the preceding poems: (a) What effect does the
poet's breaking the line (second strophe) after "a child" have in the poem "A Haven
from the Storm"? (b) In the same poem, by breaking the line "Be patient says the
lamb" after the word "lamb," what allusion can be heard in the background? Is
"lamb" emphasized? Why? Why at this season, particularly? (c) Explain why the poet
chose to break the line "In the butchershop, hanging" after the word "hanging"?

*Paul Christensen, "The Mist Over Lake Somerville," reprinted by permission of the author.

What allusion echoes here? (d) Find and explain three important line breaks in the poem "Texas in the Middle of the Nineteenth Century." (e) Have a discussion about the rhythm in five of the lines in "The Mist Over Lake Somerville." How do the line breaks create the rhythm in this poem, which is not written in regular meter?

3. Consider one more poem by Paul Christensen, and try to determine how many voice "stresses" each line gets. Is there generally a regular count of voice stresses? If so, what is it?

.... **Paul Christensen**

The Navasota Bottoms*

Follow a coon's tracks
through the razor grass,
cane, thistle, bush, and whatever
thorn the summer is growing
to a scrub oak leaning
its scrawly legs over the river.
Bless yourself three times
and give thanks to the maker
of these muddy banks,
for beyond them lie ruins
of cotton fields and a rimless
earth of smoldering prairie.

Inside every pain is an Eden
pooled like glitter, waiting
to be found. Fish slide,
and the worm balances
on a leaf's edge, a wind
plays among the fine hairs
of a spider's legs. Soft things
move in and out of plush
mosses, and the pebbles
are gleaming gems in the lace
of the river. Kneel and
be thankful the earth
pays no attention to us.

4. Write a poem of your own in which the line breaks are very important, and explain your reasons for breaking lines where you do.

*Paul Christensen, "The Navasota Bottoms," reprinted by permission of the author.

Meter

Rhythms are felt everywhere in life. As I write this, I sit near an open balcony at the edge of the Texas gulf. Sea waves crash regularly and rhythmically outside, below my door. While this is happening, I read these words by Laurence Perrine, in his book *Sound and Sense:* "RHYTHM refers to any wavelike recurrence of motion or sound."

Meter is rhythm that has been measured. People generally think of poetry as having a regular kind of rhythm. If a poem has a regular rhythm, we call that kind of poetry *verse*. Of course, we can have rhymed verse or nonrhymed verse (verse having a regular rhythm without rhyme). We call nonrhymed, metered poetry that happens to have five stressed beats per line *blank verse*. Poetry that has no fixed number of stressed beats per line is termed *free verse*.

As Perrine states, "The study of meter is a fascinating but highly complex subject. In the English language, every word with more than one syllable has at least one of the syllables heavily accented, or stressed. To measure poetry, we count the number of stresses in a line. But the basic metrical unit, or means of measuring poetry, is called a *foot*. Usually a foot is one accented syllable plus one or two unaccented syllables."

In English, a majority of two-syllable words have the second syllable accented and the first syllable unaccented: "report," "believe," "receive," and so forth. If a word has one unaccented syllable and one accented syllable, in that order, we would term the two syllables of that word an *iamb*, for example, "today."

The line length and line breaks of a poem, we have said, are crucial units of measurement in poetry. We measure a regularly-metered line by counting the number of "feet" it has within it. Yet there are a variety of kinds of feet, or ways to measure stresses or accents.

Following is a chart giving various kinds of feet: note how accented syllables and non-accented ones are marked.

Example	Name of Foot	Name of Meter
rĕ plý	iamb	iambic
áf tĕr	trochee	trochaic
iň tĕr veńe	anapest	anapestic
ẃill inğ lỷ	dactyl	dactylic
snów storḿ	spondee	spondaic

Here is a poem by Samuel Taylor Coleridge that defines and exemplifies the various kinds of metrical feet.

Metrical Feet

Trochee trips from long to short.
From long to long in solemn sort
Slow Spondee stalks; strong foot! yet ill able
Ever to come up with Dactyl trisyllable.
Iambics march from short to long.
With a leap and a bound the swift Anapests throng.

You can mark the stresses in a line of poetry by using any one of several conventions. Perhaps the easiest one is to use an accent mark (´) for each stressed syllable and an ˘ for each unstressed syllable. If you do that, you get this scheme for the first stanza of Emily Dickinson's poem "I Never Saw a Moor":

Ĭ névĕr sáw ă móor,
Ĭ névĕr sáw thĕ séa,
Yĕt knów Ĭ hów thĕ héa thĕr looḱs
Ańd wh́at ă wav́e mŭst bé.

If you were to write out the lines in partial capitals, capitalizing the accented syllables to stress the rhythm, you'd get the following:

I NEver SAW a MOOR,
I NEver SAW the SEA,
but I know HOW the HEATHer LOOKS
and WHAT a WAVE must BE.

This way of indicating the stresses is a bit confusing, because "I" is capitalized whether it is stressed or not, but the idea is clear enough.

A well-written poem that is in meter will have a majority, though certainly not all, of the same kinds of feet. We say, for example, if a poem has five feet (ten syllables, approximately) per line and if most of the feet are iambic (dă dúm) stressed feet, then the poem is in *iambic pentameter,* or in a basic iambic rhythm, with five iambs (dă dúms) per line. Certainly not every line will always have exactly five iambs. In fact, the best poems have varied feet, or else the rhythm of the poem and the poem itself become monotonous and boring.

SCANSION

Scansion is the analysis of the meter via marking the stressed and unstressed syllables in the line and in the entire poem. (I like to think of "scanning" a poem as comparable to diagramming sentences while studying grammar.) Both scanning poems
and diagramming sentences are an analytical activity, not a synthetic endeavor.

Just as learning to diagram sentences will not by itself make one a good
writer, learning to scan lines and poems will not make one a good poet. Nevertheless, it is wise for any aspiring poet to learn to scan regularly-metered verse.

After reading a poem that you are attempting to scan, the second step is to
take one line of the poem and to accent each of the stressed syllables. Next, return to the line and also mark the unstressed syllables. Beginning at the end of
the line, put a slash mark between every two syllables if the rhythm seems fairly
iambic (dă dúm) in rhythm. If the lines are in basic iambic rhythm and if you
have marked the slashes to divide the two-syllable feet, then count the number
of feet per line. This count will tell you how to name the rhythm and the line
count. Remember, not every foot will have the same number of syllables per
line, if the poem is complicated or complex. A poem in iambic meter, for example, may have only three, or even two, iambic feet in some lines. But there
should be a number of lines that are perfect iambic in rhythm in order to establish the basically regular rhythm of the poem. A perfectly regular iambic line,
then, would be all feet that are "dă dúm" in rhythm: An iambic pentameter line
would have all or the majority of its feet in this rhythm.

According to the number of feet per line, there are various names for the
lines. Here are some:

heptameter = 7

hexameter = 6

pentameter = 5

tetrameter = 4

trimeter = 3

dimeter = 2

monometer = 1

Notice that each of these terms contains the root word *meter*. (*Meter* means
"regular rhythm." The prefixes to these terms—*hept, hexa, penta, tetra, tri, di,* and
mono—are Latin words for the numbers seven, six, five, four, three, two, and one.)

EXERCISES ....

1.   If a poem has a basic iamb count and four feet per line, what rhythm is it in? The following poem has this kind of meter. Scan (that is, mark for kinds and numbers of
feet) the first stanza of the poem:

Virtue

Sweet day, so cool, so calm, so bright,
    The bridal of the earth and sky;
The dew shall weep thy fall to night,
    For thou must die.

Here are the final three stanzas of the poem. Now scan these lines.

Sweet rose, whose hue, angry and brave,
    Bids the rash gazer wipe his eye;
Thy root is ever in its grave,
    And thou must die.

Sweet spring, full of sweet days and roses,
    A box where sweets compacted lie;
My music shows ye have your closes,
    And all must die.

Only a sweet and virtuous soul,
    Like seasoned timber, never gives;
But though the whole world turn coal,
    Then chiefly lives.

2.   Try the same kind of scansion for this nursery rhyme:

Jack and Jill went up the hill
To fetch a pail of water.
Jack fell down and broke his crown
And Jill came tumbling after.

3.   What is the basic line length of each line of "Jack and Jill": 4 feet, 5 feet, or 3 feet? What is the predominant kind of foot: iambic or trochaic? What is the basic number of feet in each line? Where are the variations (the feet that are irregular)? Mark them and name them. Now try this poem:

Ride a cock horse, to Banbury Cross,
To see a fine lady upon a white horse.
Rings on her fingers and bells on her toes,
She shall have music wherever she goes.

4.   Return to the Coleridge poem "Metrical Feet" on page 149, and scan it.

5.   Answer all the questions in item 3 for this more difficult poem:

Meeting at Night

The gray sea and long black land;
And the yellow half-moon large and low;
And the startled little waves that leap
In fiery ringlets from their sleep,
As I gain the cove with pushing prow,
And quench its speed i' the slushy sand.

Then a mile of warm sea-scented beach;
Three fields to cross till a farm appears,
A tap at the pane, the quick sharp scratch
A blue spurt of a lighted match,
And a voice less loud, through its joys and fears,
Than the two hearts beating each to each!

(Here are further exercises for the Browning poem. Find all the explosive consonants, and circle the assonance. Then mark the rhyme scheme, giving each new rhyme a letter to name it: a, b, c, d, e, f. Next, note any metaphors or similes. Finally, discuss the literal subject matter (the apparent action) of the poem, and then discuss the theme of the poem (the meaning that the poem seems to be reaching for).

6. Scan the following lines, and identify the meter:

Twas the night before Christmas, and all through the house
Not a creature was stirring, not even a mouse.

London Bridge is falling down,
    Falling down, falling down,
London Bridge is falling down,
    My fair lady!

I do not love thee, Dr. Fell,
The reason why I cannot tell;
But this I know, and know full well,
I do not love thee, Dr. Fell.

7. Analyze the meter and other poetic devices that you can identify in the following poem:

Think'st Thou to Seduce Me Then

Think'st thou to seduce me then with words that have no meaning?
Parrots so can learn to prate, our speech by pieces gleaning;
Nurses teach their children so about the time of weaning.

Learn to speak first, then to woo; to wooing much pertaineth;
He that courts us, wanting art, soon falters when he feigneth,
Looks asquint on his discourse, and smiles when he complaineth.

Skillful anglers hide their hooks, fit baits for every season;
But with crooked fins fish thou, as babes do that want reason:
Gudgeons only can be caught with such poor tricks of treason.

Ruth forgive me, if I erred from human heart's compassion,
When I laughed sometimes too much to see thy foolish fashion;
But, alas, who less could do that found so good occasion?

8. Remind yourself that the poems in the preceding exercises are in regular rhythm. They can be scanned and marked and termed "verse." However, free verse poetry cannot be scanned. Often, though, at least parts of free verse poems fall back on some regular rhythm. Although the American poet Walt Whitman did not write in regular rhythm or verse, is there a line in this poem that is in regular iambic feet? If so, which one?

.... **Walt Whitman**

When I Heard the Learn'd Astronomer

When I heard the learn'd astronomer,
When the proofs, the figures, were ranged in columns before me,
When I was shown the charts and diagrams, to add, divide, and
    measure them,
When I sitting heard the astronomer where he lectured with much
    applause in the lecture-room,
How soon unaccountable I became tired and sick,
Till rising and gliding out I wandered off by myself,
In the mystical moist night-air, and from time to time,
Looked up in perfect silence at the stars.

Formal Poetry _____

> A good poem is a contribution to reality. The world is never the same once a good poem has been added to it. A good poem helps to change the shape of the universe, helps to extend everyone's knowledge of himself and the world around him.
>
> —Dylan Thomas

Formal poetry is merely poetry written in some set form. It may have regular rhythm, and/or it may have a particular number of lines per stanza. Some forms are based on syllable-counting rather than on meter. Traditional poetry tends to be in a definite verse form. Contemporary poetry, however, often departs from those forms or uses the forms with great liberty (changed or amended traditional forms). Some traditional poems that we will explore are limericks, haiku, sonnets, sestinas, and villanelles. If you are particularly drawn to form and to writing in forms, it would be useful to read about how contemporary poets use forms and how they suggest that students use them; in the Suggested Readings at the end of the book are a number of sources that discuss form.

LIMERICKS

A *limerick* is a short, humorous poem, usually in five lines. The first two and the final lines are usually fairly regular iambic trimeter (three iambic feet). The third and fourth lines are iambic dimeter (two iambic feet). The rhyme is usually based on only two sets of perfectly rhyming words. The rhyme scheme is aabba. Mark the rhyme scheme and the rhythm of the following limericks:

> There was a young lady of Lynn
> Who was so uncommonly thin
> That when she essayed
> To drink lemonade
> She slipped through the straw and fell in.

> There was an old man of Peru
> Who dreamt he was eating his shoe.
> He awoke in the night
> In a terrible fright,
> And found it was perfectly true!

See whether you can scan these poems, and also find the rhyme scheme.

Where does the humor come in these short poems? Does humor, or at least catchy lines, seem to be a prerequisite for a limerick?

HAIKU

Haiku is an ancient kind of formal poetry that originated in Japan. Short, imagistic, and lyrical poems by tradition, the original haiku had seventeen counted syllables. Initially in the Japanese language, the haiku did not have accentual-syllabic (accented or stressed) rhythm comparable to poems written in the English language. (Indeed, even poems in French and other modern Romance languages are not accentually syllabic stressed, as in the English language.)

Stephen Minot writes in his book *Three Genres,* "In English [the haiku] is usually written as a three-line poem containing five syllables in the first line, seven in the second, and five in the third." In this sense, the haiku is one form of "syllable" poem, that is, a poem in which syllables are counted in each line and often form a pattern throughout the poem.

Haiku poems, which tend to be imagistic and visual, usually name or suggest a season. There is often a contrast implied, such as between movement and stillness, or noise and silence. A haiku is very concentrated—each syllable contributes to the effect. Haiku poems are enjoyable because they suggest a kind of meditative observation that we seldom have time for. Here is a contemporary example of the form:

.... **SuzAnne C. Cole**

*Haiku**

November fields—snow
flakes drifting down to cover
the last ripe pumpkins

candle guttering
on a bare wooden table
chairs pushed away

sandy path leading
to the sea—father and child
wind blowing her hair

smoky incense drifts
through my hands to my body
Buddha breathing grace

Sometimes haiku poems are written without the 5-7-5 count; instead, such poems attempt to capture the feel of the haiku without using the pattern, which is, after all, different in effect in Japanese. Writers disagree about whether these are true haiku, but they can be interesting for their concentration. Sometimes they just present a single metaphor, as in the following:

*SuzAnne C. Cole, "November fields" appeared in *Suraga-Baiku Literary Festival Anthology,* 1999. "candle guttering" appeared in *The Thinking Post Anthology of Haiju and Zen Poetry,* Carolyn Thomas, ed., Borrega Springs, CA: Thinking Post Press, 1999. "sandy path" appeared in *Piedmont Literary Review,* 22:2 (Spring, 1999) and "smoky incense" appeared in *Potpourri* 10:3 (Fall, 1998). Reprinted by permission of the author.

Janie Grace

Haiku*

helicopter
giant mosquito
draining the clouds

SONNETS

Sonnets are a type of poem that originated in Italy. Traditionally they have fourteen lines and contain rhyme and a "rhyme scheme." Sonnets, which have meter, are most often in iambic pentameter. The Italian sonnet, which has an initial eight lines that present a "problem," referred to as the *octet*, is rhymed abba, abba. The last six lines, constituting a "resolution" to the problem, is referred to as a *sestet*. The rhyme scheme of a sestet is usually cde, cde.

The English, also called the "Elizabethan" or "Shakespearean" sonnet, written by Shakespeare and others during the reign of Queen Elizabeth I, also consists of fourteen lines, but with a different composition scheme. This type of sonnet has three *quatrains* (four-line stanzas, three of them constituting twelve lines) and a rhymed couplet at the end. The rhyme scheme of an English sonnet is often abab, cdcd, efef, gg. (Remember that each new letter labels a new rhyming sound.)

In the following sonnet, an English poet uses the Italian sonnet form:

William Wordsworth

The World Is Too Much With Us

.

The world is too much with us; late and soon,
Getting and spending, we lay waste our powers:
Little we see in Nature that is ours;
We have given our hearts away, a sordid boon!
This Sea that bares her bosom to the moon;
The winds that will be howling at all hours,
And are up-gathered now like sleeping flowers;
For this, for everything, we are out of tune;
It moves us not.—Great God! I'd rather be
A Pagan suckled in a creed outworn;

---

*Janie Grace, "Haiku" reprinted by permission of the author.

So might I, standing on this pleasant lea,
Have glimpses that would make me less forlorn;
Have sight of Proteus rising from the sea;
Or hear old Triton blow his wreathéd horn.

What is the rhyme scheme of this poem? Where is the problem, and then where is the resolution? Can you paraphrase the issues of the poem? (To paraphrase means to put the poem into prose, in your own words.)

Here is a sonnet by Robert Frost, a poet with whom we are already familiar. He divides the poem into tercets (three-line stanzas) rather than quatrains. Yet the poem uses the modified-English sonnet form, with a rhymed couplet at the end. Mark the rhyme scheme, scan the poem, and then put the poem into your own words. (While doing this, discuss whether the word "night" in the poem actually becomes a symbol, something larger than the literal meaning of the word *night*.)

.... **Robert Frost**

*Acquainted with the Night**

I have been one acquainted with the night.
I have walked out in rain—and back in rain.
I have outwalked the furthest city light.

I have looked down the saddest city lane.
I have passed by the watchman on his beat
And dropped my eyes, unwilling to explain.

I have stood still and stopped the sound of feet
When far away an interrupted cry
Came over houses from another street,

But not to call me back or say good-by;
And further still at an unearthly height
One luminary clock against the sky

Proclaimed the time was neither wrong nor right.
I have been one acquainted with the night.

Now here are two strict and traditional sonnets, one by William Shakespeare and the other by John Milton. Which is English form, and which Italian? Which one has an octave and a sestet? Which has three quatrains and a rhyming couplet?

.... **William Shakespeare**

Sonnet XXIX

When in disgrace with fortune and men's eyes
I all alone beweep my outcast state,
And trouble deaf heaven with my bootless cries,
And look upon myself, and curse my fate,
Wishing me like to one more rich in hope,
Featured like him, like him with friends possessed,
Desiring this man's art, and that man's scope,
With what I most enjoy contented least;
Yet in these though myself almost despising,
Haply I think on thee, and then my state,
Like to the lark at break of day arising
From sullen earth, sings hymns at heaven's gates;
For thy sweet love remembered such wealth brings
That then I scorn to change my state with kings.

.... **John Milton**

O Nightingale, That on Yon Bloomy Spray

O Nightingale, that on yon bloomy spray
Warbl'st at eve, when all the woods are still,
Thou with fresh hope the lover's heart dost fill,
While the jolly hours lead on propitious May.
Thy liquid notes that close the eye of day,
First heard before the shallow cuckoo's bill,
Portend success in love; O if Jove's will
Have linked that amorous power to thy soft lay
Now timely sing, 'ere the rude bird of Hate
Foretell my hopeless doom in some grove nigh:

As thou from year to year hast sung too late
For my relief, yet hadst no reason why,
Whether the Muse or Love call thee his mate,
Both them I serve and of their train am I.

Another English poet who wrote many sonnets is the Romantic poet John Keats. Decide whether the following two sonnets are English or Italian in form. Compare them with the preceding Milton sonnet.

John Keats

To One Who Has Been Long in City Pent

To one who has been long in city pent,
'Tis very sweet to look into the fair
And open face of heaven,—to breathe a prayer
Full in the smile of the blue firmament.
Who is more happy, when, with heart's content,
Fatigued he sinks into some pleasant lair
Of wavy grass, and reads a debonair
And gentle tale of love and languishment?
Returning home at evening, with an ear
Catching the notes of Philomel,—an eye
Watching the sailing cloudlet's bright career,
He mourns that day so soon has glided by
E'en like the passage of an angel's tear
That falls through the clear ether silently.

On the Grasshopper and the Cricket

The poetry of earth is never dead:
When all the birds are faint with the hot sun,
And hide in cooling trees, a voice will run
From hedge to hedge about the new-mown mead;
That is the Grasshopper's—he takes the lead
In summer luxury,—he has never done
With his delights; for when tired out with fun
He rests at ease beneath some pleasant weed.

The poetry of earth is ceasing never:
On a lone winter evening, when the frost
Has wrought a silence, from the stove there shrills
The Cricket's song, in warmth increasing ever,
And seems to one in drowsiness half lost,
The Grasshopper's among some grassy hills.

Now, here are three contemporary sonnets by contemporary poets. One of them—"Here & There," by Robert Phillips—we have already examined in another context; we will look at it now as a sonnet. Which kind of sonnet form does each poem appear to employ? How did each poet depart from strictly traditional form? (Consider the rhyme scheme and the meter.) What are the deviations in each poem from strict sonnet form? Why did the poet construct these currently-written sonnets in this way?

Ask yourself the following: Why would a contemporary poet depart from strict form? Why would the poet take such liberty? What, in your opinion, is the poetic result? Notice again, first, one poem cited earlier in another context.

Robert Phillips

*Here & There**

There was that winter a freezing of fire
and in tumbled nights the enlightening
of a pair, side by side, who were not there.
Though they shared a common bed, one flew out
west to San Diego, the other dreamed
a plaid figure on a New Hampshire mare.
From habit they slept spoon-fashion: Yin, Yang.
A transcontinental cold divided.

Their future seemed all of Manhattan's sky-
line, blacked out. Their match could not brighten that.
When spring came, oozing its thaw and its thud,
together they alone walked flowered fields,
stealing a blossom here, a blossom there,
and seeing nothing living, anywhere.

*"Here and There" by Robert Phillips. Reprinted by permission.

.... **Artis Bernard**

Cross*

Not the recognized fate of bluejays, this tidy
grave in a backyard, but what else could
we do, the boy and I? We winced to see
the startling blue wings covered with mud.

The bluejay had died among us and what we do
is bury death and then set up a sign,
so the boy and I found sticks, and he held two
against each other like a plumb line

and snapped off little pieces until he thought
he had it right, the arms of man against
man's height. Then we lashed them with a taut
string for chest and marked the grave. In defiance,

the long stick became short, the short long:
bluejay wingspan against bluejay song.

Stockyard Cafe*

The day we left my father ordered the special—
toast and steak. When the cook asked from the grill
what I'd have, I had to answer twice,
being timid and not used to eating out.

Even after we'd ordered, we stared at the menu
as if its plain speech could organize
all the dear clutter that no suitcase
could carry, that we couldn't even say was where.

Into the front door drifted the lisping cornfields,
into the back windows the bellowing cattle.
Grill, sink, tables: severe as a galley.
The cups clipped as if we were going by sea.

*Artis Bernard, "Cross" and "Stockyard Cafe" are reprinted by permission of the author.

This ship, the menu said, sails straight and hard.
What there is of love—what you have—guard.

How has the writer of the last poem departed from a strict sonnet rhyme scheme? Is there any rhyme at all? Is there any set or strict rhythm in the poem? Does each line have perfect iambic pentameter? (Note the marking by letters of each new or old rhyme, at the end of each line.) What function do the rhyming couplets have in this poem? Are they important? Are they a kind of "summing up," (as we have said that rhyming couplets usually are in English sonnets)?

SESTINA

A *sestina* is an even more difficult formed poem, consisting of exactly thirty-nine lines. Thirty-six of the lines occupy six six-line stanzas, the lines usually having no strict meter but having a fairly similar line length. The last three lines of the poem, which is thirty-nine lines long, constitute what is referred to as the "envoi."

The difficult part of writing a sestina is that all lines must end in one of six specific words, chosen by the poet. The entire sestina form, however, becomes even more complicated. The six words must come in a particular order in each stanza. A summary of the sestina form is as follows. The letters here indicate whole words, not rhymes: Stanza 1, ABCDEF; Stanza 2, FAEBDC; Stanza 3, CFDABE; Stanza 4, ECBFAD; Stanza 5, DEACFB; Stanza 6, BDFECA. The envoi does not have a required fixed pattern, but the six words must be used two per line. Some contemporary sestinas omit the envoi.

What is fun about the sestina is that it allows wordplay—if you choose "bolt" for one of your six words, for instance, you may vary its meaning and grammatical function: it can mean a bolt of lightning, the action of running out of a room, the counterpart of a "nut," or a rolled-up length of cloth—and you can change the meaning from one line to the next. When the poem is read, the repeated word holds the poem together and functions like a familiar chord.

Following are two contemporary sestinas; "High-Heeled Sestina" gives light-hearted reflections about changes in women's roles, and "Library Sestina" is about taking the bus to a certain library when the poet was a little girl. (Writers of this poetry form customarily call them "Sestina," thus making it easy to find them in an anthology's index.)

.... **Janie Grace**

*High-Heeled Sestina**

In the fifties home-ec movies, women
vacuumed carpets in stiletto heels,
slim-ankled, glided handily
across thick carpets while we girls took notes,
Future Homemakers of America, dreaming
dustless queendoms, shiny dancing shoes.

We bought the shoes,
twirled before mirrors, turning into women,
stared at toebones in x-ray boxes, dreaming
of princely hands, champagne in silver heels,
of leaving the ballroom to the wild sweet notes
of the brass band, life going handily.

we didn't know how handily
princes would turn away, the soft notes
die, leaving only the shoes,
painful, confining, bunion-causing, now women
of substance and presence, we strode on those heels
briskly down hallways. No more dreaming,

or if we kept on dreaming
it was of handily
kicking high and throwing off the heels
and walking across wet grass without shoes
high-spirited unfettered women
whistling a few notes

formless and tuneless, but still, our own notes.
(But this was only dreaming.)
We women
wore our footcuffs handily
wondering how we came to think of shoes
as freeing us, when those high heels

*Janie Grace, "High-Heeled Sestina," reprinted by permission of the author.

tapped business paths, were no champagne-filled heels
of high romance. We will take no more notes,
forever slip off shoes
for dancing and for dreaming,
having found late but handily
happier ways to show that we are women.

We can see from this sestina how this form lends itself to the narrative, or storytelling, mode of poetry. What story is the following poem, "Library Sestina," telling? What are some of the meanings of both "High-Heeled Sestina" and "Library Sestina"? What are some of the things that they are saying about childhood? Is the message about childhood in "High-Heeled Sestina" different from that in "Library Sestina"? See what you think.

.... **Sybil Pittman Estess**

Library Sestina*

(Mississippi, 1950: Age 8)

My mother always let me take the bus
to heaven for a nickel. In town I waited
with innocent breath, wondering alone where
was the nearest stop to the paradise library.
I walked some six or seven blocks away—
then the ascent up the circular, stone steps.

The Hardy Boys connived up those sky-high steps.
And Nancy Drew solved crime where the dear bus
ferried me. The Bobsey Twins played far away
from my house. Seven days I had slowly waited
to meet them Saturday. That ivy-bricked library
was not like my bookless home. It was there where

Miss librarian said "Shhhhh!" too loudly. (Nowhere
but here, I mused, could she live—so skinny!) Steps
raised me to her creaky hardwood, the library-
floors, glazed. Then green bindings boarded a bus
going slowly home with me. . . . (Each week I waited
a Genesis-creation for giant tires taking me away.)

*Sybil Pittman Estess, "Library Sestina," reprinted by permission of the author.

Every time I had to return to a plain life—away
from magic to my family—and also to where
most mysteries stayed unfixed, I still waited
to go once again to repose—up those steps
where I could see Susan B. Anthony (by bus).
Bound orange, Esther was also in the library.

And it was in the same old library
that I wrote MGM, mailed my letter away
to Hollywood and went back home by bus.
"You have made a movie of Moses, but where
is Esther's?" I composed. I had risen on steps
of stone to reach that protest. As I waited

patiently for a reply never arriving, I waited
turning new pages in the huge, high old library
still there (being renovated now)—those steps
still rising. Today, when I flee, go far away
from my own flawed house, that library is where
I yearn to reach by my mind. No, by my bus!

But I've strayed. Oh, I'm weighted, a long way away
from my lighted library with its bind. I live where
I can't wait to mount those steps. I find it won't come—that bus.

EXERCISES

1. Write out the six ending words in this sestina, and look at them—why do you think that the writer chose these words?

2. Read the preceding sestina aloud. What effect does the repetition of the end words have?

3. Write six words that you might use to create your own sestina. Choose at least one word that has more than one meaning, like "bolt" or "fly."

4. Using your six chosen words, construct a sestina of thirty-nine lines—six six-line stanzas and one three-line envoi—of your own. (Here is a tip about this process: Choose the words first, and then write them down at the right margin of your paper. Write the words as they will probably be used in your envoi. Begin to build the poem around these words in these places.)

5. This exercise is for the daring. Open the dictionary at random places, six times, and write down the six words that first catch your eye. Write them out at the side of the page in the order of the sestina pattern. Now write a sestina with these words, with or without the envoi. You are allowed to reject any totally impossible words, like "heptogenic," but keep odd ones, like "bulldoze."

VILLANELLE

Villanelle is another poetry form of definite length, rhyme scheme, and meter. Coming from the Italian word *villanella,* the term means "a rustic song or dance of a peasant." The form was introduced into France in the sixteenth century. Originally it contained a pastoral subject and the use of a refrain. Contemporary villanelles have nineteen lines. Two of the lines are repeated—the first and the third. Otherwise, the poem has a strict rhyme scheme in every line.

The villanelle is a suitable form for comic as well as serious poetry, and its lively rhythms can be moderated to provide very different emotional effects, from playful to dirge-like. Perhaps the best way to see how the form works is to troll the Internet for villanelles. Simply type the term into your favorite search engine and see what comes up. You might take your best find to share with the class.

A villanelle is a poem in form and rhyme, having nineteen lines, employing two sets of rhymed words and two entire lines that are repeated. The villanelle has five three-line stanzas and a final four-line stanza, in which both repeated lines appear at the end. *The Poetry Handbook,* by Babette Deutsch, provides the following description of how the rhyme scheme of a villanelle is often marked:

> [T]he first and third lines of the opening tercet [recur] alternately at the end of the other tercets, and both [are] repeated at the close of the concluding quatrain. With the first line as A and the third, which rhymes with it, as A′, the scheme is ABA′, ABA, ABA′, ABA, ABA′, ABAA′.

Here are four contemporary villanelles. See how they keep and also amend the traditional villanelle form and rhyme scheme. (Remember that current poems often change the forms just a bit but that they usually retain enough of the form for the poem to be recognized as written in certain forms.)

·· **Helen Frost**

*Mud, Sticks, Food**

Somewhere a house is empty of these lives,
the mother beaver dead, the pups not born.
Our hands caress the loss. Our thought contrives

to name the brown and violet parts, as if, in naming,
it revives the heart, makes loops and curves and folds less torn.
Somewhere a house is empty of these lives.

*Helen Frost, "Mud, Sticks, Food" is reprinted by permission of the author.

We lift the liquid cradles, cut them loose with knives.
Water breaks on fur, feet, tail. Watching, we forget to mourn.
Our hands caress the loss. Our thought contrives

their birth. We wrap the pups in plastic, hang them high in leaves
of willows by the river, to protect their perfect form.
Somewhere a house is empty of these lives.

We clean the inside of the mother's skin. All we do deprives
her house of mud, sticks, food—leaves her mate forlorn.
Our hands caress the loss. Our thought contrives

to find an exit. The living beaver slaps his tail and dives.
We are enclosed in widening rings of scorn.
Somewhere a house is empty of these lives.
Our hands caress the loss our thought contrives.

·· **Edward Hirsch**

*Ocean of Grass**

The ground was holy, but the wind was harsh
and unbroken prairie stretched for hundreds of miles
so that all she could see was an ocean of grass.

Some days she got so lonely she went outside
and nestled among the sheep, for company.
The ground was holy, but the wind was harsh

and prairie fires swept across the plains,
lighting up the country like a vast tinderbox
until all she could see was an ocean of flames.

She went three years without viewing a tree.
When her husband finally took her on a timber run
she called the ground holy and the wind harsh

and got down on her knees and wept inconsolably,
and lived in a sod hut for thirty more years
until the world dissolved in an ocean of grass.

Think of her sometimes when you pace the earth,
our mother, where she was laid to rest.
The ground was holy, but the wind was harsh
for those who drowned in an ocean of grass.

.... **Janet McCann**

*Child in the Science Museum**

This is the polished world without a flaw.
The bars and pistons waltz before your eyes.
Your shadow prances like a great macaw.

In this electronic temple, nature's law
Is banished. Only metal speaks and sighs.
This is the polished world without a flaw.

The distant forms diverged, but those you saw
Were not quite there, were neither truths nor lies.
Your shadow dances like a great macaw

Across the screen. I look at it in awe.
(You squint now, push a lever, fantasize.)
This is the polished world without a flaw.

Here nothing is unfinished, unplanned, raw.
This is a space where nothing ever dies.
Your shadow dances like a great macaw

And flaps its wings, extends a gentle claw;
Steel cylinders refuse to compromise.
This is the polished world without a flaw.
Your shadow prances like a great macaw.

*Janet McCann, "Child in the Science Museum" published in *Windhover,* 1999," reprinted by permission of the author.

*Survivor's Song**

All my good friends have gone away.
    The boisterous flight of stairs is bare.
There's nothing more I want to say.

First was Jean—she thought she was gay—
    drunk nightly on *vin ordinaire.*
All my good friends have gone away.

And where is Scotty B. today?
    So Southern so doomed, so *savoir-faire*?
(There's nothing more I want to say.)

Sweet Hermione was third to stray.
    How her monologues smoked the air!
All my good friends have gone away.

Daniel, our beer-budget gourmet,
    no longer plays the millionaire.
There's nothing more I want to say

Except: My world's papier-mache.
    I need them all—weren't they aware?
All my good friends have gone away.
There's nothing more I want to say.

E X E R C I S E S

1. Write your own villanelle. Keep to iambic pentameter rhythm, as well as to the strict rhyme scheme and to the correct scheme of repeating lines.

2. Write an experimental, loose villanelle—keep the repetitions and rhymes, but use off-rhymes and vary the meter.

*"Survivor's Song" by Robert Phillips. Published in *Personal Accounts,* Ontario Review Press, 1986. Reprinted by permission.

PANTOUM

A *pantoum* is a complicated form of poetry. The form is written in quatrains—any number of them, and in any meter. The stanzas are linked together, since lines 2 and 4 of each stanza become lines 1 and 3 of the next. The lines that move as a pair (1 and 3, and 2 and 4) rhyme. The pantoum can end by the final quatrain's reaching back and repeating lines 1 and 3 of the first stanza. Or it can use lines 1 and 3 as lines 4 and 2, respectively, in the last stanza. Or the last stanza may be a couplet comprising these two lines, but in reverse order from the first stanza. Miller Williams writes the following in *Patterns of Poetry:*

> For a four-stanza poem, the pattern is A/1, B/1, A/2, B/2, B/1, C/1, B/2, C/2, C/1, D/1, C/2, D/2, D/1, A/2, D/2, A/1. Or if the second option is chosen for the resolution, the final stanza would be A/2, A/1.

Here are two pantoums by contemporary poets. The poem by Robert Phillips takes liberties with the traditional spacing of the poem's quatrains (four-line stanzas). All spacings are omitted.

.... **Susan Rich**

*Muted Gold**

(For Abraham Rich, 1921-1995)

My father died just as my plane touched down.
He taught me journeys don't happen in straight lines.
I loved him without ever needing words.
Is memory a chain of alibis?

He taught me journeys don't happen in straight lines.
His father sailed Odessa to Boston Harbor.
Is memory a chain of alibis?
The story I choose a net of my own desires?

His father sailed Odessa to Boston Harbor.
Dad worked beside him in their corner store.
The story I choose a net of my own desires?
I wish I'd known to ask the simple questions.

Dad worked beside him in their corner store.
They shelved the tins of black beans, fruit preserves, and almond cakes.
I wish I'd known to ask the simple questions,
He'd have stayed with me and gossiped over toast.

*Susan Rich, "Muted Gold" from The Cartographer's Tongue/Poems of the World. Reprinted by permission of the author.

They shelved the tins of black beans, fruit preserves and almond cakes.
What colors did they wear, what languages were spoken?
He'd have stayed with me and gossiped over toast,
now he's smiling but I can't summon the thought he's thinking.

What colors did they wear, what languages were spoken?
Was it muted gold, a world of shattered feeling?
now he's smiling but I can't summon the thoughts he's thinking.
I pack the clothes away, mark them *for Goodwill.*

Was it a muted gold, a world of shattered feeling?
What good will it do to dwell, I hear him say.
I pack his clothes away, mark them *for Goodwill.*
But I hold fast to one old T shirt, butter-smooth, and brilliant.

What good will it do to dwell, I hear him say.
He much preferred to glide along life's surface.
But I hold fast to one old T shirt, butter-smooth, and brilliant
and tell a story by moonlight, to try and keep him with me.

He much preferred to glide along life's surface.
I love him now with images and words,
and tell a story by moonlight, to try and keep him with me.
My father died just as my plane touched down.

.... **Robert Phillips**

Heavenly Day for a Do:
A Pantoum*

(The terrace. American Academy and Institute
of Arts and Letters. May.)

"Heavenly day for a do!"
        "Here comes the Princeton contingent."
"They got Paul here—what a coup."
        "This punch tastes more like astringent."
"Here comes the Princeton contingent."
        "Mike Keeley and Joyce Carol Oates?"

*"Heavenly Day for a Do: A Pauntoum" by Robert Phillips. Published in *Personal Accounts,* Ontario Review Press, 1986. Reprinted by permission.

"This punch tastes more like astringent."
    "That reporter's taking *notes.*"
"Mike Keeley and Joyce Carol Oates?"
    "The proceedings were much too long."
"That reporter's taking notes."
    "He looks just like Anna May Wong."
"The proceedings were much too long."
    "Look: there's Buckminster Fuller."
"He looks just like Anna May Wong."
    "A shame about Henry Miller."
"Look, there's Buckminster Fuller!"
    "Isn't there anything to eat?"
"A shame about Henry Miller,"
    "His acceptance speech was effete."
"Isn't there anything to eat?"
    "Helen's wearing a schmata."
"His acceptance speech was effete."
    "Vassar's his alma mater."

EXERCISES

1. Try writing a pantoum on a serious of subject.

2. Try writing a comic-toned pantoum.

Political Poetry

> When power leads man toward arrogance, poetry reminds him of his limitations. When power narrows the areas of man's concern, poetry reminds him of the richness and diversity of his existence. When power corrupts, poetry cleanses.
>
> —John Fitzgerald Kennedy

Sometimes poetry concerns public events or issues. Or it may take a stance on a political topic. This is not the case as much in the United States as it is in other parts of the world—especially Eastern Europe, Africa, South America, the Middle

East, and the Far East. For some reason, perhaps because we are more affluent and therefore more politically complacent in America, poems about political topics are not accepted here as much as in the places just mentioned. Often, political poems are thought to be at best didactic or at worst preachy. Some journals even shun poems that have public or political overtones. Nevertheless, we humans are not totally private beings, and the public, social, and even political world does affect us. Our own and others' political stances involve our lives more than most of us want to recognize.

In times of public stress or crisis, poets often write on the topics of the day in the public world. This has been the tendency since ancient times. American poets of today are sometimes criticized for having narrow political stances or not reaching toward some universal kind of experience in their public poems.

Eighteenth-century British verse often took strong social and political stances—even sometimes sacrificing what we contemporaries would call inspiration or universality.

In the text *The New Princeton Handbook of Poetic Terms,* edited by T. V. F. Brogan, the editor comments,

> The history of poetry . . . is full of different kinds of successful political poems in every period of literary distinction: medieval peasant's songs, [Dante's] *Divine Comedy* . . . Milton's political sonnets, Dryden's "Absalom and Achitophel," Blake's "London" . . . Yeats's "Easter 1916," Davie's "Remembering the Thirties". . . . Political subjects churn at the center of poetry. . . . we may say, all that can be changed by social consensus or external authority is properly called political.

So, where is the boundary between the personal and the political? Where does "I" merge with "we"? Many would claim that the personal is political, that whatever we say or even think of ourselves comes from political forces invisibly at work. But we are concerned here with the writing of poetry that has deliberate social content and wishes to effect social change.

As we are moved to write about social conditions, we must be very aware of our own conditions and privileges, if we are to be effective. A poem about poverty in Mexico or India, for example, written by a Mexican or an East Indian poet, is probably not perceived in the same way that it would be if it had been written by an American poet living in our affluent, complacent, and democratic society. As poets, we must be concerned with focusing attention on unjust conditions without seeming to appropriate others' experiences for our own use.

Two noted contemporary American female poets who have written much political poetry are Adrienne Rich and Denise Levertov. Rich tends to write about women's and feminist topics, as well as poems that critique our Western and American capitalist economy and culture. Levertov wrote about topics and crises such as the Vietnamese war. Here is one of Levertov's political-type poems.

.... **Denise Levertov**

Greeting to the Vietnamese Delegates to the U.N. *

Our large hands
Your small hands

Our country's power
Our powerlessness against it

Your country's poverty
The power of your convictions

Our corrupted democracy
The integrity of your revolution

Our technology and its barbarity
Your ingenuity and simple solutions

Our bombers
Your bicycles

Our unemployed veterans
Your re-educated prostitutes

Our heroin addicts rotting
Your wounded children healing

Our longing for new life
Your building of new life

Our large hands
Your small hands

Some beetle trilling
its midnight utterance.

Voice of the scarabee,
dungroller,
working survivor . . .

*"Greeting to the Vietnamese Delegates to the U.N." by Denise Levertov, from *Life in the Forest,* copyright © 1978 by Denise Levertov.

I recall how each year
returning from voyages, flights
over sundown snowpeaks,
cities crouched over darkening lakes,
hamlets of wood and smoke,
I find
    the same blind face upturned to the light
    and singing
    and one song,

    the same weed managing
    its brood of minute stars
    in the cracked flagstones.

In this free verse poem, what is the poet's main lament? What are her central methods of creating rhythm? How does the repetition, and the creation of rhythm here, fit the content of the poem? Do you apprehend the poet's political stance on this war? What is it? What are the two final strophes of the poem about? How do they fit both the content and the protest of the poem?

Here are other poems that are on either overtly social and political topics or more subtly social ones. The subject matter of two of the poems concerns issues outside the United States. The first poem "Four Women" by Sally Ridgway Proler, confronts the problem of homeless people, which could be anywhere in the United States. Study the poems, and consider the following questions:

What is the subject matter of each poem? What is the theme of each poem? What kind of political stance is the poet taking? Who is the audience? Is the poem didactic? If so, does the didacticism get in the way of the effectiveness of the poem?

.... **Sally Ridgway Proler**

*Four Women**

Hard things come in threes
and feel like messages from gods.
The first one is simple, earthly.
How a beached blue man-of-war, curled in, dying,
was like a woman off a street, curled in a blue blanket.
I lingered over the fish but nearly ran from her.

*Sally Ridgway Proler, "Four Women," reprinted by permission of the author.

I wrote eloquently of it but not of her.
I watched its death from all angles. (Her image was first of three.)
They reminded me of each other; it was the curling, the blue blanket.
I'm ashamed I scrutinized the fish like a god.
Shouldn't it be allowed some privacy in its dying?
Or was it a public thing, earthly?

Creatures without shelter are of the world, earthly.
But next time revenge was hers:
I wanted my own public privacy. No one was dying;
I was communing with a church's St. Francis when the second of
    three
thrust her open palm between me and my god.
I ran away, again, yet it's her face I see as I sleep under my blanket.

She didn't carry a bag or blanket.
What if she isn't one of the needy earthy?
She scared me in my quiet, and I was angry in that place of god.
I keep wondering what I'm supposed to do about her.
She wasn't starving. I'm so cynical about these three.
Is something in me dying?

Maybe something in me's being born, not dying,
a sense of where I fit with women under blankets.
The one with women's magazines, last of three—
literate and discerning while earthy—
couldn't see her head, the *W, Mirabella, Vogue* on the ground beside
    her.
Our commonality exposed, could hear the chuckling of the gods.

Each time closer to some truth from gods?
The magazine reader wasn't dying.
Was it free choice for her,
a Central Park shade tree, a rust-colored blanket?
Still the dumb earthy
questioning. What am I to learn from these three?

Maybe only questions come from such threes under blankets,
not about dying but about my own freedom as I study theirs
in our earthly encounters under gods.

EXERCISES   ....

1. In what form already discussed is this poem written? What are the six ending words? How does the poet vary them slightly?

2. To whom is the poem addressed? (Or to whom is the poet speaking?)

3. Who are the four women mentioned in the title?

4. What is the social or political message here?

.... **Paul Christensen**

African Elegy*

In west Africa, the e-coli bacteria
is nothing to the AIDS gnawing at the center;
in Rwanda the Hutu have learned
to kill more quickly, without the paperwork.
The Tutsi are expert at reprisal,
and in the camps the murderers eat first.
In Angola, the land's outcrop is a freighter port
for oil and contraband, and the heavies
have been killing over it for decades.

Listen. It's the first wind of the rainy season.
It comes over the red powder like a ghost,
darkening noon. The streets go pink
with whirs, and the trees, limp and
punctured by bats, flap like old women.
A man sleeps in the shadow of a death house.

The water in the ditch is for drinking,
and the boys with round, drum-tight bellies
scoop their pots above the gray silt.
The smell of taro meal rises out of thatch
to mix with the bitterness. A pepper burns
unattended in the skillet. Someone pukes
blood into his palms and wipes the strings
from his mouth. He will not be hungry.

*Paul Christensen, "African Elegy," reprinted by permission of the author.

Lie down with me, Africa, and be still.
The only danger is resentment, anger.
The ruins are all a western diary of greed
written in your blood, your wandering spirits.
The mock-nations evaporate like shadows
from the map. This violence, this mayhem
of Lagos and Mogadishu, the Congo
of blood cascading like Victoria Falls
upon the future, is all a consequence
beyond repair. Let it occur without remorse,
and lay fresh straw, prepare for birth.

EXERCISES

1. To what or whom does the poet attribute the problems of Africa?

2. How is this assertation a political statement?

3. Would you say that the poem is for or against the past imperialism of the Western world?

4. What does the poet admonish Africa to do with her pain?

5. How is this a political poem?

Sybil Pittman Estess

The Massacre at the Mosque*

(Tomb of the Patriarchs, Hebron, West Bank, Israel: 2/25/94)

His gun shoots on the day that Kerrigan
Skates. His gun shoots when we have said about peace
"It is finished." His gun shoots by one man, one mind.
His gun shoots by a Jew, an American. . . .
His gun shoots by a finger on a hand
On a body, a masque, which says he adheres
To God. His gun shoots in an ancient place
I have seen where Rachel the mother of each
Race is not interned. She burned in Ramah where

*Sybil Pittman Estess, "Massacre at the Mosque" is reprinted by permission of the author.

Scripture declares she wept for her dead, dead children.
She cried for her kids because they were no more.
They were no more because of war. Oh Why
Have we not beat our swords into hooks for
Pruning? Why had he not pruned his hate? Why
Have we not heard Rachel wail? In this state
Of our end, this endless century, since near
Sixty silent surrounding one mosque in Ramadan,

How shall we
Now, like her, for them sing our sad, sad songs?

EXERCISES

1. What actually happened in the event described in the poem?

2. Which races are in conflict?

3. Does the poet take sides?

4. What is the tone of the poem?

5. What is the political nature of "The Massacre at the Mosque"?

If you are moved by injustice and suffering, you will write about these things, and your challenge will be to write about them without losing the poetry entirely to the lesson you wish to teach. Your images will move the reader to feel as you do; your style will persuade. Here are three political poems by Phyllis Rachel Larrabee. What methods do they use to move and persuade?

Phyllis Rachel Larrabee

*She**

She used to be
a field of anemones

red purple sepals
flung over
yellow hills

*The poem, "She" is reprinted with the author's permission from her chapbook, Old Leaflets for Shopping Lists and Rashly Written Poems, published by Stone Soup Poetry, Boston, MA 02114, copyright 1974, 1975.

Now
She is a potted plant
set in the groves
of polished marble
domesticated so well

she can reproduce
in captivity.

My Answer to the Reagan/Bush/Clinton Budget*

IF MY RAGE
COULD BE LIQUIFIED
AS TEARS
THICKENED INTO PASTA
AND SLICED
AS SPAGHETTI
THERE WOULD BE
ENOUGH
TO FEED
THE EARTH'S
CHILDREN.

The Hundred and First Flower*

When a dictator says
let a hundred flowers bloom

Beware!

He can always announce
anemones are not allowed
(you didn't read the fine print)

and roses will be banned
till their thorns can be
expurgated

*The poem, "The Hundred and First Flower" is reprinted with the author's permission from her chapbook, *Old Leaflets for Shopping Lists and Rashly Written Poems,* published by Stone Soup Poetry, Boston, MA 02114, copyright 1974, 1975. "My Answer to the Reagan/Bush/Clinton Budget" is reprinted with the author's permission.

the freckles of the tiger lily
will be cursed as
blemishes on the social fabric

and so on—

Or simply
a decree will be
issued

saying to all poets:

you are the hundred and first
      flower

and we'll be rounded up
in a bouquet
of the damned . . .

Political poetry tends to be more up-front than other poetry, but good poetry of social justice uses many of the devices of contemporary poetry to move readers. A key distinction seems to be, does the poem find favor only with those who are already committed to the cause, or does it have a wider audience?

Meaning and Ideas in Poetry _____

> The poet is the priest of the invisible.
>
> —Wallace Stevens

A poem may be originally constructed by a seminal feeling, an image, or an idea. But by the time a poem has fully discovered itself, that is, come to the end of its contruction—at least for this time period—a poem's meaning is a compilation of a sum of its parts: image, words, rhythm, form, and the like. Even if the poem is seemingly built around some central idea, all elements of the poem combine together to give the poem's meaning. Earlier we discussed "reading poetry as a poet"; now we are looking at the poem not for its structures or its devices, but for its total impact—how the poem fully experienced lives for the reader.

Even seemingly clear and direct poems have vibrancies of meaning that make them interesting and stay with the reader. We shall begin with the following poem by K. C. Elliot.

.... **K. C. Elliot**

*I still get calls from bill collectors**

They ask if I know where you are,
where you're working. I always tell them
I've not seen you since January 1995,
but they never believe me.

"But lady, he used you for a reference
last year, now I know
You've seen him since then . . ."

I haven't.
"Come on, lady, I know you're hiding something."

I guess I am, it's just nothing important.
I just remember the days when all we needed
Was a cup of coffee and a plate of french fries.
Betting the bill on Star Wars pinball
I still paid anyway.
I guess all I really know is that
When you said we'd keep in touch,
I didn't believe it, but now, I keep tabs on you.

I know you have long distance charges,
A broken lease in Dallas
And a missing cellular phone.
Ford Motor Credit is wondering if I've seen
A black '97 Mustang.
There's a private investigator in Florida
Looking for a girl named Jill that was
Last seen with you. Her parents are worried.

I imagine you driving down I-10
Back to Texas, your hair dancing through the wind
As Jill drinks a Coke and puts her feet up
On the dash and calls Mom and Dad
to tell them she's all right.

*K. C. Elliott, "I still get calls from bill collectors," reprinted by permission of the author.

It is hard to write a "relationship-gone-wrong" poem that isn't corny, but this one by Elliot is a winner. It contains a bit more than its interesting surface—for instance, the speaker's ambivalent attitude about the former friend comes through in the final imagined scene. There is some wordplay with the phrase "keep tabs" and the notion of various kinds of unpaid debts. But this is an example of a poem that's easy to get into and yet not "facile" or too easy to satisfy. The meaning of the poem also involves the hearer of the poem. In her book *To Be a True Poem*, the poet and literary critic Elizabeth Sewell writes the following:

> [P]oems always [also] have to be constructed . . . by reader or hearer, . . . warmed into activity if they are not to be just blobs. By that act we . . . the non-poets . . . construct and reconstruct our own minds, lives, acts. This activity is not a literary technique or a whimsy. It is a way of learning, a great system of education, almost wholly forgotten or ignored now, to our dire peril. One could call it imagination.

So the imaginative response of the reader also helps to create the meaning of the poem or, in current literary critical parlance, to "deconstruct" the poem, or whatever literary piece the reader encounters.

In the introduction to his book *How Does a Poem Mean*, the noted critic John Ciardi writes some of his beliefs about where the real meanings of poems lie:

> Analysis is never in any sense a substitute for the poem. The best any analysis can do is to prepare the reader to enter the poem more perceptively. By isolating for special consideration some of the many simultaneous elements of the poem, analysis makes them more visible in one sense, and less interesting in another. It is up to the reader, once the analysis is completed, to re-read the poem in a way that will restore the simultaneity and therefore the liveliness and interest of the poetic structure. The only reason for taking a poem apart is that it may then be put back together again more richly. . . . What one must always comprehend of poetry is that it is an experience the reader must re-live.

Ciardi's discussion of "The Poem in Countermotion" in the final chapter of the same book is worth quoting in full:

> [A]ll the elements of a poem are engaged in a series of countermotions. Meter and rhythm are only two of the elements that may be involved. Diction, imagery, rhyme, line length, vowel quantities, consonant sequences, and grammatical structure are some of the other principal elements. From these elements the poem builds complexes of poetic structures, each related to all the others. The motion of these poetic structures, each against the others, is what ultimately determines the poem's performance. One simple rule seems to apply to the play of all such countermotions: whenever in the course of a poem the poet changes either his tone or his attitude, some change will occur in the handling of the technical elements. That change in the technical handling of the poem may be slight or it may be marked, but some change must occur. Conversely, any change in the handling of the technical elements in the course of the poem will indicate that a change has taken place in the poet's tone or attitude. Attitude . . . is taken to signify "the way the poet takes his subject"; tone, "the way he takes himself."

Use both Sewell's and Ciardi's claims about the reader constituting the meaning of the poem and the writer's constructing the "countermotion" of the poem when you study the following poems. First, analyze all formal elements. Then ascertain what the "countermotion" of the poem is, according to Ciardi's defintion of countermotion that the poet created. Last, talk about the meaning of the poem for you as reader. (In doing the latter, you are "deconstructing" the work.)

But remember that your idea of the meaning of the poem has to be based on all of the poem's formal elements. It is crucial to understand the elements of poetry, which we have discussed in this chapter, in order to attempt to understand poems. Interpretation may be larger than, but must include, the text of the poem itself, with all the multiplicity of its facets.

··· **Robert Phillips**

*Everywhere the Same**

(For Daniel Stern)

Little League in the park afternoons,
the railroad through the bad part of town.
Cities are about the same everywhere.

Love asserts importance Saturday nights.
More important than a mountain or tree.
Little League in the park afternoons.

All Delaware roads wend to Wilmington.
All roads in Germany lead to Ausfahrt.
Cities are about the same everywhere.

You go to the empty river to fish.
You wander down to the bar to brag lies.
Little League in parks afternoons.

All Delaware roads wend to Wilmington.
All roads in Germany lead to Ausfahrt.
Cities are about the same everywhere.

*"Everywhere the Same" by Robert Phillips. Published in *Spinach Days,* Johns Hopkins Univ. Press, 2000. Reprinted by permission.

You go to the empty river to fish.
You wander down to the bar to brag lies.
Little League in parks afternoons.

There's a pool hall where only black men play.
Here's a country club that admits no Jews.
Cities are about the same everywhere—

Unless your friends and family are there:
People with your face remember your name.
Sad rapists in park afternoons.
Cities are about the same everywhere.

Personal*

I'm honest, discreet, and no way a lech.
Staying home with a rented video is just fine.
I'm seeking a friend first, we'll see what happens next.

My definition of fun is not very far-fetched:
Enjoy fishing, four-wheeling, casinos and wine.
I'm honest, discreet, and no way a lech.

Want face-to-face conversation, no phone sex.
Non-smoking, drug-free women—the old-fashioned kind.
I'm seeking a friend first, we'll see what happens next.

I like a lady to let her hair down, get a little wrecked.
I have brown hair, brown eyes, am built along trim lines.
I'm honest, discreet, and no way a lech.

I'm 37, white, have two teenagers by my ex-.
Looking for a lady, any age or race, similarly inclined.
I'm seeking a friend first, we'll see what happens next.

No psychos! (My ex- didn't play with a full deck.)
I live on the northwest side, near the refinery.
I'm honest, discreet, and no way a lech.
I'm seeking a friend first. We'll see what happens next.

*"Personal" by Robert Phillips. Published in *Spinach Days,* Johns Hopkins Univ. Press, 2000.
Reprinted by permission.

E X E R C I S E S ....

In what traditional form are the preceding two poems written? Does it shock you as a reader that the poet has used this form for the subject matter of these poems? Why or why not? Analyze the image, rhythm, and other elements. Now, as reader, interpret the meaning that the poem has for you.

The following poem is written in the same form. How are the subject matter and the meaning of the poem different from each other?

.... **Sally Ridgway Proler**

*Seeking Prickly Magic**

(After Jean Shinoda Bolen)

We're spiritual beings on a human path
to mid-life journeys spiralling in
where divinity quickens the self at last.

First incarnation was Gaia, Earth.
In her grandeur we're humbled, connect with divine;
we're spiritual beings on an earthly path.

Seeking the numinous in life's second half
we look to what heals, makes whole, we turn in
where divinity quickens the self at last.

What was dismembered, in unconscious left,
needs remembering—the childish, the juicy within
where divinity quickens the self at last.

Divine's prickly magic sought in earth's heart
sacred sites shared by guides and companions
We're spiritual beings on a human path

of temenos, self's sanctuary, where we can laugh,
be foolish, open, innocents again.
We're spiritual beings on a human path
where divinity celebrates the self at last.

*Sally Ridgway Proler, "Seeking Prickly Magic," reprinted by permission of the author.

The following poem by the same poet as the preceding is intended as a sestina, with no three-line envoi. How do you like the poem? How do you interpret it? Do you like the fact that the poet departed from the full traditional form? Why did she do so? Did the departure work?

.... **Sally Ridgway Proler**

Exorcizing Angelica*

A shiny aluminum ladder leans against the wall,
poised for painting, beside the bed
in the room where wallpaper now
climbs in teal bouquets across the ceiling,
a march of white peonies in unlikely
resonance of her. I must repaint

the room. Fresh paint
to free our walls
from her arrogant Chilean presence, our unlikely
menage a trois. Our bed's the bed
he bought for her. The ceiling
ripples, pool reflections dapple now

in wavy memories—now
hungry for new paint.
Primrose wraps us, doors and ceiling,
vinelike over trellis walls,
ninety yards of floral fabric for curtains and bed skirt.
I claimed the house, all but this unlikely

room—the rest is taupe and white—then this unlikely
riot of bouquet. Downstairs chocolate carpet's white now,
gone the brown metallic look in the house below the bed.
We must repaint
this confection of a room, the last wall
beween us—I imagined her watching the ceiling,

the pool dappling on the ceiling.
Still, she would find it unlikely,
such bother about walls.

*Sally Ridgway Proler, "Exorcizing Angelica," reprinted by permission of the author.

As if what I do will change things now.
It's a question of home, of place. When I repaint
will I retake my room, my bed?

Well, of course, I'll buy a new bed,
closer to the ceiling.
But what is this drive to repaint,
this unlikely effort to move on?
Mims' old chaise creaks now
from all this foolishness with walls

The poem's meaning may hide itself slightly, its center requiring a nudge to reveal itself. Often in such poems, humor is blended with seriousness, so that the reader needs to tease out the meaning and decide just where the poet stands behind the masks. Part of the pleasure of these poems is in the unraveling. John Donne said of his difficult intellectual style, "Wee are thought wits, when 'tis understood." Here is such a poem, from Rachel Loden's book *Hotel Imperium*:

.... **Rachel Loden**

*Revenge, Like Habanero Peppers**

Revenge, like habanero peppers, clears
the sinuses, presses the errant

sweetness into every flower. I'd swear
the trees were giddier than usual

today, all that leaf-glitter trembling
to give away such money. I graze, oh

I shall graze long and affectionately
on the fiefdom I survey, though I am

no seashell-gatherer, nor do I wander
cluelessly among the darling buds

of May (etc., etc.). On this plane
for the duration: loyal and doddering

like some old stooped family retainer
with a plot-twisting identity, I remain

the rhapsodist of cunning, blithering
songbird of iniquity, and while-u-wait

the law I love moves through here
like a wall of fire, and it is leaving

everything exactly as it stands, and
saving nothing standing in its wake.

The poem wants to reveal itself, but it wants to engage the mind in doing so. The poem wants to play with you, and if you engage in the game, you both win. To enter this poem, you might begin with the title idea: habenero peppers being so hot that the unknowing muncher feels burnt clear through, senses smoke and fire coming out of the ears and nose, believes himself or herself entirely consumed by the fiery pepper. And yet, people eat these peppers deliberately—there is a sense of release from this flame. Now, consider that revenge = the peppers = the wall of fire. But there is a playful tone in the poem too—playful, though, like a cat playing with a mouse. What do all these attributes add up to?

Then a poem may appear to be about something else. Joanne Lowery has written a sequence of strange, moving poems about a folktale, Jack and the Beanstalk. Folktales derive their power from the unconscious—they evoke the shared images and stories in what psychologist Carl Gustav Jung called "the collective unconscious," that stratum of shared experience that reveals itself in dreams. Here is one of the Jack poems, from the middle of the sequence:

·· **Joanne Lowery**

Continuity*

After sixty seconds of much-needed shut-eye
Jack woke to find himself
webbed to the stalk.

*Joanne Lowery, "Continuity" was published in *Northwestern Review,* 2/1999. Reprinted by permission of the author.

Some spider had strangled him
with silky bond anyone could leave
behind. Jack would flex,
stretch and climb from their tatters.
But first he yielded
to the spider's work
let it hold him elastic
as she shifted head down
to watch fireflies make evening
on earth alive—for heaven's sake—
with on-and-off starlight.

Then his toes got itchy
for more to do.
He righted himself
in a linear story.
Spider said: boo hoo.
Stars said: *ad astra per aspera.*
Fireflies said: gold here, green there,
green and gold everywhere.

"Ad astra per aspera" means "to the stars though effort." To get into this poem is to imagine, as the poet has done, what it is like to be Jack, climbing up this infinite pole toward the heavens, foolish but aspiring, listening to what nature tells him. The reader is invited to consider what it means to be Jack, to what extent she or he is Jack.

The following two poems by Paul Christensen are written in what in our discussion we called free verse. Discuss this aspect of the poem—why the lines are broken where they are. Discuss the images and metaphors of the poems. Then discuss the meanings that the poems have for you.

·· **Paul Christensen**

*Doors**

There are doors that are always locked.
One never bothers to try them;
they have sealed themselves to their jambs
and are thicker than the walls, harder

*Paul Christensen, "Doors" and "The Horse" are reprinted by permission of the author.

than the house they guard and diminish.

Many have wept against them, with bloodied
fists left to tremble after knocking.
Behind them have stood the last survivors
of despair, giving up in the mirror
with a razor blade or a bottle of pills,

and the living have stood on the far side
with the cry still emerging from their throats.
Doors have a will and an importance larger
than the trees they are cut from, darker
than the nails or screws that bind them

to the hinge. The locksmith has a knowledge
of their purposes and sets the tumblers
with a cold logic. The door will not live
until the lock goes in, and not rest
until the key is turned in it.

Then, with quiet rigor and attention,
the door seals another passage to the world.
The house suffers and goes dark, a light
ebbs beneath the crack and is the sign
of withering and fright, the mark of doom.

The Horse

An old woman studies the mind
of a horse. Her window looks out
on the gray pasture, the black
horse standing in the morning dazzle.
She is ninety, a brittle,
weightless object in a white room.

She imagines the horse
under her, her legs feeling
the body's response to earth,
a heft sliding easily from joint
to joint as they edge
toward the uncertain road.

To be ninety is to be held
by weak strings
to the heat of the sun.
One moves in a glass firmness,
at the limit of breaking.

The horse is a beginning,
the doorway to a temple
where the Buddha sits
in contemplation among
the white lotus blossoms;
a world of flowing and silence
begins in renunciation,
where the horse emerges.

What are the main ideas in the preceding poems by Rachel Loden, Joanne Lowery, and the two by Christensen? How do you find these ideas?

J. Pittman McGehee

*Ring the Broken Pail**

Retell the story once again not
for those who did not hear, but
for those who never knew.

How the silent hand grasped the
nail and fell across the tree.
How the Eden vine was cut and
tore the tattered veil. How
upon the Holy Grail the wine
was shed by drops. Pause beneath
the wounded wing and ring the
broken pail.

Who will thorn the bird and
scream the song as sung?

*J. Pittman McGehee, "Ring the Broken Pail" and "The Years Are Many Now" are reprinted by permission of the author.

Where's the warming fire this
night to burn denial's tongue?
Grow the rose once more and
pull its petals bare. Climb
upon the singletree and
tell of truth's despair.

Consider in the preceding poem where the line breaks are and why the poet breaks lines as he does. Do you agree with these? Would you change some? Where, and why?

J. Pittman McGehee

The Years Are Many Now

This is the timorous season.
Irreversible continuum of time
star crossed thoughts of Christmas eve driving home alone.

The incense of sky is stippled
silent lights. The streets
are wet ash. Now shadows
dream misty joy and lonely

grief. A crocus to be delivered
as a midnight sachet sits
beside me now lush
and come of age. Eyes

are apertures, every sight
a memory and a dream. The
silhouettes intersect to
circulate the intervals and

oscillate the time as birth
and when alone to know
that every year, and there are
many now, moves us closer

to the shameless sunrise coming
from a sleeping source resting
still in a rough hewn bed waiting
for the sacred fire to light.

In what form is the following poem written? How does the form contribute to the experience of the poem? What are some of the poem's meanings? "Cross" has been examined previously in another context.

.... **Artis Bernard**

Cross*

Not the recognized fate of bluejays, this tidy
grave in a backyard, but what else could
we do, the boy and I? We winced to see
the starling blue wings covered with mud.

The bluejay had died among us and what we do
is bury and then set up a sign,
so the boy and I found sticks, and he held two
against each other like a plumb line

and snapped off little pieces until he thought
he had it right, the arms of man against
man's height. Then we lashed them with a taut
string for chest and marked the grave. In defiance,
the long stick became short, the short long:
bluejay wingspan against bluejay song.

Consider the final four poems. The first poem is a short pantoum. Do you see how the repeated lines work?

*Artis Bernard, "Cross," reprinted by permission of the author.

.... **Janet McCann**

*Gift**
(A Chocolate Rose)

In German "gift" means "poison." Here:
Open your mouth and close your eyes,
And I will give you a big surprise.
But I never liked roses.

Open your mouth and close your eyes.
Pricked, she slept a hundred years.
But I never liked roses.
How bright a red!

Pricked, she slept a hundred years.
You may bite off the bud and swallow it.
How bright a red!
A kiss with bleeding lips.

Pricked, she slept a hundred years.
You may bite off the bud and swallow it.
How bright a red!
A kiss with bleeding lips.

You may bite off the bud and swallow it,
And I will give you a big surprise:
A kiss with bleeding lips.
In German it means "poison." Here:

In the next poem, be sure to ask yourself what role the rhymed lines play and also why the poet does not capitalize the beginnings of sentences. What effect and what purpose does this technique have?

*Janet McCann, "Gift," published in *Windhover* 1999. Reprinted by permission of the author.

Janet McCann

*Looking for the Buddha in the Barbed-Wire Garden**

into the barbed-wire garden I learn to stare
looking for the Buddha, surely he must be there,
the others can see him, the trick is not to care.

the trick is to move the picture slowly away
while concentrating on not looking astray
to fool the eye. hand is subtler you say

than eye. all the others have found him,
sitting in the field, flowers around him.
oh, the cool jade of his sides!—their eyes have bound him.

they are prancing over the fields, I lose the trace.
a page of flat green flakes without a face,
a letter in some strange language. In this place

cynics balk at the margin of belief,
at the missed pleasure of the perceived motif
feeling frustration, maybe even grief.

(I say, the blur in the center, that must be him,
you say, a shoddy construction, anyone can see him.)

Does it change your perception of the poem to know that on the surface, this poem describes the attempt to experience one of those pictures that look like senseless scribbles unless looked at from a certain angle? These pictures were popular a few years ago. The viewer stared at chaotic lines and curves while you brought the drawing closer and closer to your eye, until, just when you thought you were surely going blind, there was a three-dimensional scene.

The final two poems are written in verse that is counting approximately ten syllables per line. Why are the lines broken where they are? How does the rhythm of the first poem differ from the rhythm of the second, even though the line lengths are about the same? Does the poet try to create a kind of breathless rhythm in the first poem? How does that rhythm fit the content of the poem? How is the rhythm and pace of the second poem different? Is it slower? How or why do you feel that it

---

*Janet McCann, "Looking for the Buddha in the Barbed-Wire Garden" published in *Looking for Buddha,* Avisson Press, 1996. Reprinted by permission of the author.

is so? Interpret both of the poems, considering all of the elements of poetry that you can recall. Consider the repetitions in the first poem. In what part of the Bible is the rhythm of the language built upon rhythms in just this same way?

.... **Sybil Pittman Estess**

*Daughter, Can You Hear Me, What I Say?**

> At fifty, when I talk to my twelve-year-old son
> we talk about air guns, basketball, rock music,
> once in a while grades, if I'm lucky. Girls. . . .
>
> When I speak with my husband, it's books, meetings,
> what's for dinner, how tired he is. Tomorrow.
> Christmas vacation. What all our son means to say.
>
> When my husband talks to his mother, he hardly
> talks about anything except relatives, who's sick
> or who died. Sometimes recipes. Not my politics,
>
> not things of my soul. And when he talks to his
> Dad, it's always football or baseball—who passed
> and made it or missed. What the score might have
>
> been. What comes on soon and they wonder what time
> and when. Daytimes, I never talk to my father, who
> silenced it all thirty years ago, dying too soon. . . .
>
> And when I call my mother, it's about triglycerides,
> church, sometimes scripture or prayer. Or her
> neighbors, the flowers, freezes, cold air. Yesterday
>
> she had been to her doctor and driven back by herself
> forty miles. What we talked about was something
> urgent, something she desperately wanted to tell
>
> me, something she had not anyone else, not even her
> husband to tell. It was the sunset, she said, and
> the white cloud she had seen—how huge it was, and

*Sybil Pittman Estess, "Daughter, Can Your Hear Me, What I Say?" Reprinted by permission of the author. Published in *The Adobe Anthology,* 1994.

how strange. How she watched it for thirty-some
miles. Saw all the shapes it took, all the pink glow
it became. How she had never seen anything like it

until now. How she had thought of little else since.
How she had dreamed of it, how she thanked God.
How she had wanted me to see, exactly, that scene.

*Blowing Sand May Exist**

My husband who was driving thought it had
been written by a frustrated philosopher.
He came straight home and wrote an essay—
forty pages—on all its possible meanings. . . .

I had been meditating as we whizzed by.
I didn't even see it. "It may
exist," he reasoned, "it also may not."
All I knew was that grit got in my eye.

We were out on the desert, like life.
We were out where you need reminders
and signs. And after reading them you think
of heeding. . . . Warned, you wait for the wind.

"The poem is the priest of the invisible," as Wallace Stevens said. Speak it.

Perhaps a fitting conclusion to this chapter on writing poems is the poem "Advice to a Young Poet" by Kelly Cherry. As we can see, Cherry's poem alludes to the ultimate mystery, complexity, and "tenderness" as it were, necessary to write poetry.

---

*Sybil Pittman Estess, "Blowing Sand May Exist." Reprinted by permission of the author. Published in *The Paris Review,* 1998.

Kelly Cherry

*Advice to a Young Poet**

To catch a poem
   to seize it
like something falling

   or flying,
   word-wings—

   and it slips
through your fingers,
   a piece of light
   or shadow—

   alertness,
   you need, and
   patience.

   The poem,
   when trapped,
   must be treated tenderly.

It may be observed and tagged.
   Then release it
   into freedom,
   let it live

   on its own terms.

*Kelly Cherry, "Advice to a Young Poet" reprinted by permission of the author.

Revising

Short Stories and Essays

> **W**riting isn't hard. It isn't any harder than ditch-digging.
>
> —Patrick Dennis

You finish your story or essay, and the last line slides in as smooth as silk. You heave a happy sigh. You've finished. You're thinking now about what journal might publish a story like yours.

But you haven't finished, of course. What comes next is revision. Revision is the hard part—and if you don't revise, you will not have a good product. Revision is sweat, irritation, and boredom. But if it is done conscientiously, you may end up with a real thrill upon reading your final draft and may find yourself asking, in bemused contentment, Did I really write that?

Workshopping is one way of beginning to revise, and it has both benefits and limitations. Among its benefits are that it gives you another perspective and it tells you what someone else, a reader, is getting out of what you wrote. You may be surprised at how your work may be read. Drawbacks include the fact that you are getting someone else's biases, too, and your assigned reader will not be your ideal reader. It is good to have more than one person workshop your writing. It is also good to respond open-mindedly to workshop critiques, learning as you go along which to trust and which to disregard. At the end of this section are some workshop forms that may help facilitate workshop discussion.

The alternatives to workshopping include having an "expert reader," often your instructor, critique your first draft, and simply setting aside the finished work and coming back with a more critical vision later. Your instructor's comments are likely to be the most helpful of any, of course, because your instructor has training in the field and knowledge of you and your work.

The areas considered here for revising may also be considered as workshop topics or as focal points for your analysis of your own work.

For a story or an essay, read the piece from beginning to end. Then ask, what was the writer's goal in creating this piece, and how did the writer attempt to achieve it? The short story may have begun with an actual event, but it was shaped to convey some meaning—a theme. What is this theme, and how does the story express it? It is good to ask this question of your own story, because often in the beginning, you aren't quite sure of the answer, but the answer becomes clearer as you write.

These suggestions are mainly given with fiction in mind, but most of them are equally applicable to creative nonfiction essays. In creative nonfiction, you generally also have a main character, a setting, a sequence of events, and a chosen point of view. You may also have dialogue and other elements of fiction. Since you are representing a literal truth, you have less freedom in revision than the fiction writer has, but you will be making many of the same kinds of changes. You may find yourself in odd conflicts with creative nonfiction—for instance, someone may use a word that no one would expect to be in this person's vocabulary. If it is fiction, the solution is simple—substitute a word that the character would be more likely to use. If it is creative nonfiction, you might not feel right doing this, even though you don't know how this character would have acquired the word. In such cases, you may want to remember that it is not necessary to be absolutely true in every detail and also that the goal is to make the essay persuasive.

Now look at the beginning: is it appropriate to the story's goal, characters, plot, and so on? Beginnings are important; only endings are more important. Is this beginning a real and an honest hook? A common flaw in first stories is starting too soon—piling up irrelevant details before introducing character and action. Usually the beginning needs to be spare, direct, and intriguing. The title and the first sentence have a lot to do with whether the reader will continue. Stephen Crane's famous story "The Open Boat" begins, "None of them knew the color of the sky." The reader is caught, wonders why not, in an open boat? And so reads on. If Crane had begun with a heavily detailed passage about preparation for the journey, the same result would not have been achieved. At the beginning, there is nothing for detail to be relevant to. The importance of opening details might be established later—but not if the reader has stopped reading.

Ask whether the story after the first paragraph continues to run smoothly. Usually it doesn't. That is, the first draft generally has awkward passages. There are all kinds of ways things can go amiss. The pacing can be off—transitions not neatly handled, so that the reader gets jerked rather than led from one scene to another. In a short story, there can't be many scenes. Often there is one main scene and then a shorter one that shows what happened, although there are many other arrangements. Previous information may be given through memories—flashbacks. Sometimes the flashback isn't well integrated into the scene. And sometimes the scenes are too short, giving the impression that things are happening too quickly. If you read over the work thoughtfully, you can see whether the pacing is good enough to maintain the sense of time passing. If there are problems, fix them with transitions.

Many problems are caused by the need to get across information to the reader in a way that seems natural; you were aware of these difficulties when you wrote the story. Sometimes the need to inform can ruin dialogue. If you have a character saying, "Hey, Bill! I haven't seen you since you got caught cheating in high school chemistry and unfairly involved me in the scandal, getting us both thrown out," the chances are you need to do some revising. Much of revision has to do with arranging for information to be telegraphed rather than announced. See whether you can find "dead lines," usually lines of dialogue or narrative that are important to let the reader know something but that sound "lugged in"—artificially placed there to give the reader information, rather than growing naturally from the developing story. This kind of revision has a lot to do with the old "show, don't tell" advice given for poetry and prose. Work to make things indirect.

Look at your characters: is your main character consistent? The chances of a major character change taking place believably in the length of a short story are slim. Behavior may change, in response to strong provocation, but the person is likely to be pretty much the same. Is everything that the main character does and says in character? Does this character produce the effect you want him or her to? That is, if you intend the character to be sympathetic, does the reader like him or her? Occasionally the writer intends to create a sympathetic character, but the reader finds this person self-indulgent and whiny. Workshopping helps here.

Essays as well as short stories have the element of pacing—of having the sequence of events that are described seem to happen in a natural time frame. You may have seen movies that are so filled with events that your sense of the passage of time does not accept the rapid changes. This effect happens even more frequently in stories and narrative essays. Another effect is that an event is described in such detail it seems to happen in slow motion. Check to make sure the passage of time seems natural and that the scenes are neatly sewn together with smooth, unobtrusive transitions.

Is the detail all relevant? It is easy to get carried away with description. It is common for writers to take down every detail they can think of from an intriguing scene, thinking that the material can be used later. And indeed it can. But since the detail in a short story needs to develop character and advance the plot, the passage usually cannot be taken whole from a journal and plunked into the story. It has to be trimmed to fit.

Endings have to be earned—is yours? Sometimes we start stories with some kind of slam-dunk conclusion in mind, a final speech, perhaps, by a defeated or victorious main character, or with a symbolic gesture that sums up the theme neatly. We tend to remember these from favorite stories—that final image of the discarded flowers of Steinbeck's "Chrysanthemums," for instance, suggests that the woman herself has been discarded. But when your story is finished, the set piece you had in mind for the ending may not quite work any more. Then you have to rewrite for a more natural ending. Someone said of writing, "We have to murder our darlings." For the sake of the story as a whole, we may have to strike passages that in themselves are exemplary, and then to create a conclusion that is more persuasive though less rhetorically effective.

Then, you need to check your dialogue. Read it aloud. Dialogue is hard to do realistically in any case; often a realistic-sounding dialogue parts company with the story. But ordinarily the dialogue is not just there for local color. Every line of it needs to characterize and/or advance the action. See whether it does. Make sure you haven't gone so far in the direction of "realistic" dialogue that you have included every haw and hum, every clearing of the throat, and thus made the interchange boring. If you think that the dialogue drags, strike out those parts of it that are least relevant. Read it aloud again; it should sound no less realistic, but more concentrated.

Tone needs checking too. Does the story sound as though the same person wrote all of it? Is the level of diction, the word choice, consistent? Has the point of view been maintained? If you started with limited omniscient, for instance, did you stay with this perspective all the way? Is the symbolism subtle and consistent? We analyze stories for symbolism: the stopped clock that may stand for death, the thrown-away flowers that may stand for a discarded or violated woman. What about the symbols in your stories—are they persuasive?

The mechanics of composition must be observed. Yes, you may want sentence fragments for emphasis. But every violation of the grammar rules must be purposeful, and the writer should be ready to justify it. Not only should you use your spell check program, but also you should read your work over carefully one last time for errors that the program cannot catch.

When you are critiquing your own piece, it is useful to print a copy of the draft that not only is double-spaced but also has a wide—perhaps three-inch—left margin. Then, you can add comments or even short passages right on the page. It isn't ideal to critique on the screen, because the experience of screen reading is not the same as of book or even manuscript reading. You need to be able to leaf back and forth at leisure.

When you workshop, if the critique is to be of use to the writer, you must make contact with that person—you have to make it clear what you are looking for, what your criteria are, so that the writer will be less likely to take offense or dismiss the critique. It helps to look at each work as something that is in progress—that is, it is best not to rave enthusiastically or to reject the work totally. If you like it, by all means say so, but don't let the writer feel that the piece is untouchable. If you find the work bad, you will need to communicate the problems you see in it—but you will need to make your critique palatable.

1. Give the writer a general sense of what you believe she or he is doing in this story. If some unintended impression is coming across, the writer needs to be made aware of this problem.

2. Make some general comments about the overall presentation. These may be along the lines of, "Good use of detail to show what Padre Island is like over spring break!" or "The character Katy does not seem consistent—she is stingy

in the first scene, but generous in the second, for no particular reason." You may ask questions: "What does Bill look like? I don't get a sense of his appearance, but his appearance seems to be important in the story." Sometimes a question is the friendliest way to frame a critique that indicates problems.

3. Go through the work, and write comments in the margins. Focus on points that seem inconsistent or on actions or words that don't seem motivated.

4. Look at beginning and ending, since these are of major importance. Does the story get on its way quickly enough? Is the ending satisfactory on all levels?

5. Now, get small. Look for little things that could be improved. Are there too many adjectives and adverbs? Say so. The writer then may attempt to get more of the story into verbs and nouns. Are there vague words used when a more specific word would advance the story? Does the dialogue always sound natural? Is there any detail that doesn't seem natural?

6. You may conclude your critique with some directions for the writer to think about. Maybe you feel that the setting doesn't have enough detail, and you know where the writer could find some good authentic material to make it more convincing. Say so.

7. If you can, make sure that your review of the work has some positive feedback as well as the constructive criticism.

The following two workshop sheets may be used in or out of class. The longer, more detailed one serves to remind you of some of the things that you are looking for and therefore might be used first. However, only the first one is really applicable to creative nonfiction as easily as to fiction. To see how these sheets might be used, you could begin by looking at a professionally written short story in terms of these questions.

PROSE WORKSHOP WORKSHEET 1—SHORT VERSION

1. What do you consider to be the theme—or themes—of this story or essay?

2. How well do the elements of the story, plot, dialogue, tone, character, and setting fit together? Is there a deficit in any of these elements? If so, discuss it.

3. Is the main character developed and believable? What about the minor characters? Does the main character do anything that you see as out of character?

4. Is this essay or story traditional or experimental? If experimental, does the structure suggest that the writer knows the elements of the traditional story or essay but has chosen to write otherwise? What is the purpose of the experimental elements? Do they work for you? Why, or why not? If the story is traditional, how are the traditions followed?

5. What specific advice would you have for this writer? You may write comments on the work itself.

PROSE WORKSHOP WORKSHEET 2— EXTENDED VERSION

I. *Character:* This is perhaps the most important aspect of the story.
   A. Was the character dynamic (did she/he experience change) or static (did she/he remain the same from beginning to end)? How did this treatment affect the overall impact of the story?
   B. Was the character's behavior believable? Was it believable in specific instances (with regard to what the reader knows about him or her?) Is this behavior consistent with (i.e., does the character respond appropriately to) both the internal and the external motivators in the story?
   C. Can the reader identify with the main character? Was the audience supposed to identify with the main character? How is this accomplished (or not accomplished)?

II. *Plot:* Is the story mostly centered on plot or on character? How is or isn't this treatment successful?
   A. Are any of the events in the story random or illogical? (In the case of experimental fiction, the events may seem illogical, but the writer must have provided the reader with some reason to accept them. The easiest way to judge this matter is, after reading the story, to ask yourself whether or not you thought, at any point while reading the story, "This just isn't possible.") Do the events fit together to form a believable whole?
   B. The events of the story should have some impact upon the main character—do they? Are there any extraneous events? Can their existence within the story be justified?

III. *Perspective:* The point of view should be considered.
   A. Is the story told in the first person or the third person? If the third person, is the point of view limited omniscient, omniscient, or objective?
   B. Does this perspective work in terms of the story's impact upon the reader? Could a different perspective achieve a greater impact? A common effective revision involves changing the point of view to achieve greater consistency.

IV. *Language:* This is the main element of what is referred to as "style."
   A. Was the language of the story consistent? Why, or why not? Can any lack of consistency be justified within the context/events of the story?
      1. Is the language appropriate for the intended audience?
      2. Is the language flat? vivid? boring? fluid? clear? How can it be improved?
   B. Are there problems with word usage or sentence structure? Your positive answer to this question must be supported by examples.

V. *Miscellaneous:* These are other questions to consider.
   A. Is the setting too vague? Does the setting "take over" and obscure the events of the story? Does the setting suit the story?
   B. Does the dialogue seem realistic (with regard to the way dialogue is composed in fiction) or stilted? How?

C. Do there seem to be any other problems with this story? Be sure to give a very thorough and detailed explanation of any problems that seem to present themselves.

After you, your instructor, and/or the other students have critiqued your work, you need to read or review everything that has been said about the piece and then to begin the laborious work of rewriting. Cross out passages, write additions in the margins or on separate sheets, cut and paste if you can, and then reread. You will develop your own little quirks of revision; some writers will boldface or highlight all the sections that they wish to query or change. After you have rewritten the work, ask the most useful of your readers to have another look, then tinker some more. This is the third draft, now—surely it must be finished? Maybe, maybe not.

Poetry

Some poems take one careful draft to achieve final form, whereas some take twenty drafts. Poems, like prose pieces, need careful rereading before decisions are made about what to change and what to leave. The poet is even more prone than the fiction writer to feel electrified by the poem that he or she has just written and to think of it as a finished work. This outcome is quite likely because one does not usually write a fiction piece in a single sitting, so that the fiction writer has been over the material numerous times already, whereas the poet was simply struck by something—and sat down and wrote about it—and now here it is, that wonderful thing, a poem.

But even a good poem can be improved. It is worthwhile to let a poem ripen a few days after writing it—then reread it, with an eye toward getting the deadwood out, sharpening the language, and making sure that the poem is accessible to the reader at the level of understanding you want. Not all poems need to be completely understood; certainly not all poems can be paraphrased. But the reader needs to think that she or he has got something out of the poem.

Elements to examine, once you pull the poem from its hiding place and scrutinize it, include freshness of language, precision, conciseness, coherence, accessibility level, and elements of sound.

Freshness of language is a major concern, and expertise in spotting clichés comes with reading a lot of poetry. This area is a good one for workshopping, because different class members tend to be attuned to different clichés. There are the most obvious ones, golden-memories red-as-a-beet heart-of-gold clichés that people who like to read know, but then there are many less well-known, worn phrases that may slip by. Moreover, because writers tend to become defensive if others point out clichés, workshop members may be reluctant to point them out. However, clichés damage literary poetry, and since all of us use them now and then, the best thing to do is to raise our awareness of them and be ready to substitute fresher language when we—or our readers—find them.

Precision and conciseness are important elements of poetry, too. A literary poem is a compressed message, with part of the meaning under the surface. Minimalists want to put as much of the meaning under the surface as possible: "Less is more." You may not want to write heavily elliptical poetry, but you don't want to include deadwood or overexplanation, either. Ask whether each line, each word is necessary. If not, cut.

Coherence and accessibility level are important factors that need fine-tuning as well. You want your readers to understand your poem—perhaps not completely, not in a "logical" sense so that they can fully paraphrase the poem, but at least on an emotional level. So you want to make sure that there are enough hints so that your reader can get into the poem. Moreover, you want your poem to do one thing—to cohere—even if it does its one thing in a highly complex manner. To help achieve your accessibility level, ask what your most trusted readers think that you are doing in the poem. If their answers are far from your intention, see what can be done to telegraph your theme more effectively.

Finally, read your poem aloud to catch all the sound effects and to see whether the rhymes, sound echoes, alliteration, assonance, onomatopoeia—all the poetic sound devices that you use—have their desired effect.

Poet John Krajicek went through a number of revisions of a short poem: Following is the last revision of that poem. See whether you can tell what his principles of revision were.

··· **John Krajicek**

Kemp's Ridley (Revised)***

> They leave footprints in moonlight;
> heavy bodies driving slowly,
> kicking sand, dripping saltwater
> from gnarled domes, assaulting the shore
> in a procession made sacred
> by time. Their mothers walked
> this beach, this beach, and their grandmother's
> ancestors, wearily digging
> the holes, letting fall the eggs
> of sons and daughters, pearls of bone
> in the wet earth.

*Kemp's Ridley is a species of sea turtle found off the Atlantic coast of the United States.

**John Karjicek, "Kemp's Ridley" Revised and Earlier Draft are reprinted by permission of the author.

The little planets open and slow
green children emerge from sand
to fly in frenzy to salvation
in the sea.

Kemp's Ridley (Earlier Draft)

They leave footprints in the moonlight;
heavy bodies driving slowly,
kicking sand, dripping saltwater
from gnarled domes, assaulting the shore
in a procession made sacred
by time. Their mothers walked this beach,
and their grandmother's mother's ancestors,
wearily digging
the holes, letting fall the eggs
of sons and daughters, pearls of bone
white creation in the wet earth.

By the time the eggs open and
slow green children emerge from the sand,
the footprints long will be washed
into the constant mother sea.

Note that the final version is shorter, more polished, a little less direct. It implies a greater proportion of its meaning than in the earlier version. The author has decided that most of his readers won't know what Kemp's Ridley is, and although the poem is clearly about a sea turtle, the name is not meaningful without some explanation—so he provides a note. (T. S. Eliot provided multiple notes for "The Waste Land"—it would be enjoyed by fewer people without his notes.) How does the change from "the eggs" to "the little planets" widen the possibilities of the poem? The poem is superficially about the life of the sea turtle that it describes, but what else is it about?

Following are three workshop forms for poetry, including one that is especially for performance poetry. Remember that although you may want to be positive, you don't want your review to be a mere compliment.

POETRY WORKSHOP WORKSHEET 1—SHORT VERSION

1. What does this poem attempt? By what means does it attempt to convey this thought or theme?

2. If this poem is intended for the sophisticated reader of literature, in what ways does this poem work?

3. In what ways does this poem fail to work?

POETRY WORKSHOP WORKSHEET 2—EXTENDED VERSION

1. Read the poem through, and consider your initial reaction to it.
   a. Now read the poem again carefully. Does your initial reaction change in any way?
   b. What is the poem attempting to do? Lecture you? Make you feel some emotion? Share an experience? Cause you to reflect on a circumstance? Something else?
   c. How accessible is the poem? If it is very accessible, do you find that anything is left to the imagination? If it is not very accessible, do you feel an emotional response to the poem despite not knowing exactly what the poem means?
   d. What kind of surface does the poem have? How are its images related? Are the images original—do they provide a new perspective?
   e. What about the sound of the poem? Is it linked to its sense?
   f. Do the last lines provide a sense of closure? Are they satisfying? Has the writer avoided the temptation of an unwarranted slam-dunk conclusion?

2. Now, in your response, write the following.
   a. What you think the poet is attempting—what you believe the poem is about.
   b. What you think the best features of the poem are. (Sound? A particular image? An unexpected association?)
   c. Where you think the poem could be improved. (Weak lines or clichés? Overall considerations?)
   d. Anything else you think might be useful to the poet; and comments on the poem itself.

POETRY WORKSHOP WORKSHEET 3—PERFORMANCE POETRY

1. Take turns reading the poems aloud. Ask someone in the group to read your poem aloud, so that your poem is read both by you and by another person.
   a. What is there about the poem that makes it a performance poem?
   b. Are you happy with how it sounds when you listen to someone else read it?

2. Listen to a poem that another person in the group has written.
   a. What is the writer attempting? What is the poem's theme?

b. What does the poem do with images? How has the writer mingled images with elements of sound? How much of the poem's effect is there "on the page" when you look at it, and how much must be communicated in the reading?

c. Performance poetry should be workshopped orally as well as in writing. Discuss the poem. Then write down any suggestions that cannot easily be remembered, and give the notes to the poet.

Experimental Writing

6

Understanding Experimental Writing _____

Experimental writing undermines the traditions and definitions of writing, and it does so on all levels from tweaking them to blowing them up. The most experimental pieces may appear to the uninitiated reader as word salad. Other kinds of experimentation are clearer about what they are sending up, and

> "I don't know what you mean by 'glory,'" Alice said.
>
> Humpty Dumpty smiled contemptuously. "Of course you don't—till I tell you. I meant 'there's a nice knock-down argument for you!'"
>
> "But 'glory' doesn't mean 'a nice knock-down argument,'" Alice objected.
>
> "When I use a word," Humpty Dumpty said, in rather a scornful tone, "it means just what I choose it to mean—neither more nor less."
>
> —Lewis Carroll, *Alice in Wonderland*

how. Although we could discuss experimental poetry and prose separately, they often overlap—as violating the conventions of the genre is a major component of literary experiment. Thus, experimental poetry may have prose characteristics, and vice versa.

There has always been an avant-garde, even when it was not called that. Emily Dickinson's slant rhymes found little favor with the editors of her day, who believed that rhymes should be exact. In his free verse and his choice of "unpoetic" subject matter, Walt Whitman too was an innovator. At the beginning of the century, Ezra Pound urgently sought to "resuscitate the dead art of poetry," as he said in *Hugh Selwyn Mauberly*, and he led poetry through a series of new directions, discarding manifestos as soon as he thought so many had joined his bandwagon that it was no longer an elite conveyance. In a time when few areas have been left unexplored, experimental writing takes many forms. Knowing that there is always new ground (and there are always new rules) to be broken makes the imaginative writer want to make the attempt.

It may be best not to begin by writing experimental poetry and prose, because you need to be acquainted with the basics first. Some of the work that was written in the second half of the twentieth century deliberately violates our expectations and makes fun of tradition. You need to have a clear sense of what is expected and what is traditional before you start deconstructing.

That being said, it might be useful to look at what experimental writing generally is and does. Contemporary experimental literature is often called postmodern. Postmodernism is identified with certain kinds of innovative writing from World War II on, whereas the modernist period is thought of as the period between the two world wars. Both modernist and postmodernist writers use experimental techniques, but the modernist tended to use them to approach a unity beneath the surface that the global disaster they then called the Great War had fragmented, whereas the postmodernist writer tends to deny the very notion of unity, coherence, even meaning. But you as a writer may want to use experimental techniques for any number of reasons. Moreover, there's no clear-cut line between experimental poetry and other forms of contemporary poetry—we all want to experiment in some way. Poets don't want to rewrite the same poems that they have been writing and that everyone else has been writing. But the cutting edge of experimentalism has always been extreme, difficult, challenging. It is up to poets, and then to readers, to decide how far in that direction they should go.

Experimental writing tends to blur boundaries, cross them, or deny their existence. This tendency goes for all boundaries—between prose and poetry, self and other, male and female—the experimenter wants to see how far she or he can go and so pushes past barriers set by convention or tradition. Free verse at one point was experimental, and now it is standard. The new avant-garde poetry violates the conventions of free verse.

Experimental writing is likely to include bits and pieces of other things. The modernist writers did this; chunks of Dante and Baudelaire find their way into T. S. Eliot's "The Waste Land," as well as of the Bible and other works of literature. The postmodernists often appropriate without identification from both common and obscure sources. Sometimes their appropriations assume a specific area of knowledge on the reader's part, thereby giving you as reader the choice of "researching" the poem or abandoning it.

There is often an element of play in experimental writing. Words sound like other words, suggesting strange likenesses: James Joyce's phrase "whirled without aimed," for instance, contradicts or deconstructs the notion of "world without end" of the original phrase.

Many people are familiar with William Carlos Williams's poem "The Red Wheelbarrow," which appears earlier in the text and has been explained almost out of existence. This modernist poem, of course, was itself innovative. It pulls at the imagination without declaring itself. It blends suggestions of Eastern and of Western writing: being haiku-like and suggesting intuitive knowledge, it is also a sort of argument. Here it is again:

William Carlos Williams

The Red Wheelbarrow

so much depends
upon

a red wheel-
barrow

glazed with rain-
water

beside the white
chickens.

See what a graduate student poet did with that poem:

K. C. Elliot

*The Dead Teal Sparrow**

no such amends
dead swan

a lead bone
marrow

hazed with pain
slaughter

decide the right
pigeons

Elliot's version plays with the sounds of the words and substitutes a blank deadness for the vitality of the original. Instead of a suggestion of rural peace composing its own art, there may be a suggestion of urban violence, but she is

*K. C. Elliott, "The Dead Teal Sparrow" is reprinted by permission of the author.

mainly playing a postmodern game with words, deconstructing the poem, taking it away from its writer, making it mean something else. (For an exercise in pure postmodernism, take a short well-known poem and substitute words that sound sort of like the originals. Do not worry about meaning. See what happens.)

PARODY AND PASTICHE

Parody and *pastiche* are popular. A parody takes a well-known work, maintains its form, and substitutes a different content. Often a trivial or a silly subject is substituted for the original lofty one. Good parodies may last longer than the originals; Lewis Carroll's "You Are Old, Father William" has far outlasted the trite wisdom poem that it parodied. Pastiches are works made up of pieces of other works; the word comes from an Italian word for "main-dish pie"—a savory mixture of odd ingredients. A pastiche assignment might be to take an old copy of some journal and a pair of scissors, and then to cut out words and phrases—images too—and stick them on a page to represent the world and values of that journal. Collages are pastiches.

There is often an arbitrary element. That is, something outside the poem may determine its form. A poem may be in the form of a triptych, or the days of the week may be woven through the poem without respect to any meaning, or part of the poem may be in pig Latin. The words may be oddly broken up into syllables according to some principle that has nothing to do with the poem's apparent meaning. Words may be played with as though they were things like blocks rather than "signifiers."

In experimental fiction, character development, often the center of traditional fiction, is very different. Sometimes the tone is deliberately flat, and unsympathetic, undifferentiated characters may be presented to convey a theme rather than to create sympathy for or even antipathy toward a character.

Natural laws may be suspended; the story may present metaphor as reality. To see how these processes might work, read some stories by Isabel Allende or Franz Kafka. Kafka's weird, sad story "Metamorphosis," which describes a man's awakening one morning as a giant cockroachlike insect, has a lot to say about how people react to and treat one another.

In writing prose, the author may step into the story as a character or may call attention to the narrative conventions by violating them. The point of view may shift. You have always been told that it is important to establish a point of view and to stick with it; therefore, the postmodernist may be now omniscient, now first person. However, the postmodern writer makes all changes purposefully, with an awareness of the traditions, in order to undo the traditions or make fun of them. (Playing with the narrative conventions is not new. Cervantes did it in *Don Quixote*, for instance, when he had the characters Don Quixote and his sidekick Sancho Panza critiquing their story. Chaucer does it in *The Canterbury Tales,* when he presents himself as a character who is much more naive than the real Chaucer who created the character.)

Sometimes behind the wordplay and parody there is as a goal the notion of undoing the received definitions of poetry and fiction, as well as the standards of what poets and writers have held to be good and bad work.

Any kind of serious discussion of postmodernism, though, is beyond our scope; however, for those who would like to go further into this area, there are many fine websites to visit. Go to google.com and type in "postmodern literature," and see what you can find. Alan Filreis's Home Page at the University of Pennsylvania contains some key readings on postmodernism. You might begin with Albert Gelpi's essay on where these current directions come from, and then might follow the links into specialized areas of postmodernist theory and practice.

Experimental writing, a broader concept than postmodernism, will be considered here so as to offer the new writer a few alternatives to traditional writing. The story "Some of Us Had Been Threatening Our Friend Colby" is experimental in a mild way; read it again to see how it violates narrative convention. How do you expect the story to turn out? Are you fully involved with any of the characters? If not, wherein lies the interest of the story?

Italo Calvino's widely read novel *If on a Winter's Night a Traveler* is even more experimental. A passage at the beginning shows the blurring of "literature" and "life": "The novel begins in a railway station, a locomotive huffs, steam from a piston covers the opening of the chapter, a cloud of smoke hides part of the first paragraph . . . The pages of the book are clouded like the windows of an old train, the cloud of smoke rests on the sentences."

Calvino calls attention to the conventions of the novel by exploding them. The fictional sequence of events blurs into the narrative about writing the story. "The lights of the station and the sentences you are reading seem to have the job of dissolving more than of indicating the things that surface from a veil of darkness and fog." Even the convention of the narrator is described self-reflexively and thus erased: "I am the man who comes and goes between the bar and the telephone booth. Or, rather: that man is called 'I' and you know nothing else about him."

As the narrative progresses, it details and undermines all the beliefs that we hold about the novel, as well as the received definitions of reader, author, plot, and character.

FOUND POEMS

In poetry, experimentalism follows the same general directions as in prose. The poetry may question the definition of poetry in a number of ways. Consider the *found poem*, for instance. A found poem is simply a piece of writing that wasn't originally a poem, recast as a poem by the "finder." It can be an apartment lease, a news story, a list of exemptions on your insurance policy—anything.

Here is an entertaining found poem that was created by an undergraduate poet.

Found Poem: My Ex Just Called*

Text adapted from *Cosmopolitan*, January 1998, p. 46

Q: My ex just called . . .
he "found RELIGION" and
must confess SINS—
includes writing my Mother,
devout CATHOLIC,
a letter detailing our
SEXUAL experiences and
asking her FORGIVENESS.
What am I to do?

A: He found RELIGION &
lost JUDGEMENT. tell mother—
in all HONESTY—
your ex gone NUTS (why
you don't see him anymore)
tell her NOTHING he
says can be TRUTH.
generally, I advise against lying.
but in this case . . .
it will PROTECT mother.
she'd probably prefer NOT to KNOW.

One tends to think at first that this isn't poetry—why do this? But then, why isn't it poetry? The placement of the words in the appearance of a poem makes it, on one level, a poem. What the recasting does is make us read the original as if it were a poem—as if we were supposed to ponder its significance, appreciate its metaphors. Doing this can result in serious or lighthearted ironic treatment. There is plenty of paradox and irony in the advice column of Gina Pierce's poem, but the complexities and layers of the social issues discussed are emphasized by putting the original text into the form of a poem.

The source for a found poem need not be printed. Writer Shannon Nolte stated that she found a poem by "writing down a bit of phone conversation, word for word." The result is this:

*Gina Pierce, "My Ex Just Called" is reprinted by permission of the author.

*Always Wear a Hat**

The owl will attack.
When I was young
An owl hooted and came closer
When I hooted back!

The owl will attack.
At night, when out walking,
Always wear a hat.
Better than a bloody gash
On your head, wear a hat;
Let him take that!

He doesn't care, you know.
An owl will just attack!

Observe how Nolte uses her line breaks to emphasize the "a" sounds in this poem.

Another way to experiment is to mix prose into poetry. William Carlos Williams did this in *Paterson;* he took letters and reports and other documents and interspersed his lyrical or narrative passages with them. *Prose poems* are a form midway between poetry and prose, with the intensity of poetry but with the form, on the page, of prose. Toni Morrison's Pulitzer prize–winning novel *Beloved* has poetrylike passages of interior monologue. The blurring of the boundaries between genres creates redefinition. The prose poem is especially suited for dream narrative. If you would like to try writing one, take a notebook and pen to your bedroom tonight and when you wake up, write out your dream, providing as much detail as possible. Do not indicate it is a dream, and avoid ending it with a giveaway statement like "And then I woke up." Describe exactly what happened: "You walked through the wall of my room, carrying roses. You opened your mouth to speak, but no sound came . . ." End it with the last event you remember happening in the dream. You will have a surreal paragraph of some interest, with intuitive rather than logical coherence—a prose poem.

But not all experimental work is free form. Here is a different sort of found poem:

*Shannon Nolte, "Always Wear a Hat" is reprinted by permission of the author.

.... **R. S. Gwynn**

*Approaching a Significant Birthday, He Peruses the Norton Anthology of Poetry**

All human things are subject to decay.
Beauty is momentary in the mind.
The curfew tolls the knell of parting day.
If Winter comes, can Spring be far behind?

Forlorn! the very word is like a bell
And somewhat of a sad perplexity.
Here, take my picture, though I bid farewell.
In a dark time the eye begins to see.

The woods decay, the woods decay and fall—-
Bare ruined choirs where late the sweet birds sang.
What but design of darkness to appall?
An aged man is but a paltry thing.

If I should die, think only this of me:
Grass casualty obstructs the sun and rain
When I have fears that I may cease to be,
To cease upon the midnight with no pain

And hear the spectral singing of the moon
And strictly meditate the thankless muse.
The world is too much with us, late and soon.
It gathers to a greatness, like the ooze.

Do not go gentle into that good night.
Fame is no plant that grows on mortal soil.
Again he raised the jug up to the light:
Old age hath yet his honor and his toil.

Downward to darkness on extended wings,
Break, break, break, on thy cold gray stones, O sea,
And tell sad stories of the death of kings.
I do not think that they will sing to me.

*R. S. Gwynn, "Approaching a Significant Birthday, He Peruses the Norton Anthology of Poetry" from *No Word of Farewell,* Selected Poems, 2001. Reprinted by permission of Story Line Press <www.storylinepress.com>.

Gwynn provides one selection criterion in the title: what is it? As you read this poem, you can easily figure out what other considerations were made in selecting lines from *The Norton Anthology* besides the one suggested by the title. Could you, having the *Norton* in hand, add a quatrain? What might be more interesting would be to think what other considerations, both in content and in form, might be used to select lines, and from what source. A true postmodernist might simply make an arbitrary choice of every third line on every third page. You might take the title, "On Considering _____, I open a copy of _____," fill in the blanks, and start copying.

In a sense, once some new direction has been labeled, it has already slipped into tradition, so that the most experimental of texts can rarely be named. But some of the experiments have included collage poems—snippets of photos, advertisements, and texts pasted together; concrete poems—popular in the sixties and seventies, the concrete poem is made to resemble a thing on the page; and all kinds of arbitrary poems, for which something outside the content dictates the form. For an "arbitrary poem" assignment, see the exercise called "Recipe Poem," on page 236 of Chapter 7, the recipe being an arbitrary assemblage of parts. There are a number of experimental exercises in that chapter.

Other experimental wordplay games involve collaboration. If you supply some "if-clauses," and if a classmate independently supplies some "then-clauses," and if next you stick them together without even reading them, you may have an intriguing experimental poem. Janet McCann once found she had written an overly sentimental poem; radical revision resulted in the excision of every other line, removing the sentimentality (and the coherence). She published the poem, whereupon another poet, Alan Catlin, read it and then supplied the missing lines. The final result was a sequence of three poems, a collaboration between two poets who had never met or spoken with each other.

Janet McCann

*Poem with Alternate Lines Missing**

> Contemplating the unshaded bulbs
> the Jardin des Tuileries at evening
> one thinks of the meaning of
> Could it all be do you think
> a green plant? And yet the moss
> is not homicidal. Who would ask to live
> in the three-sided house, the fourth wall

*Janet McCann, "Poem with Alternate Lines Missing" published in *New Letters*, 1984, and Poem with Alternate Lines Supplied" are reprinted by permission of the author.

coming in at night with a murderer's stealth
and yet we cannot live at peace together
here in the garden, that's flat; even now
On the beach the plump pink tourists
are exploding one by one into dark
in the sky the first stars
are gathering to spell out one word:

.... **Alan Catlin**

*Alternate Lines Supplied**

the dimming lights reflecting
as stark as forced Impressionism
shadows, of night.
a mere Prolegomena of False Reasoning,
that grows inside invoking blood but
outside the laws of logic
a nightmare of geometry, a vision
walking as dreaming lovers do, possessed
torn from trellis as twined vines
our limbs, our thoughts are inseparable.
unsuspecting, open boxed lunches,
mushrooming clouds.
are tainted by an unnatural haze,
Gotterdammerung.

.... **Alan Catlin and Janet McCann***

Poem with Alternate Lines Supplied

Contemplating the unshaded bulbs
the dimming lights reflecting
the Jardin des Tuileries at evening
as stark as forced Impressionism

*Alan Catlin, "Alternate Lines Supplied" and "Poem with Alternate Lines Supplied" are reprinted by permission of the author.

one thinks of the meaning of
shadows, of night.
Could it all be do you think
a mere Prolegomena of False Reasoning,
a green plant? And yet the moss
that grows inside invoking blood but
is not homicidal. Who would ask to live
outside the laws of logic
in the three-sided house, the fourth wall
a nightmare of geometry, a vision
coming in at night with a murder's stealth
walking as dreaming lovers do, possessed
and yet we cannot live at peace together
torn from the trellis as twined vines
here in the garden, that's flat; even now
our limbs, our thoughts are inseparable.
On the beach the plump pink tourists
unsuspecting, open boxed lunches,
are exploding one by one into
dark mushrooming clouds.
In the sky the first stars
are tainted by an unnatural haze,
are gathering to spell out one word:
Gotterdammerung.

Collaboration can be casual or formal, playful or serious. A group of poets might start by reading Wallace Stevens's poem "Someone Puts a Pineapple Together," which consists of a list of metaphors for the pineapple. Then put some evocative form on the table in front of you, something like a cactus or a Mason jar or a strainer. Then go around the group more than once, each contributing a metaphor or simile for the item. Have a group member write these all down in the order received, and then you will have a satisfactory group poem.

PERFORMANCE POETRY

Another kind of poetry that might be called experimental, because the effect of the poem does not rely solely on the words on the page, is *performance poetry*. Performance poetry is intended to be read dramatically, to be performed. It may be accompanied by music or lighting effects or other elements of theater. The poem may be read by two individuals as a dialogue, or it may be recited with a background of moving or stationary art. A good performance piece reads well on the page too, but the performance remains an important enhancement. Here is an example:

.... **Chuck Taylor**

*Ode to a City Bus**

Oh you silver whale with bulging eyes,
I love the way you ride the hot asphalt
on waves of lolling, sturdy spring.
I love the way you mess the flow of traffic,
taking the corners wide over curbs,
you rebel, you magic dragon,
you thorn in the neck of the efficient state.

Let me dissertate on your sounds:
the low carbon GROAN that sends
the smoking fart from your rear end,
the PSSST that opens all your doors,
the CREECH of brakes, the PONG, PONG, PONG,
so deliciously, the pulling of that string
running above the windows
stops the bus, stops the bus:
the CHICK-CLING, CHICK-CLING, CHICK-CLING
of the counter coin drop.

Salute the driver, you riders!
Humble captain of the democratic ship!
How in your interior sit silent eyes
holding packages, on verge of thought.
Kids barter their balance
against your surprising sway.
The studious study the ads,
while in the back, the long seat
bouncy stateroom, the young, in laughter, flirting!

Oh bus! So ecologically sound!
So bannered proud! I buss your straining
chromium angel side!

When performed, this poem has a powerful appeal to various ages of audience, and it is heard differently by different age groups. Adults see the social criticism; children will see the bus.

*Chuck Taylor, "Ode to a City Bus" is reprinted by permission of the author.

Characteristics of performance poetry include repetition, refrain, sound games, onomatopoeia, parallel structure, and emphatic vocalized punctuation like the many exclamations of the bus poem. Much ethnic poetry, particularly Native American poetry and rap, is performance poetry. Performance poetry looks back at the oral tradition and reminds us of the figure of the scop or "maker" of Old English verse whose job it was to pass on history as well as to entertain.

Here are just a few lines from student poet Ebony Hicks's long poem "P.S., and for this I thank you." A lot of the poem's effect is in the reading of it, as it is enhanced by the poet's voice and presence.

.... **Ebony Hicks**

P.S., and for this I thank you *

Before my eyes entered your atmosphere I was blind,
But now I have divine sight. You allow me to look into
Your eyes and take tiny snapshots of your soul
My pupils love to bathe in the essence of your mind's light.

You allow your fingertips to dance upon my cheek
Like ballerinas in wild flower fields:
Creating and radiating energy, and calmly soothing
Away the uneasiness and nervousness my face speaks.

I find your scent intoxicating,
Ripe damp honeysuckle
   On
   A
     Warm
August morning—
Addictive and invigorating.

The main reason for attempting to write experimental prose or poetry in a basic creative writing class is to enlarge the definition of fiction or poetry, to allow other possibilities besides the conventional. Reading experimental writing and playing with it will give you a new perspective on literature. But a secondary reward is the fun—the sense that you are in control of the language, and that you, like the Humpty Dumpty of the chapter's opening quotation, can make it do what you want it to. You can experience the sheer joy of trying some-

*Ebony Hicks, lines from "P.S., and for this I thank you" are reprinted by permission of the author.

thing original and new and having it come out at least interesting and possibly exciting.

Here is another experimental poem, this one by Sophie Esquiff, a young poet who specializes in what might be called *domestic surrealism*. Note the music of the poem, a tune in a minor key that seems to be playing in the background throughout the poem. The narrative element makes this poem too suitable for performance.

.... **Sophie Esquiff**

*just copies**

the white sign with red letters read
today's special is feeling good
i considered the sign's message
and then someone tapped me on the shoulder
and asked me if i needed any help
i asked if she had anything else on special today
but she told me that this was the only special
so i told her what i was looking for
and she escorted me to the cosmetic counter

as i picked up the bottles of perfume
i noticed that they were all empty
except for a few bottles that had paper labels
after two hours had passed
the gray haired salesman finally acknowledged me
he asked if he could distract me
and i told him that he could
then i asked him if i could buy a new mood
but he told me that he was out of moods
he continued to examine his book of numbers
and then he offered me a new attitude
and said that it was the newest perfume on the market
i told him i was not interested
and i crawled away

then i decided to go to the electronic department
the area was filled with moving pictures and backward sounds

*Sophie Esquiff, "just copies" is reprinted by permission of the author.

a blind salesperson came up to me and asked me if i needed any help
i told her that i was interested in hearing the ocean's breeze
and that i wanted it in a portable radio
but she told me that the ocean no longer existed
so i asked for a new mood
and she informed me that she sold many moods
but that they were just copies
so i searched through the moods and
realized that i had felt them all at one time

then i walked over to the television screens
where she told me to switch to a station
then to open my mind
and adjust to my favorite mood
i clicked the remote control
but i could only feel the plastic of my life
then i heard the message roar loudly over the intercom
please return your smiles because we are running out
so i turned to the blind salesperson
handed her my smile
and purchased a copy of a used mood

THE SEQUENCE

Poetic *sequences* are not necessarily experimental or even new, but they may be experiments, depending on what kind of sequence you are writing and how you choose to go about it. The sequence may include prose in with the poetry and may include various kinds of poem. It may narrate a story, perhaps giving different perspectives: before, during, and after an event or different people experiencing the same thing. The sequence may be scenes from a tale or may be very different scenes that have something in common.

A poet may choose an arbitrary series to hang poems—or vignette sketches—on, such as parts of a ritual, dance steps, even numbers. Sequences are popular right now, because they may bring an element of focus to a collection and make the group of poems or short fiction pieces something more than a bunch of works, held together by nothing but the poet's voice. The most experimental sequences are often the most inclusive, that is, those that take in a vast variety of voices and that often use a number of different media.

Having a sequence rounds out a project and gives it a plan. Catholic poet David Craig has written several religious sequences, on the psalms, the sayings of Saint Theresa, and other elements of Christianity. Here are two of Craig's psalms:

.... **David Craig**

Psalm #6*

Do not punish me, do not
stamp my soul with the seal
of who I am.
Lift me up and I will rise,
pity me. I cannot keep
my bones, the rack
upon which I starve, knit.

Come back, rescue me.
This is what You do.

I could sing Your praises
in the lands of the dead,
but who would hear me?
Take these hands, lifted;
a person follows.

I am worn out with groaning,
my enemies, younger each year,
surround me.

Yahweh calls me back
as he always has,
with the sound of trumpets,
the breaking of expected days.

I come,
in human skin.

Psalm #7*

Yahweh, if I am to die,
let it be in the sweet scythe
of Your wood.

*David Craig, "Psalm #6;" "Psalm #7" from *Mercy's Face*. Reprinted by permission of the author.

Rise, You who demand justice
bear Your name.
Look past intention.
Look at this face, a cooling fire,
these hands, winter leaves.

God preserves what He has pierced.

Give thanks to Yahweh,
whose voice creaks in the starry wood,
the whole place alive somehow
with water. Heavy grasses, green,
dark with it, and I feel the
same night the foliage does,
recite the same verses.
My body, too, belongs to the great
material curve of this planet, sky.
It is who I am, this way and
terminus. It haunts my every
blind and faithful step with the
signature of what we are, the promise
of where we live.

Craig has taken the Psalms and provided interpretations in sequence, so that reader's experience of the Psalms is given the additional layer of the Craig interpretation. Here for comparison purposes is the Biblical Psalm 6:

Psalm 6 (English-NIV)

1 O LORD, do not rebuke me in your anger or discipline me in your wrath.

2 Be merciful to me, LORD, for I am faint; O LORD, heal me, for my bones are in agony.

3 My soul is in anguish. How long, O LORD, how long?

4 Turn, O LORD, and deliver me; save me because of your unfailing love.

5 No one remembers you when he is dead. Who praises you from the grave?

6 I am worn out from groaning; all night long I flood my bed with weeping and drench my couch with tears.

7 My eyes grow weak with sorrow; they fail because of all my foes.

8 Away from me, all you who do evil, for the LORD has heard my
   weeping.
9 The LORD has heard my cry for mercy; the LORD accepts my prayer.
10 All my enemies will be ashamed and dismayed; they will turn back
   in sudden disgrace.

Joanne Lowery has written a sequence of poems on the Jack and the
Beanstalk children's story. In the poems, the outrageous events that happen to
Jack give insight into the trials of daily life. One of the poems, "Continuity," is
printed on pages 189–190. Read the poem and consider how she has used the
old children's story.

A sequence of poems that is based on what is to you a sacred or symbolic
text may create a promising project. Is there a text that you believe has transcen-
dent power? If you have such a text, what kind of organization might it provide
for a series of meditative poems?

But even in meditation mode, do not forget imagery.

Activities for Searching Out the Postmodern Muse

ACTIVITY ONE

1. Take ten poems that are not yours. Then, with a poet friend, go outdoors
   somewhere, and take turns reading the poems aloud.

2. Adopt the persona of a well-known fiction writer whom you know something about, for example, Ernest Hemingway or Virginia Woolf. Read aloud
   one of that writer's short stories, and then talk about how you (as the writer)
   felt about the story. Then write a different ending for the story.

3. Do this activity with two friends: Bring in to class a poem or a piece of short
   fiction that you wrote. Read it aloud, and then record it. Next, have a second
   reader read it, and then a third, recording all the readings. Listen to all the
   readings, and then revise the work on the basis of what you heard.

ACTIVITY TWO

1. Write a poem that turns a repeated sequence of sounds into words: the
   sound of a dentist's drill, of the beginning of rain, of a dishwasher cycle, of
   whatever you choose.

2. Take a poem of yours that you think is bad. Eliminate every third word. For
   the missing words, substitute words taken in order from some printed
   source, such as a newspaper article or a cookbook.

3. In a story or sketch, substitute other symbols for the punctuation marks, such as # for , or % for ?.

4. Write a short piece in some language other than English: BASIC, pig latin, French, German, Morse code, or whatever you choose.

ACTIVITY THREE

1. Interpret a nonliterary text as an allegory, and explain it. Some possibilities are a lease, a list of ingredients, and instructions for installing something.

2. Explicate or analyze a situation as though it were a poem.

3. Write down word for word the next monologue you hear. (Monologues are simply speeches of which one side is reported or heard. Some examples are someone's trying to sell you something on the phone; your instructor's lecture on Charlemagne; your mechanic's explanation of what is wrong with your car.) Now write another voice in response to each sentence, so that you have a dialogue.

ACTIVITY FOUR

1. Create a poem that combines printed text with line drawings and handwriting.

2. Stare at a familiar object, like a cup or plate, for three minutes. Then write whatever comes into your head for five full minutes, without stopping to think. Don't cheat—use a timer.

3. Translate a poem from or into another language.

4. Translate an *unwritten* poem from a specific language and culture into English. (That is, write the English equivalent of what you think a typical French or Spanish poem would be like.)

5. Write a poem based on an interoffice memo, an e-mail general announcement, or some other piece of official mail sent out to a group.

6. Write a poem on something other than paper.

7. Write a dialogue between two inanimate objects.

Creative Writing Exercises

This section is a minitext in itself, for the use of creative writing students both in groups and by themselves. It provides a series of forty-four prompts that may take anything from ten minutes to several hours to respond to. Instructors may also assign the exercises. The goal is to spark ideas, break down barriers, get people writing, wake everyone up. Many of the prompts proceed from the premise that writing is fun, though some are more serious and extensive.

1. INVERTING THE CLICHÉ

Write down all the clichés you can think of, focusing especially on those that involve similes or metaphors. Start with the most obvious, "heart of gold," "sore as a boil," "happy as a clam," and the like. Now jot down all the old sayings, warnings, and platitudes that you remember: "You've made your bed, now you have to lie in it." "The devil's children belong with the devil." "Too many cooks spoil the broth." "Nobody's sweetheart is ugly." Everyone should read his or her list aloud to the class.

Now look at the saying that has most appeal for you, and read it over and over, thinking about all the possible literal and figurative meanings it might have in addition to the cliché meaning. What might it mean to have a heart of gold? It might suggest a cold, metallic organ. The cliché is supposed to suggest something just the opposite—an inner goodness that is perhaps concealed by a gruff exterior.

Write a free verse poem that involves the meanings of the cliché or saying with the exclusion of the hackneyed one. See what you come up with. If you are successful, you will have wrested a new perspective from an old saying, and you will be more aware of cliché.

2. QUESTIONS AND ANSWERS

This exercise has been kicking around in creative writing classes for so long that it is impossible to tell where it came from. Half the class should write three questions, the other half three answers—without consulting with anyone. Then the leader should collect the questions and the answers, and give one set to one reader at one end of the room, and the other to another reader—often it is a good idea to get a male and a female for the contrast in voices.

Now, have the one reader read the first question, and the other reader the first answer. Continue through the questions and answers. If there are more of one than the other, as a result of unforeseen confusion, just repeat the questions or the answers in order until all of both have been read. Discuss what happens when the random answers acquire relevance through being connected with the questions. Consider how this random relevance might spark poetry.

3. GROUP POEMS

This is an exercise that has been done for generations, probably since creative writing classes began to be taught. It has also been done in art: an "exquisite corpse" was a drawing done by a group of artists starting at the top and working down, with each artist not knowing what the previous artists had drawn. To do the group poem, invite the first student to write a line, fold the sheet of paper so that the line does not show, and pass the paper to the next student, who writes another line. When all students have added a line—with no idea what the previous students wrote—the instructor or a student unfolds the paper and reads the "poem."

Variations involve setting specific guidelines. Some possibilities are as follows:

A. All lines must be in iambic pentameter. Needless to say, the definition and practice of iambic pentameter must precede this assignment.

B. Poems are to rhyme in couplets or tercets. For couplet rhyme, the first student writes the last word of his or her line on the fold. The second student's line must rhyme with that word. The third student writes a line without concern for rhyme but writes the last word on the fold. The fourth student's rhyme must rhyme with that. And so forth.

C. Poems are preceded by a focus—looking at a Salvador Dali painting, listening to a rock song, and so forth.

D. The class is broken up into groups of three students to do this, so that each poem becomes a collaboration among those three.

4. TRANSLATION

Find a poem in another language, and attempt to make it into an English poem. If you know another language well, needless to say, this project will be easier than if you do not. But not all translators are speakers of the language that they translate. Ezra Pound, for instance, used the literal translation of another writer to create his famous poem "The River Merchant's Wife" from an ancient Chinese poem.

If you do not know another language well enough to translate, then try this: find a book that does literal translations, like *The Poem Itself* or *Contemporary*

French Poetry. The book that you choose must include both the original and the translation, because you need to look at the original even if you do not read the language. How the poem looks on the page is a part of its original effect.

You may want to play with one of the Internet translation programs to do this—since they are very inexact, they often add an element of the surreal to your translation, and in any case, they are fun to work with. Go to Altavista.com and pick the translation program; follow the instructions to use it.

5. THE POETRY KIT

(There *is* a poetry kit, which is an assortment of words on tiny magnets that you rearrange to make poems on file cabinets, refrigerators, and the like.) This is a kit that you make as a group or class. Each of you should write ten nouns, ten verbs, ten adjectives, ten adverbs, five prepositions, and five conjunctions. Add a pile of articles (*a, an, the*). Throw in an exclamation or two if you wish. Now, print each of your words on a square of paper 1″ × 1″. Put all of the group's words together face up in the middle of a table. Now, make poems from the words, taking them as you need them, until the group and/or the pile is exhausted.

6. THE DICTIONARY POEM

This is a simple exercise. Open a dictionary without paying attention. With your finger, press down on a page without looking. Read carefully the definition of the word that your finger has landed on. Write a poem about that word.

You are allowed one redo if you get an impossible word, but make sure your word is a genuine dud. A word like *of*, for instance, is fraught with possibilities. Harder to deal with sometimes are extremely technical terms—but then think, you may have discovered the makings of a wonderful metaphor.

7. PARODY

A parody is an exaggerated imitation of a work of art. It is a parasitic form, and the parody doesn't usually outlast the original—although sometimes it does. Lewis Carroll's "You Are Old, Father William" is still quoted, whereas Robert Southey's "The Old Man's Comforts," on which Lewis Carroll's "Father William" is based, is not. But parodies are fun, and they can be a vehicle for satire.

To make up a parody, take a well-known poem or part of a poem—or a famous speech in blank verse from a Shakespeare play, or another well-known speech—and change the content. Often a parody takes a poem with an exalted content and substitutes something trivial. You might look up Shakespeare's "To be or not to be" speech from *Hamlet* and then think what might take the place of "be." To a golfer, it might be "to putt or not to putt." For a man with a beard or for a woman considering the political implications of smooth legs, it might be "to shave or not to shave." Next, you go through the rest of the speech, making changes to conform with the main change, and then you have a parody.

8. INTERTEXTING

Take a well-known poem that fascinates you, and copy it, leaving lots of room between the lines. Now write yourself into that poem. That is, fill in the spaces between the lines with your own interpretations, reflections, and images. When you have finished, cross out as much of the original poem as you can, and give the new poem a new title. You may want to leave several intact lines or partial lines of the original author's in your poem. Identify these borrowed lines by quotation marks when you recopy your poem. Sometimes you can identify the poem you have used by alluding to it in your title.

9. SICK POEMS

Read some clinical descriptions of symptoms or of diseases from a medical journal or *The Merck Manual of Diagnosis and Treatment*. Find the illness you think has most potential as some kind of metaphor. Now, write a poem about the condition, using the *Merck* or the journal information as a background. You may even quote from the source, either as an epigraph or within the body of the poem.

As a variant, your instructor may ask you to make photocopies of the description of the disease and bring the photocopies to class. Then the class will put the copies in a pile, each member will take one, and each one will write a poem about the disease. If you do this, you may want to keep two copies of the material—one copy so that you can write your own poem about your chosen disease later.

10. POEM IN PARTS

Begin with two, three, or even four poems that you have written on a similar topic that you do not think worked out very well. Now, cut the poems ruthlessly until you have only what you find to be effective lines left. If a poem dwindles down to two or three lines, that's fine; keep them.

Now, think of your reduced poems as parts of a longer poem. Go back to the original subject: A personal loss? A scene that you found memorable enough to write about several times? A concept or an idea? Then write two or more short poems about it. You might make yourself some assignments: a segment that is in rhymed quatrains; a segment that is a "prose poem"; a segment that is in blank verse; a segment in which each line has six syllables. Now, give the overall poem a title, and arrange the pieces of it in what you find the most effective sequence, using numbers or asterisks to divide up the poem. Sometimes the last step of the construction is to remove the weakest segment.

11. RAISING THE UNDERDOG

Write a dramatic monologue from the point of view of an unsympathetic and a relatively unimportant character in literature, myth, or history. You might find someone like Drusilla, one of Cinderella's ugly stepsisters, or Holden Caulfield's rather disgusting friend Ackley from *The Catcher in the Rye*. Using blank verse, adopt the mask of this person, and tell his or her tale in such a way as to make "the other side of the story" clear to the reader.

Alternatively, to use this premise in a fiction exercise, write a dialogue between this person and someone else. Have your main character do most of the talking, again with the goal of making his or her side more acceptable.

12. DIALOGUE

Get a friend to agree to participate in this exercise. Take a tape recorder and turn it on; now, you and your friend should have a five-minute desultory chat about something—grades, friends, a social event, a teacher, something in the news. Now, play the tape. Is there anything in the dialogue that characterizes you and/or your friend? Type or write out a page or so of this dialogue. Is it interesting? Why, or why not?

Next, rewrite your actual dialogue as a fictional dialogue in which some information is passed on to the reader and some characterization is done. You will leave out most of the original dialogue as you do this. See whether you can come up with one or two pages of realistic, character-rich chat based on your real discussion.

13. DESCRIBING A PLACE

Choose a landscape that has a particular emotional value to you: maybe a beach you used to frequent with your friends, a mountain retreat where your spiritual values were enhanced, or a backyard where you grew vegetables with your parents. Give a physical description of the place, but try to leave out judgment words. If you are describing the mountains, for instance, don't say "magnificent," but try to figure out what physical details underlie the conclusion that the mountains are magnificent. Try to make the details as exact as you can: What kinds of trees? What kinds of flowers? What shapes? What colors?

Now, write a sentence that could be considered a thesis statement for your description, because it captures, in a few words, the overall impression of the place. Try even here to avoid the obvious.

To make your description into a poem, go through it and highlight the details. Choose the best of these, and arrange them into a pattern on the page that is pleasing to the eye and ear.

To keep your description in prose, place the thesis statement at the end— read the description through, and see whether you think the statement is needed or whether the details imply the thesis sufficiently. Pay attention to how the details are arranged—can you perceive a pattern, like background to foreground, or following some kind of time sequence?

14. THE EDIBLE POEM

This is a relaxed exercise that perhaps is more for fun than for educational profit. Bring to class two small food items of one kind: apples, bananas, chocolate bars, pickles, strips of beef jerky. Your instructor or group leader will pair you off, preferably on the basis of odd combinations of foodstuff. Now trade off your extra item with your partner. Observe the qualities of both your offering and of that of your partner; jot them down. Eat the two items. Then write a poem about each. (*Note:* if it turns out that you can't eat your partner's food for one reason or another, just make the poem describe its appearance, or use it as a metaphor.)

Here are some variations: (a) Make one poem consider the item as a symbol or a metaphor; (b) write one poem about both items; or (c) collaborate with your partner on one of the poems. If there is an odd number of students, have one group of three—or let the instructor play! The class should consider beforehand, though, that there *may* be an odd person, so provision must be made for such a case.

15. GENDER-BENDING DIALOGUE

Imagine yourself as a member of the opposite sex. Now write a dialogue in which this imagined transformed self is speaking with someone else. The other person can be of either sex. In the dialogue, have the imagined self do most of the speaking. A variation is to make this a dramatic monologue rather than a dialogue.

16. DIALOGUE WITH PLACE

Consider a place with which you are familiar that has elements of local color appeal. This could be a country-and-western bar and grill, a town with a population of two hundred, a general store, or a fishing resort. Now write a sketch in which you both describe the place and include some dialogue between its inhabitants or between a stranger and a local.

17. DESCRIBING ACTION

Write a brief scene in which some rapid and/or abrupt action takes place—a fight, an explosion, a horse race, whatever action scene you want to work into a story. Now exchange with a classmate and critique the scenes. Are the verbs good? Does the pacing of the sentences reflect the action? How do you think that the writer could improve the scene? Rewrite your action scene after considering the critiques.

18. THE PROCESS PAPER

Write a short essay in which you describe an orderly, step-by-step procedure for doing something that doesn't ordinarily have steps, such as going to sleep, falling in love, eating a pizza, or flunking an algebra test. This exercise can also be done as a poem. If appropriate, provide diagrams.

19. THE SELF-REFLEXIVE POEM

Write a poem giving instructions on how to write a poem.

20. WHODUNIT

This exercise, which is for those interested in writing formula stories, can be fun. Each member of your group should place some item on a desk or table. If the exercise is agreed upon ahead of time and if you have a chance to prepare for it, provide items that may be very strange. If you do the exercise on the spur of the moment, the items you place on the desk will be more prosaic, but the exercise will be easier! What you should do is to imagine that a murder victim has been found and had on his or her person the items now on the desk. Your job is to create a plot that uses the items on the desk to explain why the individual was killed and who did it.

21. VERB POETRY

Write a poem that uses verbs without subjects; that is, instead of "I see," use "see," "sees," or "seeing." The verbs may take objects of all kinds, but concentrate on the verbs—make them as precise and as evocative as you can.

22. RECIPE POEM

Follow these instructions:

A. Write a line beginning with a conjunction.
B. Write a line with a color in it.
C. Write a line in a language other than English. (If you don't know one, make one up.)
D. Write a line ending with a question mark or an exclamation point.
E. Write a line no more than four syllables long.
F. Write a line containing a quotation.
G. Write a line containing one or more numbers.
H. Write a line that is quoted from something.
 I. Write a line more than ten syllables long.
J. Write a line ending with a conjunction.

Now, write two separate lines of instructions. Make them as wild as possible, but still followable; that is, "Write a line in Russian" would not be fair. In your group, take these instructions in random order to create another recipe poem assignment.

23. THE MAP

Bring to class two maps, the first a local one and the second of some terrain other than your immediate location. Put the nonlocal maps in a pile on a desk; each class member should draw one out of the stack. Now, write a poem about some element of the map that you have chosen. When you have finished—allow, say, half an hour for this—return these maps to their owners. Now, take the other map that you brought, the local one, and write a poem about some aspect of that. Finally, find some way to put together your two poems—as a single poem with two sections, as one poem—whatever. Revise the poem or the poem pair.

24. THE ZOO POEM

First, read some of Marianne Moore's and perhaps some of Rainer Maria Rilke's poems about animals. Then, choose a bird or an animal to write about. Start by actually examining the bird or animal as closely as is possible. Jot down as many precise details of your chosen bird or animal as you can. On another sheet, think of as many metaphors as you can for the bird or animal: how it looks, how it behaves. Now, go research the bird or animal, finding out details of its history and natural habitat. Copy this information down in the language of your source, on a third sheet. Now take your three sheets, and combine them into a poem, using whatever you want of each, wherever you want to put it.

25. VOICES I

Tell a fairy tale from three different points of view: for instance, you might take the story of Snow White and narrate it in the voices of two different dwarfs and of the witch.

26. VOICES II

Select a fictional character from a novel, and tell her or his story from a time after the end of the novel. See whether you can both keep the character's way of speaking and also show how it might change with age and experience. Possibilities are a fifty-year-old Holden Caulfield, Huck Finn, or Edna Pontillier.

27. THE PATHETIC FALLACY

Take an abstract problem, like an example from a logic text or a simple mathematical problem. A logic problem that would work might be one of those that starts with a premise like, "Imagine an island where the natives always tell lies and non-natives always tell the truth." But any math problem with names would work: "Susan is mixing three kinds of coffee, one that costs $4.50 a pound, another that costs $7.50 a pound, and a third . . ." Now, decide that the people in your problem are real individuals. Give them names and characteristics. Write a poem about how they behave in their problem, or create a short sketch about them.

28. FORMS

Write a sonnet with absolutely metrical regularity, after consulting the definition and the examples in Chapter 4. Now revise the sonnet to give it a less exact, more natural rhythm. Which is the better sonnet, do you think? Why? Instead of a sonnet, you might do this with a villanelle or some other form.

29. REVISION

Look at the beginnings and the endings of either twenty well-known contemporary poems or twenty well-known short stories. Decide what the writers appear to be doing in their openings and closings, and ask yourself whether there are any general rules that might describe their methods. Rewrite one of the endings in a paragraph to make the story or poem turn out differently. Now, rewrite the beginning and the ending of your own most recent poem or short story.

30. SOUND

Read Lewis Carroll's "Jabberwocky" on pages 134–135. Write a poem in which you do not pay any attention to what the poem means but only to how it sounds. Make up words. Repeat sounds. Let syllables echo and invert each other. Have fun without worrying at all whether or not the poem is absolutely nonsensical. Now exchange the poem with that of your neighbor, and explicate each other's poem. Write what the theme of your neighbor's poem is, what its major images seem to be, and so on, as if the poem had been written by James Joyce or Gertrude Stein. Give your neighbor your explication.

31. MUSICAL MAYHEM

Five students should each bring in a tape or a disk of music that they like, and the tastes should be as different as possible, for instance, classical, heavy metal, country-and-western, jazz, and show tunes. Each student (including the music providers) should play either a five-minute chunk of music or a selection of about five minutes. During the playing, everybody should write—just jot down images, thoughts, ideas. After the five segments have been listened to, then take the responses, choose your favorite two, and underline the best lines and images in them. Out of class, write a poem or two based on these responses to music.

32. SCIENCE FICTION AND REALITY

Write an outline plot for a science fiction story. Now rewrite the outline as a realistic story. Discuss the differences between the two outlines. Which one has more promise?

33. JUST A POEM

Write a poem that describes what you see when you look out your window. Try to avoid words that are evaluations—concentrate on detail.

34. HISTORY POEM

Look through a history book until you find an incident that interests you, and write a poem about it. Use a quotation from the book as an epigraph, which is a quotation between the title and the body of the poem, usually shedding light on the poem's theme.

35. LETTERS AND CHARACTER

Write a brief character sketch of a friend or family member that relies at least partly on letters for its source of detail. You can do this exercise as a poem as well.

36. THE RESPONSE POEM

Many well-known poems issue an invitation or state a position. Andrew Marvell's "Come live with me and be my love" issues an invitation common to many poems, whereas William Carlos Williams's poem that begins "We cannot move to the country / For the country will give us no peace" takes a position that the reader can accept or reject. Find a poem that you disagree with or that you reject the invitation in, and respond to it.

37. ONE METAPHOR

If you were to imagine a single metaphor for yourself, what would it be? A house? A garden? An animal? Describe this image of yourself in a paragraph or as a poem.

38. AN EXERCISE IN EVALUATION

Read the following four short poems, and discuss with a group what seems to be wrong with them. Generate a definition of good poetry from your discussion of the bad poetry.

Poetry

Starving Dog devours the newborn rats
vomits them up behind the barn
pink, tiny legs, torsos, twitching.

Haiku

The yellow bird flies
Up among the puffy white
Clouds. My sad heart lifts.

Friendship

I thank you for your friendly hand
when I was like to slip and fall;
you reached for me and held me up;
I hardly noticed it at all.

Specter

> Creature of night lurks
> in the dank cave of the soul,
> hoping to slake its thirst at Beauty's throat

In what different ways can poetry fail? What does poetic failure emphasize about poetic success?

39. RECALLING CHILDHOOD

The following assignment is more a prompt for a full-length essay or story than it is an exercise, but it gives you a different way to go about storytelling. Close your eyes and think about how it felt to be a child—how things looked and how you understood or failed to understand your environment. Now think about what you understood your sex role to be—that is, what it meant to be a child who would become a man or a woman. Where did you get your idea of adult sex roles from? Was this a good place to get it? Now write a short story or an essay that re-creates a child's mind as this child thinks about manhood or womanhood.

See what a St. Mary's University student has done with this kind of speculation:

.... **Cara Ford**

Pink Car Without a Top*

I want to be Barbie when I grow up. I will have so many friends and a pink car without a top and live in a big house with three floors and an elevator and a heart-shaped bed with ten pillows and Skipper and Ken will always want to play with me. Not like you and Chris who play Atari and tell me I'm fat and make me tell Mom she's ugly so I get in trouble.

But Mom always laughs and says you're just being silly. But I tell her you're mean and you make me cry but she doesn't care because you look like a doll and are always smiling and everybody loves you because you're perfect and do everything right, and everybody hates me because I'm fat and I can't play piano and can't read like you can.

When you're at school I go into your room and try on your clothes and pretend I am you. It's fun because you aren't there to yell at me

*Cara Ford, "Pink Car Without a Top" is reprinted by permission of the author.

when I wear your green shirt with the blue people on the front. Sometimes I lay in your bed and play with your dolls. I like the one with the yellow hair. Mine is not as pretty as yours, because the hair is brown, like mine. When you are gone, I make my own roles. Like how many pillows belong on the bed, and which blanket is the best to make a tent (I like the purple one). When I'm a big kid like you, you can't tell me what to do. I can build a fort too, you know.

I color a picture from the book with the crayons you gave me after you got a new box. Mommy put it next to yours on the 'frigerator with the apple magnet. Your paper is better 'cause you got a gold star and there's an "A" with a cross on it. I try to make my own "A," but it looks like a "D" and I threw it away because it looks ugly next to yours. But it doesn't matter anyway because you have another paper with a star and Mommy kisses you and Daddy lets you go to 7-11 with him and gets you a Slurpee after school on Thursdays when he comes home early. I hate you and Mom just smiles when I cry.

When Mommy makes you play with me, you always pretend you're nice but I know you're mean because you think you're better than me just because you're seven and I'm five. You tell me to go get this and that for you and I want to say no and hit you but Mommy told me to be nice so I say yes and do what you tell me even though I still want to hit you.

Someday when I'm Barbie I will invite you to my house and let you drive my pink car without a top and everybody will tell you how lucky you are to be my sister. And you will want to go to my bedroom and sit in my heart bed and read my books and look at all of my pretty clothes.

40. REPRESENTATIVE CLOTHING

Write a poem or a one-page creative nonfiction essay on an article of clothing that to you in some way represents your origins, your genes, and your people. As an example, consider the following poem:

Monica Puri

*Saree**

> Rustling
> autumn leaves;
> silk drapes
> the brown body.
> Crisp.
>
> Cocoon.
> Metamorphosed
> into sprawling night.
> Nine yards of black silk
> shimmering.
> Night sky.

41. SEQUENCE

Take a poem you have written that you like; choose a line from that poem, and write another poem that begins with this line. Do this again—choosing a line from the second poem, or another from the first. Your poem may be either one long poem or a linked sequence of three.

42. CHARACTER DIALOGUE

All class members should bring pictures cut out from journals. Each member should name this character and narrate this person's waking up and setting forth. Then, the class should break up into twosomes (or threesomes), invent a plausible reason for these particular characters to be together (stuck in an elevator? being two "soccer moms"?), and create a dialogue for them.

43. FAIRY TALES AGAIN

This time, think of the fairy tale that most appeals to you, for whatever reason. Fairy tales, like myths, are easy to identify with, as many a bestseller writer knows. Then narrate portions of the tale in which you imply what the tale means to you. Poet Joanne Lowery has a long sequence of Jack and the Beanstalk poems, one of which is included on pages 189–190. Read the poem and then write a poem about a fairy tale that you can identify with.

*Monica Puri, "Saree" is reprinted by permission of the author.

44. RANDOM WEIRDNESS

Invent an exercise that you think will stimulate the imagination. It must be something that can be done on the spot without preparation, and that would take about fifteen minutes. (Possible exercises are to write about something that is touching your skin or to write about what you are writing with or on.) Hand the exercise to the person on your right. The person on your left, then, will be handing you an exercise.

Publishing in Journals

> *To have great poets, there must be great audiences too.*
>
> —Walt Whitman

Should you rush off to publish after finishing your first creative writing class, or even before? The answer to that is, decide whether you want to. Publishing can be addictive. You can start writing not for yourself but for the various markets. If you want to publish articles in newspapers about planting begonias or refinishing floors, writing for markets is fine. If your goal is to write a fine poem that the next generation will want to read, it probably isn't. But publishing does make contacts for you, encourage you, and give you a sense of who else is doing what you are doing. So you may want to send your work to some journals.

On the other hand, sending out your work can be very discouraging. You can publish anything. If you send your work to a members-only journal, or if you enter the kind of contest that accepts all contributions and then charges $50 for a copy, or if you subsidize the publication, you can publish your laundry list. But if you are sending to well-known or exclusive journals, the steady diet of rejection can be depressing. It usually takes a while to break into the middle-ranked college and university journals. And even after your work is being accepted, you will still receive many of those colored slips of paper that say, "We regret that your manuscript does not meet our present needs. We wish you luck in placing it elsewhere."

If you want to try publishing, the following guidelines may help you.

1. Composing a List of Possible Sources

Use a market list such as *Writer's Market* that describes the publications in detail. Then, if possible, look at a copy of the journal to which you will send your work. Sending for sample copies is a smart step because it helps the small press publishers as well as giving you a good idea of what they are looking for. But you may not have the money or the patience to do this; if you do not, go to the library.

2. Items to Search For

Note the following items in descriptions. They may help you decide which sources to send to.

Circulation

If the journal has a circulation of fifty, you might as well just pass copies around the class. For a literary journal, a circulation of one thousand and up should be suitable. Popular journals will be in the tens of thousands.

Turnaround Time

Consider how long the source will keep your manuscript before deciding on it.

Payment

For poems, often published copies are the only payment. Usually stories and essays provide some monetary payment, but not always. If a journal wants you to pay them, don't. Some journals say "no payment," which usually means that they don't even send you a copy. Avoid these sources. The slick, high-circulation journals pay quite a bit, but some of them are interested in formula rather than in literary stories, and in any case, this market is hard to break into. The literary journals, when they pay at all, usually offer only a token payment. You get the prestige of publishing and the delight of seeing your words in print.

Rights

What rights do the journals buy? *First rights* means that this must be the first time the work has been published. First *North American serial rights* means that this must be the first time the work has been published in a journal in North America. *Second rights* means that this work has been published once and that this is the second publication. *One-time rights* means that the journal has the right to publish the work once, whatever its publication history. *All rights* means that the work belongs henceforth to the journal. You have to get the editors' written permission and possibly have to pay them in order to publish the work again.

Many journals want first North American serial rights. After the work has been published in such a journal, you can have it republished in one that will accept second rights or one-time rights.

Appearance

Look at the journal or the description to see how the journal is bound. It may be photocopied and saddle-wired in somebody's garage. Or it may be perfect-bound and look like a book. Sometimes the informal journals contain the best work, though; you cannot always "tell a book by its cover."

Other Considerations

Read the whole entry in the directory carefully to see whether there is anything that would rule out your work or that would favor it. It is useful to use a directory even if you also have a copy of the journal. Some types of notation that might either lure you or send you running are no profanity, formal poetry only, subject must be Midwestern, international emphasis, and upbeat writing needed. And, of course, there is that old warning, naively issued by many journals: work of highest literary quality only!

3. Preparing Your Manuscript for Submission

First, look at specific requirements that the journals may have. Much postage has been wasted because submitters fail to note that a journal does not read in the summer or that it insists on particular format requirements that have not been met. Some journals, for instance, have blind judging, meaning that you must send a list of your submission titles and your name and address separately from the poems, so that the judge cannot identify the submitter. If you follow the normal guidelines by putting your name and address on each page, your work may not be considered. You should also note that some journals will accept "simultaneous submissions," allowing you to submit the same work to several journals at once, whereas others do not. But if you are submitting to several journals, you need to keep extremely careful records, and you should write to the other editor immediately if a piece of work is accepted elsewhere.

The Manuscript Itself

The typed prose manuscript should be double-spaced and professional in appearance, without corrections, scribbles, or stains. Many writers prefer to single-space poems, because they tend to look better that way. At the top right corner of each page should be your name and address, as well as the word count for the manuscript. All pages should be numbered; the last name of the writer is usually repeated in the header on subsequent pages: Jones—2. For poems, include your name and address with each poem. This step is important, because the journal may accept one poem and then send the others back to you. When the journal publishes your poem, if there is no address with it, the journal will not know where to send your contributor's copies.

The Cover Letter

Ordinarily, you should include a cover letter that includes the information that you are offering your manuscript (give title) for consideration for publication, and that it is unpublished and not being considered elsewhere (if it isn't). You do not want to make the cover letter too chatty, but you may include some biographical information if it is relevant to the offering. When you have published a few things, you can include a brief listing as part of this letter. For best results, send the manuscript to the editor by name, and address the editor by name in the letter. The most recent *Writer's Market* and *Poet's Market* will provide these names.

4. Preparing and Sending Envelopes

You need an SASE, that is, a stamped, self-addressed envelope, for the return of the manuscript or the response. Most editors don't like SAPs (stamped, addressed postcards), but a few state that they will accept them. If you are mailing out more than three sheets, it is best to use a large envelope that doesn't require you to fold the work. If you want the manuscript back, you need to include a large enough envelope and sufficient postage. If you are satisfied with a response, just send a business-sized SASE, but include in the letter the information that this envelope is for a response only and that the manuscript itself need not be returned. (Otherwise, some editors will cram your twelve-page manuscript into your tiny SASE, and it will arrive—if at all—postage due.)

It is usually the case that you won't be able to resubmit the same manuscript elsewhere, if anyone has actually read it, because the sheets will be folded and possibly written on. Limp, refolded manuscripts have a sad tale to tell, and most editors don't want to hear it. Therefore, it makes sense to send an envelope for "response only." On the other hand, occasionally an editor will write useful comments on a manuscript.

5. Keeping Careful Records

Be sure to keep careful records of what you sent where and when. Keep track of any comments made; if you receive any comment at all written on the rejection slip, this outcome usually means that someone at the journal liked your work. You will want to submit more to the same place—but not by return mail. Wait a week or two, but not long enough to be forgotten.

You may make up a submission log like the following:

2001 Submissions

Title	Sent To	Out	In	Comments
"Two Women"				
"Carriage House"	*Antioch Review*	5/10	6/1	"Try us with others"
"Ghosts"				
"The Yellow Cat"				
"Hen's Teeth"	*Maryland Review*	5/12	6/4	Accepted "Ghosts"!

There are a number of computer programs available to help you track your submissions, but it is easy enough to make a template of your own. Be sure to update your log promptly—and do take down any positive comments, so that the log does not look discouraging and also so that you know where your work has evoked some positive response.

6. Waiting for Responses

Two weeks to four months is the general turnaround time; if six months elapse without a response, you may want to send a follow-up letter. In this letter you ask whether the manuscript under submission (give title) is still being considered, and if it is, when a decision might be expected. Unfortunately, you need to include an SASE with *every* letter that you send to the editor from whom you expect a response. A certain percentage of submissions just disappear into the ether. After a year and with no reply to a follow-up, I always assume that these are lost and resubmit elsewhere.

Once your work is accepted, the editor may ask for a contributor's note and may occasionally send you galley proofs to be corrected and returned. Up to a year may elapse between acceptance and publication—sometimes even longer.

7. Miscellaneous Tips

You may also want to submit to on-line journals. Each of these has its own submission procedures; read and follow them carefully. It is satisfying to see your work in these journals, often very attractively illustrated. Like editors of other journals, the on-line editors run the gamut from uninformed hobbyist to literary sophisticate. Many on-line journals have a wide readership. The downside is that your publication can disappear without a trace overnight, not leaving so much as a copy in some archive. On-line journals often take somewhat shorter poems, since the on-line reading experience is different.

If you send out batch after batch and get them all back unaccepted, do not be discouraged—even poets with several books get a lot of rejection slips. Try submitting differently.

If you have been using a market directory, go to the library instead, and browse through their journals, taking down names and addresses for those that seem appropriate.

Look for student journals—these open and shut down frequently, so it would be unwise to use anything but a very current source. Of course, your college may have a student journal. Start there. Then look in the directory for other journals that feature student work or that are edited by students.

Look at the websites of Poets and Writers to find the Classified section; this is a list of journals and book editors actively seeking manuscripts. The address is www.pw.org.

Be sure your submissions are well timed. Many journals, especially those affiliated with a college or university, don't read over the summer. Fall is a good time to send to them, and also early spring—but around the first of May, many will shut down. They will either return manuscripts unread over the summer or let them pile up somewhere to be read all at once in the fall—either way, you lose.

Enter student contests! You will be competing with peers, not professional writers. There is usually no entry fee, and often there is a prize as well as publication for the winners. When you win these contests, mention the award in your subsequent cover letters.

Look at poetry society contests also—although these usually require entry fees, often the fees are only a couple of dollars, and the competition is less stiff than in other contests.

However you begin publication, you will find it a great stimulus to further writing.

Computers and Creative Writing

Using Your Computer

The web is a blank slate for you to write on, as well as an inexhaustible research resource. Technology changes so quickly that there is little use in providing a set of instructions for taking any particular action, like setting up a web page. A list of useful websites might prove profitless as well, since these disappear and are replaced frequently. The web is both useful and frustrating. Some general comments about creative writing and the web may prove helpful, both to regular browsers and to those who have not had as much access to web technology. It is assumed that you access the web and do some research already; if not, go to one of the major search engines, like Altarist, Locos, Infoseek, Webcrawler, or Yahoo, and read their search instructions carefully. The protocols differ from one search engine to another.

> *The Net is the back fence of the universe.*
>
> —Hugh McCann

Resources for Creative Writers

The web is the back fence of the universe. What you find there may be sound information, or it may be gossipy speculation. There is no quality control, and if you hunt up "poetry on a search engine, you will probably find a million pages ranging from the works of unknown writers in unknown languages to a clever fourth-grader's net page with Joyce Kilmer's poem "Trees" on it. To find anything on the net, you need to know what you are looking for and be able to frame your search with exactness. Excellent search engines include Altavista.com, Google.com, Infoseek.com, and others. But what is there for the creative writer to look for?

On-line Journals

On-line journals give you access to contemporary poetry without a fee. Many journals that are not on-line in their totality have websites with selections from the journals, so that you can decide from the sample if you want to subscribe—or to submit. There are dozens, perhaps even hundreds, of on-line journals and print journals with on-line samples.

Workshop Groups

Each genre—poetry, essay, fiction, play—has numerous groups that submit work for group critique. Some of these you must be invited to join; others are open to all who submit. Most workshop groups have requirements that you must accept, such as agreeing to critique a work a month.

Creative Writing Discussion Groups

Often but not always by genre, there are numerous discussion groups for writers and readers. These discussion groups, as well as the workshops, are very different from the "chat rooms" of the on-line services, and usually involve your subscribing by e-mail and then receiving and posting contributions by e-mail. Each group has a different tone and focus; some groups insist that all posts be directly relevant to the a particular issue or assigned topic, whereas others do not. When you sign up for a group, it is often best to listen or "lurk" for a while before posting assertively. You may find during this listening period that this group is not an appropriate one for you, and unsubscribe. It is true that e-mail-based groups require that you have a certain amount of time and room for e-mail; some groups get over a hundred posts a day.

Lists of Markets and Awards

You will find any number of lists of places to submit to, contests to enter, and awards to apply for. To begin, you might go to the Poets and Writers site at www.pw.org and click on Classifieds. But if you search for "poetry contests" or "creative writing contests," you will find other lists and individual contests, including many for students that do not have entry fees.

On-line Contests

Such contests are easy to enter and usually require no fee. Some of them have no prizes besides publication in a webzine, but they do usually produce attractive web publications. Read the journals before entering these contests; you will get a clear idea whether these are the right venues for you.

Links Pages

A search for "poetry" or "fiction" will, among the thousands of other options, provide you with some links pages that keep up-to-date on poetry or fiction resources.

Research Resources

The net can find you directories of quotations, rhyming dictionaries, searchable great works, bibles, real and just-for-fun translators (Alta Vista translation services, dialectizer), dictionaries, encyclopedias, reviews, and so forth. Some encyclopedias and other reference works require you to pay to subscribe, but many do not. The easiest way to begin is to go to the Yahoo! site, the Altarist site, or another such site and to try their simplified searches. Remember that for most of the search engines, you need to put what you are looking for in quotation marks: "Emily Dickinson," for instance. Otherwise, you will get all the Emilys and all the Dickinsons.

Particular Works and Writers

You can often find a copy of a poem of which you have forgotten all but one line. On a search engine like Google, just type in the line in quotation marks: "And miles to go before I sleep." You are likely to find both poem and author. (Of course, if you don't remember your line exactly or if the poem is not that well known, you won't. But it is worth a try.) You can find quick and casual information about any poet you can think of. But evaluate your find carefully—that Emily Dickinson web page may be some junior high school student's class project, and it may be all wrong. Regarding older popular works no longer under copyright, many are on-line.

A great resource is Poetry Daily, which provides an accessible and exciting poem each day from one of the many new collections that appear. Go to www.poems.com. You'll find useful links here too.

Book Buying

Check out Amazon.com and Barnesandnoble.com for any book you might want to buy; you may well find additional information and reviews about the book. You can briefly review books that you have bought from Amazon.com and post the reviews on their site. Barnes and Noble's on-line store also provides helpful information, and there are numerous other sellers of both new and used books on the web.

What You Can Do with the Computer

Collaborate

You can work together on a poem or fiction piece—perhaps an epistolary novel or a short story in which your character writes one sequence of letters and another comes from your friend, with another character. You can do haiku sequences together, or if you are truly ambitious, you can create a crown of sonnets. This undertaking can be done simply by using e-mail, but there are websites devoted to collaborations. Search for "collaborative padre."

Workshop

Besides using the established lists, you can establish your own informal workshop group. One person posts a work to the others, and they respond. You may be able to have a list set up for you, depending on your institution. If you have a listserv. list, then all responses are automatically circulated to all members. If you just have an informal list, only the persons to whom you actually send the message receive it. But if it is a small group, say ten or fewer participants, it is easy to send to all listmembers yourself.

Use Creative Writing Programs

Many programs have been developed for creative writing that can be purchased and used. These include the numerous programs put out by Hale Chatfield, including PoetryStar. These programs include teach-yourself exercises and collaborations with the computer to produce poems. For example, the Haiku section allows you to write as much of the haiku as you want, and the computer will write the rest. More for fun than for the production of serious poetry, these programs are nevertheless stimulating. Other programs offer help and formatting to writers of short stories, novels, plays, and screenplays. Some programs offer a demo for a token fee or even free; it is best to try these programs before buying, as some are expensive and may not be what you want.

Use a Shared Computer

You can use a shared computer to build a long poem, novel, or story with participants stopping in at different times to add material. Be sure to make a backup disk after each addition, in case of accident (or mischief).

Publish Your Work

You may publish your work by making a web page. You may enjoy setting up a website with your work on it; you can add graphics, animation, and sound to your page. Many of the major web centers like Yahoo.com and Go.com offer free websites, and you can build your web "dwelling" in a "neighborhood" of other writers. Services such as ALL and CompuServe also offer free websites to their customers and give very simple instructions on how to set them up. You may also be able to create a web page using your college or university account; look over the instructions that you received for setting up your account, or ask your computer help facility for information.

If you are going to use Yahoo!'s Geocities, then it is worth your time to explore others' web pages in the writers' neighborhoods, to see what kind of thing can be done. You can make of your poetry a multimedia presentation, with music and animation, without knowing anything about html—hypertext markup language. If you do know html, you can do almost anything.

Consider These Additional Ideas

1. Use the translation programs for fun and enlightenment.
2. Find resources for graduate programs.
3. Take more creative writing courses on-line.

As mentioned, there are also on-line journals and contests that publish the winners on-line. The computer is a wonderful aid to writing, but it doesn't, of course, replace pencil and paper.

Suggested Readings

I. TEXTBOOKS AND OTHER RESOURCES FOR THE BEGINNING CREATIVE WRITER

These are books that students may use to teach themselves. They include textbooks and a few useful reference books that have been chosen for the student who has taken a creative writing class and wants to explore the field further.

Altabernd, Lynn, and Leslie, Lewis *A Handbook for the Study of Poetry*. New York: Macmillan, 1966. (86 pages). Is an old but useful handbook. It provides clear, exact descriptions of poetic forms.

Baldwin, Michael. *The Way to Write Poetry*. London: Elm Tree Books, 1982. (111 pages; index). Although old, is a lucid and insightful guide for beginning poets. At the beginning of Chapter 1, Baldwin proclaims, "This book is for poets, would-be poets, teachers of creative writing, teachers in general, and . . . student philosophers of the creative process."

Behn, Robin, and Chase Twichell, eds. *The Practice of Poetry*. New York: HarperCollins, 1992. (299 pages; appendices, index). Contains exercises for all levels of poetry writing, described by professional poet-teachers who use these exercises in their own teaching (and often, their own practice). The book can be used by everyone from beginners to professional poets with a case of writer's block.

Bently, Peter, ed. *The Dictionary of World Myth*. New York: Duncan Baird Publishers, 1995. (240 pages; foreword, bibliography, illustrations, indexes). Is an excellent reference for any writer. In alphabetical order are listed all international historical and current mythological/religious characters and main events, including creation, heaven, hell, and death. This book would serve well as a highly recommended reference or as a cotext in a graduate level writing class. The book allows the creative mind a universal touch.

Bernays, Anne and Pamela Painter. *What if? Writing Exercises for Fiction Writers*. New York: HarperCollins, 1990. (230 pages; bibliography, introduction). Contains over eighty exercises "useful for people who have begun to publish and for those who have never written a word of fiction." The exercises, which could be used in any order and alone or among other exercises, focus on beginning a work, using memories, characterization, perspective and point of view, dialogue, plot, story elements, resolution and meaning, transformation, mechanics, brainstorming and creative inspiration, and style. The readings in this text include extensive writings from students. The final section of the text is a collection of short stories.

Bickham, Jack M. *The 38 Most Common Fiction Writing Mistakes (And How to Avoid Them)*. Cincinnati: Writers Digest Books, 1992. (117 pages; index). Is written by a knowledgeable author/professor of fiction. The book has a positive approach to the negative aspects encountered while writing fiction and offers sound, relevant advice. It helps streamline, strengthen, and focus one's work, making it more readable and enjoyable. This is an elementary-level book.

Bishop, Wendy. *Thirteen Ways of Looking at a Poem: A Guide to Writing Poetry*. New York: Longman, 2000. (437 pages; bibliography, index). Is an excellent text for a poetry-writing class. The book has an imaginative and fun approach, good for beginning and intermediate poets. It can be used by students on their own.

Brogan, T. V. E., Alex Preminger, et al. *The New Princeton Encyclopedia of Poetry and Poetics*. New York: MJF Books, 1993. (1383 pages). Is a most useful encyclopedia covering all the movements, terms, and major figures.

Burroway, Janet. *Writing Fiction*. 3rd ed. New York: HarperCollins 1992. (397 pages; preface, appendices, index, bibliography). Is a textbook suitable for college and junior college students. The book contains in-depth explanation of aspects of narrative craft and includes generative discussion questions and writing prompts. The tone of explanatory materials is generous and accessible. Some readings are from the canon, but most selections are contemporary, and include readings from a variety of cultures.

Carroll, David L. *A Manual of Writer's Tricks*. New York: Paragon Press, 1990. (127 pages; suggested readings). Gives useful tips on development, style, and problem solving through revision. Easily read, this book is valuable for aspiring authors as a secondary source. Insightful tips, not found elsewhere, are provided.

Ciardi, John. *Ciardi Himself: Fifteen Essays in the Reading, Writing, and Teaching of Poetry*. Fayetteville and London: University of Arkansas Press: 1989. (141 pages). Contains informed, intellectual, but accessible advice on the creation of poetry. The essays stress that a poet must commit to using precision in rhythm, diction, image or metaphor, and form; these essays also underscore that a successful poem is emotionally precise, contains multiple and interdependent ideas, and depends on the language more than on the subject.

Dacey, Phillip, and David Jauss. *Strong Measures*. New York: Harper & Row, 1986. (492 pages; bibliography, glossary, index). Is an excellent anthology-text of formal poetry that provides clear definitions and contemporary examples of the forms.

Dillard, Annie. *The Writing Life*. New York: Harper, 1989. (111 pages). Is a short and informal book. Dillard's relaxed language makes some difficult abstractions accessible. Dillard explains the time commitment involved in writing, two to ten years, and what makes that time commitment worthwhile for her. She talks about the kinds of things she does to keep going, to keep writing. The book is accessible for college students.

Falk, K. *How to Write a Romance and Get It Published*. New York: Penguin Books USA, 1990. (515 pages; index, illustrations, introduction). Takes a lighthearted look at becoming a romance novelist. The book details the how-tos from beginning to write a romance novel to publication with tips and information from the leading romance novelists currently on the bestseller list. For those who want to write romances, this is a good self-help book.

Friedman, Bonnie. *Writing Past Dark: Envy, Fear, Distractions, and Other Dilemmas in the Writer's Life*. New York: Harper, 1993. (146 pages; introduction). Examines some of the issues that writers face: fear, envy, jealousy, isolation. The purpose of the text is to help writers circumvent the solitary aspects of writing and perceive psychological alienation in terms of experiences shared by all writers.

Gioia, Dana. *Can Poetry Matter?* Boston: Atlantic Monthly Company, 1991. (206 pages). Is a key reading for all who want a sense of what is happening in contemporary poetry. The central essay, "Can Poetry Matter," can be found on the Atlantic's on-line site.

Goldberg, Natalie. *Writing Down the Bones: Freeing the Writer Within.* Boston and London: Shambhala, 1986. (171 pages; introduction). Offers writers inspiration from Goldberg's accounts of personal writing frustrations, through proposed exercises, and via the strain of Zen philosophy that runs throughout the text. The book concentrates on starting writing projects more than on polishing writing projects; and it emphasizes harmonizing routinized writing with inspiration and written expressions with our overall behavior toward the world, others, and the lives we lead.

Hickey, Donna J. *Developing a Written Voice.* Calif.: Mayfield, 1993. (260 pages; preface, appendix, bibliography, index). Includes thorough explanatory material, writing prompts, group exercises, and discussions of student and professional writing. The book works with a wide range of levels of voice. The text is rhetorically aware without being theory-bound or encumbered with excessive theoretical terminology.

Kirby, David. *Diving for Poems.* Tallahassee: Word Beat Press, 1985. (90 pages; bibliography, introduction). Is a short guide for students. The author states: "The first part of this book deals with the raw material of poetry, and the second part deals with the shaping of that material into finished poems. As examples I use poems by well-known authors but also ones by my students and myself."

Kubis, Pat, and Bob Howland. *The Complete Guide to Writing Fiction and Nonfiction and Getting It Published.* 2nd ed. Englewood Cliffs, N.J.: Prentice-Hall, 1990. (292 pages; index). Is for beginning writers intent on publishing. The first half of the book considers the basics with publishing in mind: plot; viewpoint; opening; full characters; effective dialogue; and developing good style, settings, and time sequence. The second half is directly concerned with the practicalities involved with the publishing industry.

Livingston, Myra Cohn. *Poem-Making: Ways to Begin Writing Poetry.* New York: Harper-Collins, 1991. (162 pages; index, introduction). Is a convenient guide to many of the basic elements of poetry, including point of view, poetic devices, rhythm and metrics, figures of speech, and forms.

Lodge, David. *The Art of Fiction.* New York: Viking, 1992. (240 pages; preface, bibliography, index). Is a suitable text for an advanced college-level class in which the focus will be fiction, or for personal exploration. This cleverly written guide to fiction writing contains intense, thorough, and demanding discussions of the aspects of narrative craft. Each chapter uses sizable samples of literature, primarily from the canon, as the basis for discussion.

Minot, Stephen. *Three Genres: The Writing of Poetry, Fiction, and Drama.* 3rd ed. Englewood Cliffs, N.J.: Prentice-Hall, 1982. (326 pages; appendices). Presents the technical aspects of the three major genres. This is a teaching book with examples in each genre section and with extensive coverage of revision and self-criticism.

Mueller, Lavonne, and Jerry D. Reynolds. *Creative Writing: Forms and Techniques.* Chicago: NTC Publishing Co., 1990. (250 pages; introduction, appendices, bibliography, index). Assumes the premise that students in creative writing classes want to be in the class and want to write. Having taken that premise, this college textbook works through beginning exercises to making work public. The limitation may be that the text attempts to cover too much: poetry, short story, one-act plays, and nonfiction, at various levels of expertise.

Oliver, Mary, and Mary Cliver. *Rules for the Dance: A Handbook for Writing and Reading Metrical Verse.* 1998. (194 pages; index.) Is a useful handbook for poets to possess and consult.

Peacock, Molly. *How to Read a Poem and Start a Poetry Circle.* New York: Riverhead Books, 2000. (209 pages). Is essential book for a poetry novice. It takes the reader through a dozen or so of the author's favorite poems and shares her enthusiasm with the reader. Then practical instructions are supplied for passing on to others this love of poetry.

Plimpton, George, ed. *Poets at Work: The Paris Review Interviews.* New York: Viking, 1989. (439 pages; introduction, notes on contributors). Features interviews with only the famous. This secondary source provides some stimulating reading on the lives, ambitions, and frustrations of poets. There are some sample poems, drafts, and notes included, as well as interesting sidelights on the writing life.

Ross, Elizabeth Irvin. *How to Write While You Sleep.* Cincinnati: Writer's Digest Books, 1985. (228 pages; bibliography and index). Is a resource of method. This book provides a comprehensive method for bringing forth creative writing ("Write-Now" method). The emphasis is on increasing creativity, decreasing hindrances, reducing stress associated with writer's block, maintaining effective time management, and understanding the production of publishable material.

Turco, Lewis. *The New Book of Forms: A Handbook of Poetics.* Hanover, N. H.: University Press of New England, 1986. (280 pages; preface, introduction, appendix, index). Is a reference book for poetics that is suitable for junior college to advanced writing classes. The text presents a study of poetics from the Middle Ages to the present. The handbook section discusses typographical, sonic, sensory, and ideational levels. It explains prosodic and metrical systems, and clarifies poetic terms. The form section of the book is organized and cross-referenced by rhyme scheme, meter, and number of lines. Although the focus is on English language forms, the text includes such culturally diverse forms as Middle Eastern and Malayan.

Turner, Alberta T. *Poets Teaching the Creative Process.* New York: Longman, 1980. (221 pages; introduction). Is a collaboration of thirty-two established teachers of creative writing. The text is composed entirely of student poems to which the poet-teachers respond. Also, the text sharply enacts various pedagogical positions and considers their implications for poetic theory and their effects on the writing of students.

II. ANTHOLOGIES FOR STUDENTS TO CONSULT

Andrews, W. L., ed. *Classic Fiction of the Harlem Renaissance.* New York: Oxford University Press, 1994. (403 pages; bibliography, illustrations, introduction). Combines popular Harlem Renaissance writers with definitive works to illustrate the movement. Each short story is prefaced with an author introduction giving the reader some additional background information about the period. A glossary of common phrases of the time is included further to acquaint the reader with the period.

Birmingham, John, Laura Gilpin, and Joesph F. McCrindle. *The Henfield Prize Stories.* New York: Warner Books, 1992. (291 pages; short notes on authors and editors). Includes the twenty-three "finest" Henfield prizewinner from 1980 through 1990. The book features contemporary writers exploring the depths of the American short story with creativity, vigor, and "new styles." This is a good book for contemporary fiction classes to view up-and-coming authors.

Bloom, Lynn Z., ed. *The Essay Connection: Readings for Writers*. 3rd ed. Lexington, Mass., and Toronto: D. C. Heath, 1991. (753 pages; index). Contains short, mostly twentieth-century essays by students and professionals in many disciplines. In addition, the anthology represents men and women, and majority and minority, essayists. Bloom divides the text into sections that focus on particular rhetorical strategies and composition techniques.

Field, Edward, Gerald Locklin, and Charles Stetler, eds. *A New Geography of Poets*. Fayetteville: University of Arkansas Press, 1992. (324 pages; index, introduction). Organizes the poems of contemporary American poets according to the part of the country in which each poet lives. In the introduction, the editors explain their purpose: "An anthology that sets out to demonstrate that poets—good poets—are to be found, not just in a few cities and cultural centers but everywhere in America."

Finch, Annie, ed. *A Formal Feeling Comes: Poems in Form by Contemporary Women*. Ashland, Oreg.: Story Line Press, 1994. (308 pages; indices, introduction). Provides appealing poems in loose and tight forms by a variety of women of many cultural backgrounds. This anthology is an excellent tool for teaching forms and learning about them.

Frosch, M. ed. *Coming of Age in America: A Multicultural Anthology*. New York: The New Press, 1994. (274 pages). Gives voice to new writers who concentrate on the trials of youth. The collection touches on a number of cultures and religions. This anthology would be an important addition to a creative writing course because it deals primarily with experiences that young people can relate to, write about, and create their own stories from.

Gillan, M. M., and Gillan, J., eds. *Unsettling America: An Anthology of Contemporary Multicultural Poetry*. New York: Penguin Books USA, 1994. (406 pages; index, introduction). Provides a forum for poets of all ethnicities. By offering a different type of stage, the editors have allowed for the "conception of other American identities" that have been otherwise neglected. The poems included address cultural conflict, self-hate, coming of age, and other issues that affect America's youth regardless of ethnicity. Also, there are short biographies of each author at the end of the text. This book would be a wonderful addition to any class planning to include poetry in its curriculum.

Goss, L., and Barnes, M. E., eds. *Talk That Talk: An Anthology of African-American Storytelling*. New York: Simon & Schuster, 1989. (521 pages; index, bibliography, introduction). Contains well-rounded examples of most aspects of African-American literature. This anthology includes value-building bedtime stories for children, stories filled with historical content, sermons (which are a very important part of black folklore), tales, and commentaries. This thorough collection is a necessary piece of any ethnic literature class as well as a wonderful source of inspiration in a creative writing course.

Green, Veronica, ed. *The Rhythm of Our Days: An Anthology of Women's Poetry*. Cambridge: Cambridge University Press, 1991. (136 pages; introduction). Is an inclusive collection of modern women's poetry. In the introduction, the editor states: "I have included women writers from as far around the world as I can, writing about all sorts of things from which they cannot escape. All the women are 'modern' in that they have all written since the 1950s."

Hirschberg, Stuart, ed. *The Many Worlds of Literature*. New York: Macmillan, 1994. (1093 pages; glossary, plus geographical, author, and title indexes). Is a multicultural anthology of contemporary poetry, fiction, and nonfiction. Inclusions are diverse, taken from around the world, and they are divided into common themes such as family and cultural heritage, coming of age, gender, and spirituality. Although this is an excellent multicultural text, for a creative writing class, an instructor may prefer to choose particular entries rather than the whole text.

Hoeper, Jeffrey D., and James H. Pickering, eds. *Poetry*. New York: Macmillan, 1990. (455 pages; introduction, handbook of terms, bibliography, index). Is suitable for both college and junior college level students. With the poetry there is provided extensive explanatory material of all aspects of poetic forms, concepts, and terms. Each section has questions that prompt writing and thinking. The poetic selections feature lesser-known poets and are gender balanced, but they lack cultural diversity.

Knowles, Horace, ed. *A Treasury of American Writers: From Harper's Magazine*. New York: Bonanza Books, 1985. (696 pages; introduction, index). Contains the best of *Harper's* articles since 1850. This very diverse collection of both poetry and prose is very good for creative nonfiction in either lower- or upper-level or graduate writing courses, and can be used independently to stimulate thought. The selections were chosen for their reader interest and for their literary excellence, and they represent ninety authors—some little-known writers and others internationally renowned authors, whose works are arranged into eleven broad categories. *Harper's* ideal standards were used in the selection process: deals primarily with ideas; provides a highly selective kind of news coverage; seeks an independent assessment of public issues; welcomes controversy; and provides a vehicle for the artists in literature. Among the contributors are E. B. White, K. A. Porter, S. Lanier, and A. G. Winslow.

Lehman, David, ed. *Ecstatic Occasions, Expedient Forms: 65 Leading Contemporary Poets Select and Comment on Their Poems*. New York: Macmillan, 1987. (256 pages; bibliography, introduction). Is an extremely interesting and valuable book, which Lehman calls "a forum on form that has itself become a form." Lehman asked sixty-five contemporary poets to explore the elusive topic of poetic form. He explains: "Each contributor was asked to provide a poem accompanied by a statement on the decisions that went into its making. . . . I wanted merely to create an expedient occasion for various poets to ruminate variously about a common concern."

Lopate, Phillip, ed. *The Art of the Personal Essay*. New York: Anchor Doubleday, 1994. (777 pages; introduction). Is a useful tool for those interested in creative nonfiction. This book contains a sound introduction and well-chosen examples from classical times up to the present.

Martin, Janet. *The Voice of Reflection: A Writer's Reader*. New York: HarperCollins, 1995. (416 pages; preface, bibliography, index). Is suitable for a junior college or college audience. The book contains fifty-eight expressive essays that are directly or indirectly autobiographical. The essays serve as models for reflection and writing. The text is divided into eight sections: autobiography, family, friendship, self-portrait, country and city life, life in America, and illness and death.

Pack, R., and J. Parini, eds. *American Identities: Contemporary Multicultural Voices*. Hanover, N.H.: University Press of New England, 1994. (173 pages; introduction). Displays a great diversity of authors. The editors selected works that highlight the "multiplicity of well-maintained identities" rather than emphasizing the "obsolete idea of the American melting pot." Both short stories and poetry are included in the anthology. Short biographies of the contributors are helpful to the reader.

Pickering, James H. *Fiction 100: An Anthology of Short Stories*. 5th ed. New York: Macmillan, 1988. (1533 pages; preface, biographical notes, glossary). Includes 110 short stories. A reader's guide serves as an instructional booklet for short story writing, analysis, and criticism writing. This text includes a diverse group of writers from Alice Adams to Richard

Wright, including Susan Glaspell and Isaac Bashevis Singer. It is a great selection for upper-level and graduate writing courses, and it is useful for students who want a broad range of stories and styles to pursue.

Wolff, Tobias, ed. *The Vintage Book of Contemporary Short Stories*. New York: Random House, 1994. (558 pages). Is an anthology of contemporary fictional short stories. Many of the stories tackle today's problems. The book contains serious subject matter, such as sex, drugs, and rape. The well-written, thought-provoking stories are appropriate for adult classes related to fiction; however, the subject matter may still prove controversial.

Index